W9-AOW-442

500

Freshwater Aquarium Fish

Consulting Editor
Greg Jennings

A Visual Reference to the Most
Popular Species

FIREFLY BOOKS

A FIREFLY BOOK

Published by Firefly Books Ltd. 2018

Copyright © 2006, 2018 Brown Bear Books Ltd

All rights reserved. No part of this publication may be reproduced, stored in a retrieval system, or transmitted in any form or by any means, electronic, mechanical, photocopying, recording or otherwise, without the prior written permission of the Publisher.

First printing

Library of Congress Control Number: 2018931667

Library and Archives Canada Cataloguing in Publication

500 freshwater aquarium fish : a visual reference to the most popular species / consulting editor, Greg Jennings.
Previously published: 2006.
Includes bibliographical references and index.
ISBN 978-1-77085-919-7 (softcover)
        1. Aquarium fishes. 2. Freshwater fishes. 3. Aquarium fishes--Identification. 4. Freshwater fishes--Identification. 5. Aquarium fishes--Pictorial works. 6. Freshwater fishes--Pictorial works. I. Jennings, Greg, 1955-, editor II. Title: Five hundred freshwater aquarium fish.
SF457.F48 2018   639.34   C2017-902810-3

Published in the United States by
Firefly Books (U.S.) Inc.
P.O. Box 1338, Ellicott Station
Buffalo, New York 14205

Published in Canada by
Firefly Books Ltd.
50 Staples Avenue, Unit 1
Richmond Hill, Ontario L4B 0A7

Printed in China

First published by Brown Bear Books Ltd
First Floor
9-17 St Albans Place
London N1 0NX
www.brownbearbooks.co.uk

For Brown Bear Books Ltd:
Project Editor: Graham Bateman
Editor: Virginia Carter
Design: Steve McCurdy, Martin Anderson
Photo credits
Front cover: Photomax/Max Gibbs
all other Photographs:
© Hippocampus Bildarchiv
www.Hippocampus-Bildarchiv.com

Front cover: Dwarf Gourami
(Colisa lalia)
Spine: Blue Gularis
(Aphyosemion sjoestedti)
Back cover (top to bottom): Siamese
Fighting Fish (Betta splendens)
Leopard Ctenopoma (Ctenopoma acutirostre)

Page 1: Green Discus, solid turquoise
form (Symphysodon aequifasciatus).
Pages 2–3: Leopard Danio
(Brachydanio rerio var. frankei).

baac

500
Freshwater Aquarium Fish

CONTENTS

Right: Shoal of Swordtails (*Xiphophorus helleri*).

184–241
CYPRINIDS

242–319
CHARACOIDS

388–401
RAINBOWS AND BLUE-EYES

402–421
KILLIFISH

WHAT IS A FISH?

THERE ARE WELL OVER 24,000 SPECIES OF FISH known to science, and that number appears to be increasing daily. With so many thousands of species in existence—from whale sharks to minnows—we should all know what a fish is. However, things are not that simple, since there is no categorical definition of the term "fish."

Identifying combined characteristics associated with fishes, such as an aquatic lifestyle and the possession of gills and fins, might seem to bring a definition a little closer—but other animals such as cuttlefishes (*Sepia*, etc.) and squids exhibit the same characteristics.

In broad terms there are two groups of fishes:
Cartilaginous fishes (Class Chondrichthyes)
Sharks, rays, and chimaeras (about 700 species).

Bony fishes (Class Osteichthyes)
A large class of species ranging from guppies to seahorses (over 23,000 species).

Of these two categories, the one that is encountered almost (but not quite) exclusively in aquaria and in ponds is the Class Osteichthyes, the bony fishes. It is possible, with difficulty and numerous exceptions and qualifications, to list the characteristics that, in combination, allow us to recognize a bony fish as such.
Bony fish:

- Possess a braincase and limb (fin) skeleton consisting, at least in part, of bone.
- Possess fins, usually with spines and/or rays.
- Breathe through outwardly directed gills covered by an operculum (gill cover) that appears externally as a slitlike aperture.
- Have bodies totally or partially covered in scales (with some important exceptions).
- Possess an air/gas swimbladder used in buoyancy control (with a few exceptions).
- Possess a sensory mechanism called the lateral line system, which runs in a head–tail direction.
- Are poikilothermic (cold-blooded): their body temperature is determined by that of the environment.

Left: Angel (*Pterophyllum scalare*).

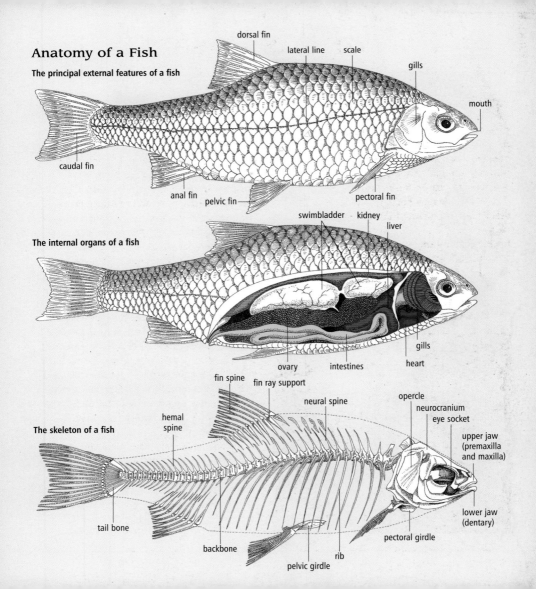

Anatomy of a Fish

The principal external features of a fish

dorsal fin
lateral line
scale
gills
mouth
caudal fin
anal fin
pelvic fin
pectoral fin

The internal organs of a fish

swimbladder
kidney
liver
ovary
intestines
heart
gills

The skeleton of a fish

fin spine
fin ray support
neural spine
opercle
neurocranium
eye socket
hemal spine
upper jaw (premaxilla and maxilla)
tail bone
backbone
pelvic girdle
rib
pectoral girdle
lower jaw (dentary)

FISH HABITATS

Fish can be found in almost every aquatic habitat, from Arctic wastes and the darkest recesses of midocean abysses to mudpools and the brightly illuminated warm shallows of coral reefs. Very little of the planet's surface is covered by freshwater (lakes, rivers, and steams). Yet these habitats contain a myriad of unique fish species. While many regions of the world contribute fish to the aquarist hobby, a large number come from the Amazon Basin and Africa's Rift Valley lakes.

FISH CONSERVATION

Like many animals, fish are under threat from human activities, for example, through habitat destruction and pollution. Numbers of some fish in their natural habitats have decreased dramatically as a result of collection for the aquarium trade. However, international trade in particular species is often restricted or banned now, and the recent increase in the captive breeding of aquarium fish to satisfy the boom in demand from the aquarium hobby has resulted in a reduction of the pressures on wild specimens. An estimated 90 percent of all freshwater aquarium and pond fish are now bred in captivity.

Left, from top: Sailfin Molly (*Poecilia latipinna*); Leopard Ctenopoma (*Ctenopoma acutirostre*); Red Aphyosemion (*Aphyosemion sjoestedti*). **Opposite:** Redhook Pacu (*Myleus rubripinnis*).

500 FRESHWATER AQUARIUM FISH

This book illustrates and describes a range of freshwater fish that are kept in the freshwater aquarium. For the most part they are tropical species that require the water to be heated, but also included are some that survive quite happily at room temperature. Over 500 species, strains, or varieties are illustrated, in most cases accompanied by a brief description of interesting aspects of their biology and classification. The information is suported by fact boxes that describe their origins, form, behavior, as well as the aquarium conditions required.

Every attempt has been made to use the latest scientific names for all species. However, the level of acceptance and frequency of use varies among scientists, aquarists, and countries. For this reason, synonyms are included wherever relevant.

SPECIES'
PROFILES

Left: Shoal of Cardinal Tetras
(*Paracheirodon axelrodi*).

CICHLIDS

Family Cichlidae

The cichlids are a large family (Cichlidae) comprising at least 2,000 species. In fact, some authors believe that, depending on the way in which a species is defined, Lake Malawi in Africa alone may contain 1,600 different species. They occur mainly in freshwater in Central and South America, the West Indies, Africa, Madagascar, Syria, the coastal areas of the southern half of India, and Sri Lanka.

The northernmost species is the Texas Cichlid (*Herichthys cyanoguttatus*). The largest species—at a length of 36in (90cm)—is *Boulengerochromis microlepis* from Lake Tanganyika. The smallest cichlids belong to the genus *Apistogramma* and grow no bigger than $1\frac{1}{2}$in (3.5cm).

While the overall form of cichlids varies immensely, there are common features. Cichlids have only one nostril on each side of the head rather than the normal two; the lateral line is often split, the front (longer) section being located higher up the body; most species have brown-tipped teeth; and the dorsal fin is divided into a spiny, unbranched (hard)

Left: *Maylandia fainzilberi.*
Opposite: *Steatocranus gibbiceps.*

front section and a branched (soft) rear one supported by rays.

Spawning behavior in cichlids is very varied, although parental care is characteristic. Spawning strategies include depositing the eggs on rocks, leaves, and so on; incubation in the mouth by females (mouthbrooding); and a few feed their young on body secretions during the first weeks of life.

Cichlids will eat a wide range of foods and are therefore not generally difficult to keep. There are so many species available within the hobby that, once basic aquarium keeping has been mastered, most aquarists interested in cichlids begin to specialize.

Blue Acara

Andinoacara pulcher (previously Aequidens pulcher)

Other common name:
Blue-spot Cichlid

Synonyms: *Aequidens latifrons, A. cf. latifrons, A. caeruleopunctatus*

Distribution: *A. pulcher* found in Panama, Trinidad, and Venezuela; *A. latifrons* and *A. caeruleopunctatus* in Colombia.

Size: Up to 8in (20cm) reported; usually smaller.

Behavior: Relatively peaceful, except during breeding. Although this species burrows, it does not eat plants. Roots should nevertheless be protected.

Diet: All commercial and livefoods accepted.

Aquarium: Open areas, hiding places, and some flat or smooth, rounded rocks. Plants must be robust and/or artificial. Water chemistry not critical but quality must be good. Temperature range: 64–77°F (18–25°C); slightly higher for breeding.

Breeding: Eggs are laid on a precleaned rock, and they and the fry are guarded by both parents. Hatching takes 2–5 days.

Despite the Blue Acara's long history in the hobby (it was first introduced into Europe in 1906), there is still considerable debate regarding its correct scientific name. As a result, the various names given above are often used interchangeably, with some authorities regarding the Colombian Blue Acaras as valid species in their own rights—*A. latifrons, A. cf. latifrons* or *A. caeruleopunctatus*—and the others as *A. pulcher*. There are certainly observable differences between these, but some other authorities believe them to be insufficiently significant to warrant separation.

Green Terror

Andinoacara rivulatus (previously Aequidens rivulatus)

Other common names:
Silver Seam, Silver Saum,
Gold Seam, Gold Saum

Distribution: Green Terror
and Gold Saum found in
Ecuador; Silver Saum in
Peru.

Size: Up to 10½ in (27cm)
reported; usually smaller.

Behavior: Territorial and
aggressive, particularly at
breeding time. Only equally
large, robust tankmates
recommended.

Diet: Substantial commercial
foods, e.g. granules, tablets
and, particularly, livefoods.

Aquarium: Large and as for
A. pulcher, but temperature
range: 68–75°F (20–24°C);
slightly higher for breeding.

Breeding: Eggs are laid on a
precleaned rock, and they
and the fry are guarded by
both parents. Hatching
takes 2–5 days.

This relatively large fish has distinctive cheek markings that are similar to
those found in the Blue Acara. However, the head, particularly in males, is
considerably larger, with a noticeable "forehead." The Gold Saum and
Silver Saum have golden/reddish and whitish/silvery edges to the dorsal
and caudal fins respectively.

Pearly Compressiceps

Altolamprologus calvus

Synonym: *Lamprologus calvus*

Distribution: Lake Tanganyika, between Kapampa (D. R. Congo) and Cape Chaitika (Zambia).

Size: Males 6in (15cm); females 4in (10cm).

Behavior: Should be kept with equally robust species. Has been reported to "steal" eggs from mouthbrooders. Intolerant of its own and other *Altolamprologus* species.

Diet: Livefoods preferred.

Aquarium: Well-lit and properly constructed backgrounds with numerous boltholes; at least one sandy area and one large snail shell or small cave for female. Water should be hard and alkaline (pH 7.5–9.5), and well filtered and oxygenated. Temperature range: 73–81°F (23–27°C).

Breeding: Eggs are laid in a cave or shell that should be too small for male to enter. Female undertakes most brood-guarding responsibilities, with male predominantly responsible for guarding territory.

Altolamprologus species are easily distinguished from the related genus *Neolamprologus*—including *N. brichardi* (the Fairy Cichlid)—by their deeper (i.e., higher, or "altum") body and dorsal fin. These fin characteristics make *Altolamprologus* appear considerably more robust and predatory. Other *Altolamprologus* regularly available are: *A. compressiceps*, 6¼in (16cm); and the much smaller *A.* "Compressiceps Shell," with a maximum length of 3in (8cm). Females of both species are smaller than the males.

Midas Cichlid

Amphilophus citrinellus

Distribution: Nicaragua and Costa Rica.

Size: 13³/₄in (35cm); usually smaller.

Behavior: Territorial and aggressive, particularly during breeding time; likes burrowing.

Diet: Wide range of substantial commercial foods and livefoods accepted.

Aquarium: Large, with well-protected, robust plants, shelters (caves or bogwood), and some flat or rounded rocks. Rocks should be well bedded to prevent them from being toppled over. Water chemistry not critical. Temperature range: 70–77°F (21–25°C).

Breeding: Eggs are laid on a precleaned rock, and they and the fry are guarded by both parents. Hatching takes 2–5 days.

This large fish is available in several color forms, including "Gold," "Marble," "Red-head," and "Tiger," which are all naturally occurring morphs. There are also some commercially produced varieties. In all varieties mature males develop a distinctive "bump" (nuchal hump) on the forehead.

Red Devil

Amphilophus labiatus

Other common name:
Thick-lipped Cichlid

Distribution: Nicaragua.

Size: 13³/₄in (35cm); usually smaller.

Behavior: Aggressive, territorial; active burrower.

Diet: All large foods accepted, e.g. tablets, granules.

Aquarium: Large, with well-protected, robust plants, shelters (caves or bogwood), and some flat or rounded rocks. Rocks should be well bedded to prevent them from being toppled over. Water chemistry not critical. Temperature range: 70–77°F (21–25°C).

Breeding: Eggs are laid on a precleaned rock, and they and the fry are guarded by both parents, although the female takes greater responsibility for the fry. Hatching takes 2–5 days.

As one of the common names for this species indicates, one of the main characteristics is the thick lips possessed, particularly by adult males. While red specimens occur in nature, this is by no means the only naturally occurring morph of this variable species. Several cultivated color varieties are also available.

Blood Parrot

Unknown hybrid

Other common names:
Bloody Parrot, Blood Parrotfish, Jellybean Parrot, Red Parrot

Distribution: Man-made hybrid, therefore no natural distribution.

Size: Up to 8in (20cm).

Behavior: Usually peaceful, shy fish; can be territorial.

Diet: A variety of foods accepted, e.g. tablets, flakes, frozen foods, and krill.

Aquarium: Large with plenty of rock formations and shelters, especially caves. Plants not essential. Temperature range: 70–82°F (21–28°C).

Breeding: Generally infertile unless paired with a nonhybrid fish.

The Blood Parrot is the result of interbreeding between two unknown species of cichlids—although the South American Severum (*Heros severus*) and a Central American cichlid, such as the Midas Cichlid (*Amphilophus citrinellus*) or the Red Devil (*A. labiatus*) are often cited as the parents. This hybrid fish occurs in a range of colors, from orange to red or purple. The most common morph is the Red Blood Parrot, which, despite its name, is gold to orange in color with a pink patch on the throat. The main characteristics that distinguish the Blood Parrot from other cichlids are its beaklike mouth and unusually large, bright yellowish-green eyes, often with an oddly shaped iris.

African Butterfly Cichlid

Anomalochromis thomasi

Other common name:
Dwarf Jewel Fish

Distribution: Coastal freshwater habitats in Sierra Leone, Guinea, and Liberia.

Size: Male 4in (10cm); females considerably smaller.

Behavior: Territorial, but tolerant of other species.

Diet: Wide range of foods accepted; both vegetable and livefood components recommended.

Aquarium: Well planted, with hiding places and flat-topped or smoothly rounded pebbles. Water chemistry not critical, but soft, slightly acid conditions are best for breeding. Temperature range: 73–81°F (23–27°C).

Breeding: Eggs are laid on a precleaned broad leaf, or on a flat or rounded pebble. Both parents guard the eggs and fry. Hatching occurs after about 2 days.

The second of the above common names for this species is rarely encountered these days, but it reflects the fact that this beautifully marked fish was once considered a *Hemichromis*, the genus to which the "true" Jewel Cichlids belong. It is hard to differentiate between the two sexes, but adult females generally have stronger black markings and their bodies are more rounded just before spawning.

Agassiz's Dwarf Cichlid

Apistogramma agassizii

Distribution: Wide distribution in southern tributaries of the Amazon.

Size: Up to 4in (10cm) reported; usually smaller; males considerably larger than females.

Behavior: Peaceful toward other species, but intolerant of its own in a confined space.

Diet: Most commercial formulations accepted, but livefoods preferred.

Aquarium: Thick planting, plus other forms of shelter, e.g. caves. Dark, fine-grained substratum recommended. Soft, acid water required. Temperature range: 72–77°F (22–25°C).

Breeding: Eggs are (usually) laid on the roof of a cave. Female takes on main responsibility for guarding both eggs and fry, with male defending territory. Hatching takes 3–5 days. If several females are kept in a sufficiently spacious aquarium with well-spaced-out caves, each will establish its own territory and may spawn with the same male.

This is an exceptionally beautiful dwarf cichlid. Agassiz's Dwarf Cichlid was first imported into Europe in 1909 and is available in numerous naturally occurring color morphs, as well as in some commercially developed ones. Typical of its genus, *A. agassizii* demonstrates sexual dimorphism, with the males being much larger than the females, and the two sexes often exhibiting completely different coloration.

Borelli's Dwarf Cichlid

Apistogramma borellii

This is a slightly deeper-bodied species than *A. agassizii*. Several naturally occurring color forms exist. In all forms, mature males have some blue coloration and quite splendid dorsal fins when expanded. Occasionally young males in a group will adopt the same coloration as the females, and are thus not regarded by older males as rivals.

Other common name: Umbrella Dwarf Cichlid

Synonym: *Apistogramma reitzigi*

Distribution: Mainly Mato Grosso (Brazil), Pantanal (Paraguay).

Size: Males up to 3in (8cm); females considerably smaller.

Behavior: Peaceful toward other species, but intolerant of its own in confined space.

Diet: Will accept some commercial preparations, but prefers livefoods.

Aquarium: Thick planting, plus other forms of shelter, e.g. caves. Dark, fine-grained substratum recommended. Temperature range: 72–77°F (22–25°C); slightly higher for breeding.

Breeding: Eggs are (usually) laid on the roof of a cave. Female takes on main responsibility for guarding eggs; male and female both involved in fry protection, with male defending territory. Hatching takes 4–5 days. If several females are kept in a sufficiently spacious aquarium with well-spaced-out caves, each will establish its own territory and may spawn with the same male.

Macmaster's Dwarf Cichlid

Apistogramma macmasteri

Other common names:
Red-tailed Dwarf Cichlid,
Villavicencio Apistogramma

Synonym: *Apistogramma
ornatipinnis*

Distribution: Mainly Río
Meta drainage system,
Colombia.

Size: Males up to 4in (10cm);
females considerably smaller.

Behavior: Typical
Apistogramma, i.e. generally
peaceful but intolerant of its
own in confined space.

Diet: Strong preference for
livefoods; sometimes
difficult to wean off
livefoods and on to
commercial diets.

Aquarium: As for other
Apistogramma species, but
very soft, acid water
recommended. Temperature
range: 73–86°F (23–30°C).

Breeding: As for other
Apistogramma species.
Hatching takes upward
of 2½ days, depending
on temperature.

Although the alternative name, *A. ornatipinnis*, was most frequently used during the 1970s, it is still encountered from time to time today.
To confuse matters further, *A. ornatipinnis* is considered a synonym of *A. steindachneri* (Steindachner's Dwarf Cichlid). Macmaster's Dwarf Cichlid shows marked differences between males and females of the species. Males are larger than females, and their dorsal membranes are slightly longer. Some males may have a forked tail, whereas females' tails are always rounded in shape.

Panda Dwarf Cichlid

Apistogramma nijsseni

Distribution: Mainly Río Ucayali and Río Yavarí, west of Iquitos, Peru.

Size: Males up to 3¹/₂in (9cm); females smaller.

Behavior: Typical *Apistogramma*.

Diet: Prefers livefoods, but may also accept commercial preparations.

Aquarium: Layout as for other *Apistogramma* species. *A. nijsenni* is less demanding than most of its closest relatives in its water chemistry requirements. Temperature range: 75–82°F (24–28°C); slightly higher for breeding.

Breeding: Breeds in typical *Apistogramma* fashion. Peat filtration and soft, acid water recommended. Hatching takes 3–4 days. Experiments have shown that at 68–73°F (20–23°C) all eggs develop into females; the ratio of males begins to increase from 73.6°F (23.1°C), with 100 percent male offspring being produced at 84.4–89.6°F (29.1–32°C). Hatching rates are low in hard water (around 16 percent), rising to around 83 percent in soft water.

One of the most immediately recognizable features of this species is the rounded caudal fin of the vast majority of males (in most other species, there are upper and lower fin ray extensions). As in many other *Apistogramma*, several naturally occurring color forms of this species—whose sex is influenced by both temperature and pH—exist.

Convict Cichlid

Amatitlania nigrofasciata (previously Archocentrus nigrofasciatus)

Other common name:
Zebra Cichlid

Synonyms:
Heros nigrofasciatus,
Cichlasoma nigrofasciatum

Distribution: Widely
distributed in Central
America.

Size: Males up to 6in (15cm);
females smaller.

Behavior: Highly territorial;
will damage tender plants.

Diet: All foods accepted;
vegetable component
essential.

Aquarium: Spacious, with
easily defended shelters,
robust and/or unpalatable
plants, and rounded or flat-
topped pebbles. Water
chemistry not critical.
Temperature range: 68–77°F
(20–25°C).

Breeding: Eggs are laid
either in caves or in the
open, and they and the fry
are protected by both
parents. Hatching takes a
few days.

This stunningly patterned fish has been popular within the aquarium
hobby for nearly 70 years. This is, perhaps, a little surprising given that its
strong territorial instincts make it somewhat aggressive toward many of its
tankmates. However, the pleasure of keeping a well-matched pair housed
in a sufficiently spacious, well-designed aquarium, stocked with robust
species, more than makes up for the disadvantages in the behavioral
aspects of the species. An albino variety is occasionally available.

T-bar Cichlid

Amatitlania sajica (previously Archocentrus sajica)

Other common name:
Sajica's Cichlid

Synonym: *Cichlasoma sajica*

Distribution: Costa Rica.

Size: Males up to 4³/₄in (12cm); females smaller.

Behavior: Territorial, but generally more tolerant of other fish than some similar-sized cichlids, except during breeding.

Diet: All foods accepted.

Aquarium: Spacious, well planted, with hiding places, shelters, and caves. Water chemistry not critical. Temperature range: 72–77°F (22–25°C).

Breeding: Eggs usually laid in caves. Female generally cares for eggs and young (which hatch out in several days), with male guarding territory.

Although the second of the above scientific names is now ceasing to be used, it is included here because it still appears in print from time to time, particularly in articles. Several naturally occurring forms of this species are available, the color and patterning depending on locality. The T-bar Cichlid is sometimes confused with the less colorful *A. spilurus*.

Burton's Mouthbrooder

Astatotilapia burtoni

Synonym: *Haplochromis burtoni*

Distribution: Lake Tanganyika basin.

Size: Males up to 4³/₄in (12cm), but usually smaller; females around 2³/₄in (7cm).

Behavior: Males are aggressive toward each other, but juvenile males may be kept together in a sufficiently large aquarium.

Diet: All foods accepted; vegetable component recommended.

Aquarium: Hiding places, an open swimming space and a fine-grained substratum should be provided. Medium-hard alkaline water preferred. Temperature range: 68–77°F (20–25°C); slightly higher for breeding.

Breeding: Maternal mouthbrooder. Males dig large pits to which they attract females. Once a few eggs are laid, the female takes them into her mouth. Hatching can take over 1 week. For a time after this, the female will guard her offspring, taking them into her mouth when danger threatens and rereleasing them later.

This species was among the early mouthbrooders to be kept by aquarists, at a time when "eggspots" or "egg dummies" were still a novelty. It is perhaps not kept as widely these days owing to the numerous, more colorful, mouthbrooders that are now available. Eggspots are markings that are present on the male's anal fin, and are thought to play an important role in reproduction. After the female has taken some of her eggs into her mouth, she pecks at the eggspots on the male's anal fin as if they, too, were eggs. This action is believed to stimulate the male to release sperm, thus ensuring fertilization.

Oscar

Astronotus ocellatus

First imported into the European hobby in the late 1920s, the Oscar is still going as strongly as ever. Indeed, with modern-day technology making it ever easier to keep large fish in aquaria, this species—which is available in numerous color forms and even in a long-finned variety—could be on its way to becoming even more popular.

Other common names: Peacock-eye, Velvet Cichlid

Distribution: Amazon, Orinoco and Paraguay River basins.

Size: Up to 13³/₄in (35cm) reported, but usually smaller.

Behavior: Territorial, especially when paired up for breeding. At other times, relatively tolerant of other equally robust species.

Diet: All large foods accepted.

Aquarium: Large, with good cover and ample, open swimming areas. Plants must be robust and protected (by making the area around the base of the stems inaccessible), or artificial. Large rounded/smooth stones and bogwood should make up most of the decor. Water chemistry not critical, but water must be well filtered. Temperature range: 68–77°F (20–25°C).

Breeding: A strong bond is established between the pair after numerous "trials of strength," after which the pair remains loyal. Broods of around 1,000 eggs are laid on a precleaned site. Eggs and young are protected by the parents.

Above: Wild form.
Left: Plain Red Blackfin.
Opposite: Tiger.

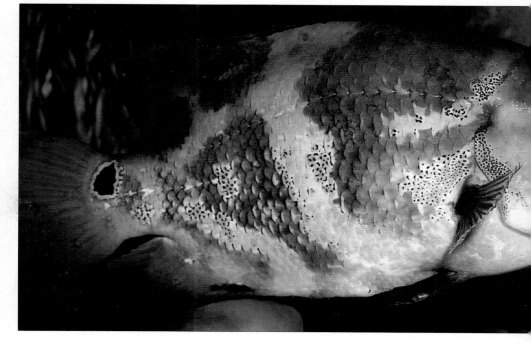

Left: Big-spot Wild form.
Far left: Wild form.
Below: Marble.
Right: Plane Gray Blackfin.
Below right: Albino.

Yellow Peacock

Aulonocara baenschi

Other common names:
Sunshine/Nkhomo-
Benga/Baensch's Peacock,
Aulonocara Benga

Distribution: Around
Nkhomo Reef in Lake
Malawi.

Size: Males around 3½in
(9cm) in the wild, but can
grow larger in aquaria;
females smaller.

Behavior: Territorial, but
relatively peaceful toward
other fishes.

Diet: Livefoods and
commercial diets accepted.

Aquarium: Properly
constructed backgrounds
that reach almost to the
water surface, with plenty
of boltholes. Must be
well lit and well filtered.
Medium-hard, alkaline
water required. Temperature
range: 72–77°F (22–25°C).

Breeding: Typical maternal
mouthbrooder (see
Astatotilapia burtoni).

Two of this species' common names, Yellow Peacock and Sunshine
Peacock, accurately describe the resplendent colors of males in full
breeding condition. There are at least three different color morphs—
the blue-yellow is the one that is bred most often. Females, however,
are relatively drab.

Butterfly Peacock

Aulonocara jacobfreibergi

Other common name:
Malawi Butterfly

Distribution: Widely
distributed in Lake Malawi.

Size: Males up to 5in (13cm)
in the wild, but can grow
larger in aquaria; females
considerably smaller.

Behavior: Territorial and
aggressive toward other
conspecific males (i.e. males
of the same species); more
tolerant of other species.

Diet: Predominantly livefood
based, but will also take
some commercial
formulations, particularly
deep-frozen diets.

Aquarium: Properly
constructed backgrounds
that reach almost to the
water surface, with plenty
of boltholes. Must be
well lit and well filtered.
Medium-hard, alkaline
water required. Temperature
range: 72–77°F (22–25°C).

Breeding: Maternal
mouthbrooder, but male
does not dig a pit; attracts
females to his cave instead.

Although the base body color of males is blue, individuals differ in
patterning and fin coloration, depending on locality. However, all are
brilliantly colored when in full breeding regalia. The male is larger than
the female, with long pelvic fins. Its dorsal and anal fins are pointed.
Females have a red stripe on the dorsal fin.

Pastel Cichlid

Callochromis pleurospilus

Other common name:
Redspot Callochromis

Distribution: Shallow water throughout Lake Tanganyika.

Size: Up to 6in (15cm).

Behavior: Active shoaler and digger that should be kept in small groups.

Diet: Sinking formulations and livefoods preferred.

Aquarium: Shelter, plus ample sandy areas, must be provided. Medium-hard, alkaline, well-filtered water recommended. Temperature range: 73–77°F (23–25°C).

Breeding: Maternal mouthbrooder. Males excavate pits to which they attract females.

This interesting and attractive slender fish is one of the sand-sifting African Rift Lake cichlids that have become progressively more widely available from the early 1990s onward. Although they vary significantly in color, most male Pastel Cichlids have a light green and pinkish metallic sheen to each of the scales on the sides, and the anal fin is often tinged with pink. The heads of the males are bluish-green, and their lips are bright blue. The females are less spectacular, being plain silver in color.

Peacock Cichlid

Cichla ocellaris

Other common names:
Peacock Bass, Eyespot
Cichlid, Eyespot Bass,
Tucunaré

Distribution: Central and
northern South America.

Size: Up to 24in (60cm); may
be slightly larger in the wild.

Behavior: Aggressive
predator.

Diet: Large livefoods
and commercial diets
(freeze-dried, deep frozen,
pellets, etc.).

Aquarium: Large, with
ample open spaces,
bogwood, and large, robust
plants. Water chemistry not
critical, but water must be
well filtered. Temperature
range: 75–82°F (24–28°C).

Breeding: Difficult in
aquaria. This is a substrate-
spawning species with
typical parental protection.

Although it looks superficially like a bass, *C. ocellaris* is a true cichlid in
every sense. It is a variable species, particularly attractive during its
juvenile phase. It soon outgrows most aquaria. A closely related species,
C. temensis, which is even larger, is also occasionally available.

Brown Cichlid
Cichlasoma portalegrense

Other common names: Brown Acara, Port Cichlid, Port Acara

Synonyms: *Cichlasoma portalegrensis*, *Aequidens portalegrensis*

Distribution: Argentina, Bolivia, Brazil, the Guianas, Paraguay, and Venezuela. However, owing to confusion regarding some lookalikes, e.g. *C. bimaculatum*, *C. dimerus*, and *C. boliviense*, distribution details may be inaccurate.

Size: Up to 6in (15cm), but usually smaller.

Behavior: Peaceful and hardy.

Diet: All foods accepted.

Aquarium: Well planted (with robust plants), with open spaces and flat-topped or smooth-rounded pebbles. Water chemistry not critical, but soft to medium-hard, slightly acid water preferred. Temperature range: 66–79°F (19–26°C).

Breeding: Eggs laid on precleaned site and guarded by both parents who also share in the defense of the fry.

There is still some debate about the identity, as well as the correct spelling, of the species name of this relatively subtly colored but lovely cichlid. The "Acara" part of one of the common names reflects the fact that this fish is still also referred to as *Aequidens portalegrensis* in some quarters.

Haplochromis Quads

Copadichromis mbenjii

Synonym: *Haplochromis quadrimaculatus*

Distribution: Mbenji Island in Lake Malawi.

Size: Males up to 6in (15cm); females smaller.

Behavior: Males territorial, while females and juveniles tend to shoal.

Diet: Wide range of foods accepted, but livefoods preferred.

Aquarium: Properly constructed backgrounds that reach almost to the water surface, with plenty of boltholes. Must be well lit and well filtered. Medium-hard to hard, alkaline water essential. Temperature range: 75–79°F (24–26°C).

Breeding: Males construct semicircular sand nests to which they attract females; female broods eggs orally.

Despite its common name (an abbreviated form of its synonym, *Haplochromis quadrimaculatus*), *Copadichromis mbenjii* is a totally separate species from *C. quadrimaculatus* (whose common name is Haplochromis Mbarule). Unlike the latter, *C. mbenjii* does not migrate and is confined to a very specific area of Lake Malawi. It is also considerably smaller than *C. quadrimaculatus* (which can grow to over 8in/20cm).

Nicaragua Cichlid

Hypsophrys nicaraguensis (previously Copora nicaraguense)

Synonyms: *Cichlasoma nicaraguense, Copora nicaraguensis, Herichthys nicaraguense, Hypsophrys nicaraguensis*

Distribution: Nicaragua and Costa Rica.

Size: Males up to 10in (25cm); females somewhat smaller.

Behavior: Territorial digger, but not overaggressive in sufficiently large aquaria.

Diet: All foods accepted.

Aquarium: Large, with adequate shelter and robust or unpalatable plants (both of which must be protected by making base of stems inaccessible). Water chemistry not critical, but quality must be good. Temperature range: 73–79°F (23–26°C).

Breeding: Eggs are laid in deep pits or in a cave. Egg and fry care usually performed by female, with male guarding territory.

The two main attractions of this species are its rounded head and the body patterning or coloration of both male and female. Males have dark-edged scales toward the back of the body, while females have metallic golden dorsal fins and a more intense coloration. The disadvantages of the species are its large size and its tendency to eat succulent plants.

Two-spot Cichlid

Crenicichla lepidota

Other common name:
Comb Pike Cichlid

Distribution: Brazil and Bolivia.

Size: Occasionally reported up to 18in (45cm), but usually 6–8in (15–20cm).

Behavior: A predator that stalks its prey; can only be kept with fish too large for it to swallow.

Diet: Mainly meat-based, i.e. large livefoods, deep frozen, freeze-dried, etc.

Aquarium: Large, well covered, with open areas and adequate shelter. Water chemistry not critical, but quality must be good. Temperature range: 73–80°F (23–27°C).

Breeding: Quite difficult in aquaria. Eggs, laid on the roof of a cave, are guarded by female while male defends territory.

The genus *Crenicichla* probably contains around 175 or more species. Some of these have yet to be described scientifically, but many are available under a variety of trade names. *Crenicichla lepidota* is one of the most widely encountered species within the hobby, though not the most spectacularly colored.

Striped Pike Cichlid

Crenicichla strigata

Synonym: *Crenicichla lugubris*

Distribution: Brazil.

Size: Up to 15in (38cm).

Behavior: A predator that stalks its prey; can only be kept with fish too large for it to swallow.

Diet: Mainly meat-based, i.e. large livefoods, deep frozen, freeze-dried, etc.

Aquarium: Very large, well covered, with open areas and adequate shelter. Water chemistry not critical, but quality must be good. Temperature range: 73–80°F (23–27°C).

Breeding: Not reported in aquaria, but eggs are probably laid on the roof of a cave and guarded by the female while the male defends territory.

In this species, it is the body patterning in juveniles that is particularly interesting and gives a most striking appearance: in addition to the red and black coloration of the dorsal, caudal, and anal fins set against a fawn-colored background, the juvenile has several thin, black lines running the length of the body.

Blue Flash

Cyprichromis leptosoma

Distribution: Throughout Lake Tanganyika, except the extreme north.

Size: Wild-caught specimens around 3in (8cm); aquarium specimens can grow considerably larger.

Behavior: A generally peaceful, active species, but males show some aggression toward each other.

Diet: Wide range of foods accepted, but livefoods preferred.

Aquarium: Large, open swimming areas and properly constructed backgrounds that reach almost to the water surface, with plenty of boltholes. Must be well lit and well filtered. Medium-hard, alkaline water. Temperature range: 73–77°F (23–25°C).

Breeding: Unusually, spawning takes place in midwater or just under the surface, with female picking up eggs as they begin to sink. Mouthbrooding females will tend to ignore fry once they are released some 3 weeks after spawning.

There are several *Cyprichromis* species available. All are slender bodied and most contain some blue and yellow on their fins and/or bodies. Males are usually brown in color, with bright yellow tips to their pelvic fins, and with blue dorsal and anal fins. The females are more drab, usually gray, with silver markings on the sides of the head. These active fish look at their best when kept in a shoal.

Malawi Blue Dolphin

Cyrtocara moorii

Other common names: Blue Lumphead, Moorii

Distribution: Throughout Lake Malawi.

Size: Up to 9in (23cm) reported, but usually smaller.

Behavior: Usually follows sand-sifting species around; while males show territorial behavior—in that they defend the space around their host—this "territory" is not fixed in the traditional sense.

Diet: Some commercial formulations, e.g. tablets, accepted, but prefers livefoods.

Aquarium: Spacious; properly constructed backgrounds that reach almost to the water surface, with plenty of boltholes. Must be well lit and well filtered. Medium-hard, alkaline water. Temperature range: 72–79°F (22–26°C).

Breeding: Typical maternal mouthbrooder.

The alternative common name of this species, Blue Lumphead, derives from the pronounced "lumphead" (nuchal hump) of mature males, which resembles that of a dolphin. Its distinctively shaped head makes this popular cichlid immediately recognizable. Females also develop the lump, but it may not be quite as pronounced as it is in older males.

Malawi Eye-biter

Dimidiochromis compressiceps

Other common name:
Compressiceps

Distribution: Throughout Lake Malawi and Lake Malombe.

Size: Wild-caught males about 9in (23cm); aquarium-reared specimens slightly larger.

Behavior: Predatory, particularly on small fishes; may be housed with other large species.

Diet: Predominantly carnivorous, requiring livefoods or deep-frozen/freeze-dried formulations.

Aquarium: Large, well-covered with open sandy areas and robust plants; properly constructed backgrounds that reach almost to the water surface, with plenty of boltholes. Must be well lit and well filtered. Medium-hard, alkaline water. Temperature range: 72–80°F (22–27°C).

Breeding: Maternal mouthbrooder; male attracts females to a shallow sand depression.

There's no mistaking the feeding habits of this large cichlid, whose entire body shape and head profile belie its predatory lifestyle. Its common name derives from reports that it has been seen biting other fishes' eyes, possibly in order to blind them before seizing them. Unusually, it is the only predator that is known to eat its prey tail first.

Orange Chromide

Pseudetroplus maculatus (previously Etroplus maculatus)

Distribution: Western India and Sri Lanka.

Size: Up to 4in (10cm), but usually smaller.

Behavior: Generally peaceful.

Diet: All foods accepted; vegetable component recommended.

Aquarium: Well planted, but with open areas and a flat or rounded rock. Although medium-hard, neutral to alkaline freshwater is acceptable, the addition of a teaspoonful of good-quality marine salt to every 1 gallon (4.5 liters) is beneficial for fungus-free egg development, though not for general maintenance. Temperature range: 68–79°F (20–26°C); slightly higher for breeding.

Breeding: Eggs are laid on a precleaned site and defended by both parents who also care for fry and transfer them between pits excavated in the substratum.

Although a golden-orange variety of this species exists, the common name refers to the numerous orange spots that are distributed all over the body of the wild type. A blue-bodied form is also available. Unusually for a cichlid, the Orange Chromide is often found in brackish water in the wild.

Green Chromide

Etroplus suratensis

Other common name:
Banded Chromide

Distribution: India and Sri Lanka.

Size: Up to 18in (45cm) reported, but usually considerably smaller.

Behavior: Somewhat intolerant of its own species, especially during the breeding season. May eat succulent aquarium plants.

Diet: All foods accepted; vegetable component recommended.

Aquarium: Spacious, basically as for *E. maculatus*, but with sturdy, unpalatable plants. Addition of salt (optional for *E. maculatus*) recommended for *E. suratensis*, particularly for breeding purposes. Acclimatization of specimens to freshwater is not difficult. Temperature range: 73–79°F (23–26°C).

Breeding: Eggs are laid on a precleaned site and defended by both parents who also care for fry and transfer them between pits excavated in the substratum.

This is a considerably larger fish than the Orange Chromide. In its native waters, it is regarded as a food fish. Although it is usually reported as inhabiting brackish water, the Green Chromide also occurs in freshwater habitats. Unlike some other cichlids, the species does not display sexual dimorphism—males and females are identical in color, and their body and fin shapes are the same.

Pearl Cichlid

Geophagus brasiliensis

Distribution: Atlantic coastal strip of Brazil, southward to the Río de la Plata, Argentina.

Size: Up to 11in (28cm) reported; usually considerably smaller.

Behavior: Territorial, but somewhat more tolerant than most of its close relatives, particularly of similar-sized tankmates.

Diet: All foods accepted.

Aquarium: Grain size of substratum should be sufficiently fine—at least in some areas—to allow for burrowing. Plants must be protected (by making the area around the base of the stems inaccessible). At least one large flat-topped or smoothly rounded rock should be provided. Water chemistry not critical, but soft-to-medium-hard, slightly acid water recommended. Temperature range: 68–81°F (20–27°C).

Breeding: Eggs are laid on precleaned site, and both they and the fry are defended by the pair.

Geophagus means "eartheater," and this species lives up to its name tag, spending much of its time rooting around the substratum and generally burrowing. It is tolerant of a wide range of water conditions, and has even been collected in oxygen-deficient, algae-laden, partially polluted water.

Jewel Cichlid

Hemichromis bimaculatus

Distribution: Southern Guinea to central Liberia.

Size: Up to 6in (15cm) reported, but usually smaller.

Behavior: Highly territorial, particularly during breeding. At other times, it will tolerate other similar-sized tankmates.

Diet: Wide range of foods accepted.

Aquarium: Well planted, with numerous shelters and at least one flat-topped or smoothly rounded rock. Some plants may need protection (by making the area around the base of the stems inaccessible). Water chemistry not critical but should be well filtered. Temperature range: 70–77°F (21–25°C); higher for breeding.

Breeding: Eggs are laid on a precleaned site and are defended vigorously by both parents who then guard the fry, moving them to previously dug pits.

First imported into Europe before 1910, this species immediately created interest owing to the intense reddish coloration of the males when in full breeding condition. Although it has subsequently been outshone in terms of color by its close relative *H. lifalili* (Lifalili Cichlid), it still remains popular among hobbyists.

Texas Cichlid

Herichthys cyanoguttatus

Other common names: Pearl Cichlid, Río Grande Perch

Synonym: *Herichthys cyanoguttatum*

Distribution: Texas and northern Mexico.

Size: Up to 12in (30cm), but usually smaller.

Behavior: Aggressive and territorial burrower that will uproot plants.

Diet: Wide range of large foods accepted.

Aquarium: Only stout, protected plants are suitable (protection can be achieved by making the area around the base of the stems inaccessible). Large open spaces with shelters should be provided. Water chemistry not critical but well-filtered water important. Temperature range: 59–77°F (15–25°C).

Breeding: Eggs are laid on a precleaned site. Parental care is not as pronounced in this species as in most other cichlids.

Besides its undoubted beauty, the Texas Cichlid is also famous for two other, totally unrelated, reasons. It was one of the first cichlids to be imported into Europe (1902), and it is the northernmost cichlid species known. A similar-looking species, the Blue or Green Texas Cichlid (*H. carpinte*) from Mexico (not Texas!) is sometimes confused with *H. cyanoguttatus*. Other *Herichthys* species are only infrequently encountered in the hobby.

Severum Cichlid

Heros severus

Other common names:
Eyespot Cichlid, Banded
Cichlid

Distribution: Northern
South America, south to
the Amazon basin.

Size: Some wild-caught
specimens reported up to
12in (30cm), but usually
smaller.

Behavior: Territorial but
not overaggressive toward
other medium-size or large
tankmates, except during
breeding.

Diet: Wide range of foods
accepted.

Aquarium: Spacious, with
substantial plants, shelters,
and at least one flat-topped
or smoothly rounded rock.
Water chemistry not critical,
but soft, acid, well-filtered
water recommended.
Temperature range: 73–77°F
(23–25°C); slightly higher for
breeding.

Breeding: Eggs are laid on a
precleaned site and are
defended——as are the fry——
by both parents. This species
is sometimes reported as
showing some signs of
mouthbrooding.

The Severum is an old favorite (first imported in 1909) that has held its
own against strong competition from other species. The species occurs in
three color forms: green, gold, and blue-green. The wild form is usually a
brownish green color. About eight or nine vertical bands appear on the
body. They are more pronounced in juveniles, but the band nearest the
caudal fin retains its dark coloration.

Rusty Cichlid

Iodotropheus sprengerae

Synonym: *Petrotilapia tridentiger*

Distribution: Southeastern arm of Lake Malawi.

Size: Around 4in (10cm).

Behavior: Relatively tolerant, even of its own species (in a sufficiently roomy aquarium).

Diet: Wide range of foods accepted.

Aquarium: Properly constructed backgrounds that reach almost to the water surface, with plenty of boltholes. Must be well lit and well filtered. Medium-hard, alkaline water important. Temperature range: 72–77°F (22–25°C); slightly higher for breeding.

Breeding: Typical maternal mouthbrooder; will breed even when quite small and relatively young (at around 3½ months).

Although some color morphs of this species undoubtedly have a "rusty" element to their body coloration, *I. sprengerae* is, nevertheless, more colorful and variable than its name suggests. This is one of the easier species of African Rift Lake cichlids to keep and breed, and it is therefore often recommended for those entering this branch of the hobby for the first time. A few other *Iodotropheus* species are available but, generally, not as widely as the Rusty Cichlid.

Dickfeld's Julie

Julidochromis dickfeldi

Other common name:
Brown Julie

Distribution: Southwestern part of Lake Tanganyika.

Size: Up to 4in (10cm), but often smaller.

Behavior: Intolerant toward its own species.

Diet: Wide range of foods accepted.

Aquarium: Properly constructed backgrounds with plenty of rock shelters and open sandy areas. Medium-hard, alkaline, well-filtered water important. Temperature range: 72–77°F (22–25°C); slightly higher for breeding.

Breeding: Eggs are laid in a cave, and they and the fry are cared for by both parents.

Unusually for an African Rift Lake species, the various Julies, including *J. dickfeldi*, are not mouthbrooders. This species, together with the Yellow or Ornate Julie (*J. ornatus*) and the Masked or Black-and-white Julie (*J. transcriptus*), are often referred to as the "dwarf" Julies, although the size difference between them and the other two species in the genus is not always as great as their "labels" might suggest.

Fuelleborn's Cichlid

Labeotropheus fuelleborni

Distribution: Throughout Lake Malawi.

Size: Male, wild-caught specimens reported up to 7in (18cm), but usually smaller; females smaller.

Behavior: Males are territorial and aggressive toward both sexes, particularly other males.

Diet: Wide range of foods accepted.

Aquarium: Roomy, with numerous caves and shelters. Should be well lit. Robust plants may be added, as well as at least one flat-topped rock. Medium-hard, alkaline, well-filtered water important. Temperature range: 70–77°F (21–25°C); slightly higher for breeding.

Breeding: Eggs are laid on a flat surface or inside a cave and are incubated orally by female.

This exceptionally variable species is restricted to shallow, wave-washed habitats. Many morphs are available, both wild-caught and captive-bred ones. Males of the species have yellow egg-shaped markings on their anal fins, and females are marbled in color. Both have a distinctive snout, shaped like a fleshy growth above the mouth.

Labidochromis Electric Yellow

Labidochromis caeruleus

Other common names:
Labidochromis
Yellow/White/Blue;
Tanganicae

Distribution: Eastern and
western coasts of Lake
Malawi.

Size: About 4in (10cm).

Behavior: Nonterritorial, not
aggressive.

Diet: Wide range of foods
accepted, particularly
livefoods.

Aquarium: Properly
constructed backgrounds
that reach almost to the
water surface, with plenty of
boltholes. Must be well lit
and well filtered. Medium-
hard, alkaline, well-filtered
water. Temperature range:
72–77°F (22–25°C).

Breeding: Typical maternal
mouthbrooder; females tend
to incubate their eggs in
caves.

This is yet another variable, rock-dwelling cichlid (mbuna), the actual
coloration and body patterning depending on locality. Some specimens
(e.g. from Kakusa), have brilliant yellow bodies, while others (e.g. from
Nkata Bay) are blue, making them appear to be distinct species. However,
both have a characteristic black band running the whole length of the
dorsal fin.

Ocellated Shelldweller

Lamprologus ocellatus

Other common names:
Golden Lamprologus,
Red Lamprologus

Distribution: Throughout
Lake Tanganyika.

Size: Around 2¹/₂in (6cm).

Behavior: Territorial, but—
owing to the relatively small
area defended (around an
empty snail shell)—may be
kept with conspecifics in a
roomy aquarium.

Diet: Livefoods preferred.

Aquarium: Properly
constructed backgrounds
with plenty of boltholes.
Must be well lit and well
filtered and include sandy
areas and snail shells.
Medium-hard, alkaline water
important. Temperature
range: 73–77°F (23–25°C).

Breeding: Eggs are laid
inside female's snail shell.
Both eggs and fry are
protected by the parents.

This is one of the smaller African Rift Lake cichlids, which, along with
some of its closest relatives, has become popular owing largely to its
interesting breeding habits (see right). The species has a brown underlying
body coloration, with violet on the sides and a whitish underside. Males
and females of the species are very similar, although males grow
significantly larger.

Auratus Cichlid

Melanochromis auratus

Other common name:
Malawi Golden Cichlid

Distribution: Southern part of Lake Malawi.

Size: Males around 4in (10cm); females a little smaller.

Behavior: Territorial; males are intolerant of rivals; one male should be kept with several females.

Diet: Wide range of commercial diets accepted, but livefoods preferred.

Aquarium: Properly constructed backgrounds with plenty of boltholes. Must be well lit and well filtered. Medium-hard, neutral to alkaline water important. Temperature range: 72–79°F (22–26°C); slightly higher for breeding.

Breeding: Eggs are often laid inside a cave and are incubated orally by female, who also protects the fry.

This was one of the early African Rift Lake cichlids to become established within the hobby. It still remains popular today, particularly owing to the attractive coloration of both males and females. At least two other "Auratus" are available: *Melanochromis* sp. "auratus dwarf" and *M.* sp. "auratus elongate," both from the eastern coast of the lake.

Pearl of Likoma

Melanochromis joanjohnsonae

Synonyms: *Melanochromis exasperatus, M. textilis*

Distribution: Native to Likoma Island near the east coast of Lake Malawi, but has been introduced around Thumbi West Island, located in the southwestern arm of the lake.

Size: Males around 4in (10cm); females a little smaller.

Behavior: Territorial; males are intolerant of rivals.

Diet: Wide range of commercial diets accepted, but livefoods preferred.

Aquarium: Properly constructed backgrounds with plenty of boltholes. Must be well lit and well filtered. Medium-hard, neutral to alkaline water important. Temperature range: 72–79°F (22–26°C); slightly higher for breeding.

Breeding: Spawning may occur in the open, but eggs are often laid inside a cave and are incubated orally by female, who also protects the fry.

As in *Melanochromis auratus*, both male and female *M. joanjohnsonae* are very attractively (though differently) marked. Coloration also varies according to locality. Males have distinctive yellow egg-shaped markings on the anal fin as well as a wide black stripe running the length of the dorsal fin.

Festive Cichlid

Mesonauta festivus

Other common names:
Flag Cichlid, Festivum

Synonym: *Mesonauta festiva*

Distribution: Amazon basin, but may exist elsewhere, e.g. Guyana.

Size: Up to 8in (20cm) reported, but usually smaller.

Behavior: Territorial at breeding time, but otherwise can be timid.

Diet: All foods accepted.

Aquarium: Spacious and well planted, with adequate shelter and at least one flat-topped or smooth, rounded rock. Water chemistry not critical, but soft, slightly acid conditions preferred. Temperature range: 72–77°F (22–25°C); slightly higher for breeding.

Breeding: Eggs are laid on a precleaned site, which can be a broadleaved plant or a rock. Eggs and fry are protected by both parents.

This is an old favorite, first introduced into Europe in 1908 and bred in captivity a year later. Despite this, there is still some doubt regarding the true identity of the species, with a school of thought leaning toward the "*festivus*" from the Río Negro being renamed *M. insignis* and those from other areas being regarded as the "true" *M. festivus*.

Zebra Cichlid

Maylandia.zebra (previously Metriaclima zebra)

Other common name:
Nyasa Blue Cichlid

Synonym: *Pseudotropheus zebra*

Distribution: Widely distributed in Lake Malawi.

Size: Up to 6in (15cm) reported, but usually smaller.

Behavior: Territorial and aggressive, particularly toward its own kind.

Diet: Wide range of foods accepted.

Aquarium: Properly constructed backgrounds with plenty of boltholes. Must be well lit and well filtered. Medium-hard to hard, alkaline, water important. Temperature range: 72–82°F (22–28°C).

Breeding: Typical maternal mouthbrooder.

This is one of the "keystone" species of the African Rift Lake cichlid hobby. Numerous morphs occur in the wild, and male coloration is very different to that of the female. Some of the types are incapable of interbreeding, and this has given rise to the belief that they may constitute separate species, rather than morphs. As a result, the collection of all these intimately related species/morphs is referred to as the "zebra complex." The new name, *Metriaclima*, was erected in 1997 and now includes several new species that would formerly have been regarded as *Pseudotropheus*.

Altispinosa Ram

Mikrogeophagus altispinosus (previously Microgeophagus altispinosus)

Other common names:
Altispinosa Butterfly Cichlid,
Bolivian Butterfly Cichlid

Synonym: *Papiliochromis altispinosus*

Distribution: Eastern Bolivia and Mato Grosso, Brazil.

Size: Males around 3in (8cm); females slightly smaller.

Behavior: Peaceful and tolerant of other tankmates; territorial during breeding.

Diet: Wide range of foods accepted, but livefoods preferred.

Aquarium: Well planted, with adequate shelter, fine-grained substratum, and a flat-topped or rounded rock. Soft, slightly acid to slightly alkaline water recommended. Raw (household) water should be avoided. Temperature range: 72–77°F (22–25°C); slightly higher for breeding.

Breeding: Eggs are laid on a precleaned site and are protected primarily by female. Care of fry (which are often transferred between pits dug by male) is undertaken by both parents.

Slightly larger than its better-known closest relative, the Ram (*M. ramirezi*), this beautiful and variable species also has a particularly striking dorsal fin when it is fully extended. Males have extended top and bottom caudal-fin rays and, generally speaking, brilliantly colored pelvic and anal fins.

Ram

Mikrogeophagus ramirezi (previously Microgeophagus ramirezi)

This spectacular dwarf cichlid has been popular in the hobby for over 50 years, and with good reason. The wild type, in particular, is one of the "jewels" of the aquarium, although many of the cultivated forms, especially the gold, are also extremely attractive. In the late 1990s, a "Jumbo" form of the Ram was introduced. Whether it ever replaces its smaller counterparts, though, only time will tell.

Other common names: Butterfly Dwarf Cichlid, Ramirez's Dwarf Cichlid

Synonym: *Papiliochromis ramirezi*

Distribution: Colombia and Venezuela.

Size: Wild-caught specimens and most cultivated forms up to 2¾in (7cm), but usually smaller; Jumbos somewhat larger.

Behavior: Peaceful and tolerant of other tankmates; territorial during breeding.

Diet: Wide range of foods accepted, but livefoods preferred.

Aquarium: Well planted, with adequate shelter, fine-grained substratum, and a flat-topped or rounded rock. Soft, slightly acid to slightly alkaline water recommended. Raw (household) water should be avoided. Temperature range: 72–77°F (22–25°C); slightly higher for breeding.

Breeding: Eggs are laid on a precleaned site or in a depression in the substratum, and they and the fry are cared for by both parents.

Red Terror

Mesoheros festae (previously Nandopsis festae)

Other common names:
Festa's Cichlid, Tiger Cichlid

Synonyms: *Cichlasoma festae, Herichthys festae*

Distribution: Ecuador.

Size: Fully mature males reported up to 20in (50cm), but usually somewhat smaller; females smaller.

Behavior: Aggressive and territorial; should be kept only with equally large, robust tankmates.

Diet: Large commercial formulations and livefoods accepted.

Aquarium: Spacious, with open spaces and substantial shelters. Rocks and other decor should be well bedded. Plants need to be protected (by making the areas around the base of the stems inaccessible). Water chemistry not critical, but well-filtered, soft, neutral water recommended. Temperature range: 77–82°F (25–28°C).

Breeding: Eggs are laid on a precleaned site (usually a rock). Female guards eggs while male defends territory. Fry are initially moved between predug pits by both parents.

Some of the color forms of this large species are truly stunning, particularly during breeding. Orange-bodied, black- or blue-banded types with iridescent scales are especially striking. Red Terrors are predators and are known to burrow during the spawning period. The common name for the species derives from its aggressive, territorial nature.

Friedrichsthal's Cichlid

Parachromis friedrichsthalii (previously Nandopsis friedrichsthalii)

Synonyms: *Cichlasoma friedrichsthalii, Herichthys friedrichsthalii, Parachromis friedrichsthalii*

Distribution: Widely distributed in Central America.

Size: Up to 13³/₄in (35cm), but usually smaller; females smaller than males.

Behavior: Aggressive and territorial; should be kept only with equally large, robust tankmates.

Diet: Large commercial formulations and livefoods accepted.

Aquarium: Spacious, with open spaces and substantial shelters. Rocks and other decor should be well bedded. Plants need to be protected (by making the base of stems inaccessible). Water chemistry not critical, but well-filtered, soft, neutral water recommended. Temperature range: 72–81°F (22–27°C).

Breeding: Eggs are laid on a precleaned site (usually a rock). Female guards eggs while male defends territory. Fry are initially moved between predug pits by both parents.

A little smaller but somewhat more elongate than *N. festae*, this is another well-marked species whose beauty is best appreciated in fully mature specimens. Color variations occur according to habitat. Males range from light gray, violet, or blue to almost black; some aquarium populations in Europe have females that are bright yellow in color.

Jaguar Cichlid

Parachromis managuensis (previously Nandopsis managuense)

Other common name:
Managua Cichlid

Synonyms: *Cichlasoma managuense, Heros managuense, Herichthys managuensis, Parachromis managuense*

Distribution: Central America.

Size: Some fully mature males reported over 18in (45cm), but usually smaller; females smaller than males.

Behavior: Aggressive and territorial; should be kept only with equally large, robust tankmates.

Diet: Large commercial formulations and livefoods accepted.

Aquarium: Spacious, with open spaces and substantial shelters. Rocks and other decor should be well bedded. Plants need to be protected. Water chemistry not critical, but well-filtered, soft, neutral water recommended. Temperature range: 73–77°F (23–25°C).

Breeding: Eggs are laid on a precleaned site (usually a rock). Female often takes on the major share of fry care and guards eggs while male defends territory. Fry are initially moved between predug pits by both parents.

The common name of this species aptly describes both the coloration and patterning of this impressive cichlid which, like other widely distributed species, occurs in several forms, depending on locality. It is difficult to tell the two sexes apart, although the male tends to be larger and has pointed dorsal and anal fins, while the female is usually the more brightly colored of the two.

Jack Dempsey

Rocio octofasciata (previously Nandopsis octofasciatus)

Synonyms: *Cichlasoma octofasciatum, Cichlasoma biocellatum, Heros octofasciatus*

Distribution: Belize, Guatemala, Honduras, and southern Mexico.

Size: Males to over 8in (20cm); females smaller.

Behavior: Territorial, aggressive burrower; will damage plants.

Diet: Large commercial formulations and livefoods accepted.

Aquarium: Spacious, with open spaces and substantial shelters. Rocks and other decor should be well bedded. Plants need to be protected (by making the area around the base of the stems inaccessible). Water chemistry not critical, but well-filtered, soft, neutral water recommended. Temperature range: 72–77°F (22–25°C).

Breeding: Eggs are laid on a precleaned site (usually a rock). Female guards eggs while male defends territory. Fry are initially moved between predug pits by both parents.

Named after legendary boxer Jack Dempsey, this pugnacious cichlid lives up to its name. However, it is a most attractively marked species that, despite its temperament, is still much sought after. Jack Dempsey's background color is blue. It has a series of white to iridescent blue spots on its median fins, head, and body, and a series of dark bars along its sides.

Salvin's Cichlid

Trichromis salvini (previously Nandopsis salvini)

Other common name:
Tricolor Cichlid

Synonyms: *Cichlasoma salvini, Heros salvini, Herichthys salvini*

Distribution: Guatemala, Honduras, and southern Mexico.

Size: Fully mature males reported over 8in (20cm), but usually smaller; females smaller.

Behavior: Territorial and intolerant of rivals, but may be kept with similar-sized fish. Unlike other members of the genus, does not uproot plants.

Diet: Large commercial formulations and livefoods accepted.

Aquarium: Spacious, with open spaces and substantial shelters. Rocks and other decor should be well bedded. Plants need to be protected. Water chemistry not critical, but well-filtered, soft, neutral water recommended. Temperature range: 72–79°F (22–26°C).

Breeding: Eggs are laid on a precleaned site (usually a rock). Female guards eggs while male defends territory. Fry are initially moved between predug pits by both parents.

This is another spectacularly colored member of the genus. Although it is a substantial fish, the adult coloration begins to develop (particularly in males) while the fish are still modestly sized (i.e. about half the full size). Males and females can be easily distinguished. Females have a patch in the middle of the dorsal fin, and a dark spot is present on the lower edge of the gill cover. Males have pointed fins and brighter coloration.

Golden Dwarf Acara

Nannacara anomala

Other common name:
Golden-eyed Dwarf Cichlid

Distribution: Northern South America and, possibly, French Guiana.

Size: Males up to 3½in (9cm); females much smaller.

Behavior: A peaceful, tolerant species, except during breeding.

Diet: Most commercial formulations accepted, but livefoods preferred.

Aquarium: Heavily planted, with ample shelter and fine-grained substratum recommended. Soft to moderately hard, slightly acid water is best. Temperature range: 72–77°F (22–25°C); slightly warmer for breeding.

Breeding: Eggs are laid in a cave, and both they and the fry are guarded by female, which develops distinctive coloration at this time.

This is a highly variable species whose coloration and patterning both differ between localities. This has led to some doubt regarding its possible presence in French Guiana, with some authorities believing that the fish that are found in this region belong to a separate species, the Goldhead Nannacara (*N. aureocephalus*). A third species, the Adok Nannacara (*N. adoketa*) from the Río Negro in Brazil is also sometimes available to aquarists.

Congo Dwarf Cichlid

Nanochromis parilus

Other common name:
Nudiceps

Synonyms: *Nanochromis parilius, N. nudiceps*

Distribution: Congo basin, particularly Stanley Pool.

Size: Males up to 3in (8cm); females a little smaller.

Behavior: Males are aggressive toward rivals and often toward unreceptive females as well.

Diet: Commercial formulations accepted but livefoods preferred.

Aquarium: Well planted, with numerous shelters and caves. Soft, slightly acid water (preferably filtered through peat or containing a "blackwater" commercial additive) is best. Temperature range: 72–77°F (22–25°C); slightly higher for breeding.

Breeding: Eggs are laid in a cave, and both they and the fry are guarded by female while male generally defends territory.

This species, along with two of its closest relatives, *N. dimidiatus* and *N. transvestitus*, is one of the relatively few dwarf cichlids from Africa (excluding the Rift Lake dwarves) that is fairly widely available in the hobby. Both sexes are beautifully, though differently, colored. Females appear to be full of eggs all the time and possess a pinkish belly flush, which reveals the relationship of this species with the other African dwarves commonly referred to as kribs.

Brevis

Lamprologus brevis (previously Neolamprologus brevis)

Synonym: *Lamprologus brevis*

Distribution: Throughout Lake Tanganyika.

Size: Males up to 2in (5cm); females smaller.

Behavior: Peaceful snail-shell dweller; tolerant of other species.

Diet: Prefers livefoods but will accept other formulations, particularly deep-frozen ones.

Aquarium: Properly constructed backgrounds with sandy areas and one cave and/or large empty snail shell per adult. Must be well lit and well filtered. Medium-hard, alkaline water important. Temperature range: 73–79°F (23–26°C).

Breeding: Eggs are laid in a snail shell. Both parents care for the brood.

This is one of the smallest African Rift Lake cichlids in the hobby. In the wild, it occurs over a sandy substratum and lives in and around an empty snail shell. While not being spectacularly colored, males are very attractive. They have a pronounced orange fringe on the upper edge of the dorsal fin, which is not present in females.

Fairy Cichlid

Neolamprologus pulcher (previously Neolamprologus brichardi)

Other common names:
Lyretail Lamprologus,
Princess of Burundi

Synonyms: *Lamprologus brichardi, Lamprologus elongatus*

Distribution: Throughout Lake Tanganyika.

Size: Around 4in (10cm).

Behavior: Peaceful shoaler; can therefore be kept in a group.

Diet: Wide range of commercial formulations accepted, but livefoods preferred.

Aquarium: Properly constructed backgrounds that reach almost to the water surface, with plenty of boltholes. Must be well lit. Well-filtered, medium-hard, alkaline water important. Temperature range: 73–79°F (23–26°C).

Breeding: Eggs are laid inside a cave. Brood care is undertaken largely by female.

This is the most widely available and most commercially bred member of the genus. Several cultivated varieties, including an albino, have been produced, and these now out-sell wild-caught specimens. *Neolamprologus brichardi* is a "must" for anyone interested in African Rift Lake cichlids.

Lemon Cichlid

Neolamprologus leleupi

Synonyms: *Lamprologus leleupi, L. longior*

Distribution: Unevenly distributed along northwestern, western, and eastern coasts of Lake Tanganyika.

Size: Around 4¼in (11cm).

Behavior: May be aggressive toward members of its own species.

Diet: Wide range of commercial formulations accepted, but livefoods preferred.

Aquarium: Properly constructed backgrounds that reach almost to the water surface, with plenty of boltholes. Must be well lit. Well-filtered, medium-hard, alkaline water important. Temperature range: 73–79°F (23–26°C).

Breeding: Eggs are laid inside a cave. Brood care is undertaken largely by female; it is advisable to remove male after spawning, leaving female to care for her brood in peace.

In terms of color, no other *Neolamprologus* can match the Lemon Cichlid. The intensity of the yellow coloration can vary between "true" lemon yellow, through more golden shades to almost goldish brown or burnished gold.

NOTE: This species must not be confused with the similarly named, but differently colored (i.e. non-yellow) Pearlscale Lamprologus (*N. leloupi*). *Neolamprologus leloupi* is also smaller (3in/8cm) and altogether more peaceful.

Five-barred Lamprologus

Neolamprologus tretocephalus

Other common name:
Tret

Synonym: *Lamprologus tretocephalus*

Distribution: Northern half of Lake Tanganyika (*N. sexfasciatus* is found in the southern half).

Size: Around 5½in (14cm).

Behavior: Aggressive toward its own species; only one pair should be kept.

Diet: Livefoods preferred.

Aquarium: Properly constructed backgrounds that reach almost to the water surface, with plenty of boltholes. Must be well lit. Well-filtered, medium-hard, alkaline water important. Temperature range: 73–79°F (23–26°C).

Breeding: Eggs are laid inside a cave and hatch after about 2 days.

This species is superficially similar to *N. sexfasciatus*, but possesses one fewer body bar (five instead of six). Both are spectacular fish in their own right, particularly during their juvenile and subadult stages. Males may be larger than females, with darker fins.

Livingstoni
Nimbochromis livingstonii

Synonyms: *Haplochromis livingstonii, Cyrtocara livingstonii*

Distribution: Throughout Lake Malawi.

Size: Up to 10in (25cm).

Behavior: Predatory; lies on the bottom feigning death and lunges at any swallowable fish that swims up to investigate.

Diet: Large commercial formulations accepted, but prefers livefood.

Aquarium: Properly constructed backgrounds with plenty of boltholes and sandy areas. Must be well lit and well filtered. Medium-hard, alkaline water required. Temperature range: 73–79°F (23–26°C) .

Breeding: Maternal mouthbrooder.

This relatively large cichlid species is exceptionally marked. In particular, the brown body patches on a light-colored base, coupled with the red tinge of the anal fin of males, make it a striking fish even among more spectacularly colored species. Livingstoni has an unusual habit of lying on its side on the bottom for long periods, feigning death. This technique allows it to seize any suitable prey that comes along to investigate.

Mozambique Mouthbrooder

Oreochromis mossambicus

Synonyms: *Sarotherodon mossambicus*, *Tilapia mossambica*

Distribution: Eastern Africa, but widely introduced elsewhere.

Size: Fully mature males up to 16in (40cm); females much smaller.

Behavior: Aggressive burrower that destroys (and eats) plants; highly territorial during breeding.

Diet: All large foods accepted; vegetable supplement recommended.

Aquarium: Large, with well-bedded decor or rocks. Well-filtered water. Water chemistry not critical and can range from soft to brackish. Temperature range: 68–74°F (20–24°C); slightly higher for breeding.

Breeding: Male excavates large pit to which he attracts females. After spawning, female incubates the eggs orally and subsequently cares for the fry.

This is a large, tough fish that is able to tolerate a wide range of conditions (even fully marine ones) and will reproduce with great facility and regularity in aquaria. A "red" variety, which is more pink than red, plus several mottled ones, are available. It hybridizes with its close relatives and is widely used as a food fish, as are the two other *Oreochromis* species that are occasionally encountered in the hobby: *O.* (*Sarotherodon*) *galileus* and *O. niloticus*.

Yellow Krib

Wallaceochromis humilis (previously Pelvicachromis humilis)

Synonym:
Pelmatochromis humilis

Distribution: Guinea, Liberia, and Sierra Leone.

Size: Males reported up to 5in (13cm), but usually smaller; females smaller.

Behavior: Generally peaceful, but territorial during breeding.

Diet: Wide range of foods accepted.

Aquarium: Well matured and well planted, with shelters (caves). Soft, acid water recommended. Temperature range: 75–79°F (24–26°C); slightly higher for breeding.

Breeding: Eggs are laid in a cave, and both they and the fry are protected by the female.

The yellow pigmentation indicated in the common name is restricted to the cheek, chest, or belly in males. Females lack this distinctive coloration, but have violet or reddish bellies. At least three naturally occurring color morphs exist. In their natural habitat, Yellow Kribs live in slow-flowing water that is rich in oxygen. Usually placid, they can turn territorial during the spawning period.

Krib

Pelvicachromis pulcher

Other common names:
Kribensis Cichlid, Purple Cichlid

Synonym: *Pelmatochromis pulcher*

Distribution: Nigeria, often in brackish water.

Size: Males up to 4in (10cm), but usually smaller; females smaller.

Behavior: Territorial at breeding time, but usually peaceful toward other species.

Diet: Wide range of foods accepted.

Aquarium: Well planted, with adequate shelters (caves) and an open swimming area. Good-quality water important; medium-hard, slightly acid water recommended. Temperature range: 75–79°F (24–26°C); slightly higher for breeding.

Breeding: Eggs are laid on the roof of a cave, and both they and the fry are guarded by female; male defends territory, though he will also participate in fry care.

This old favorite is perhaps the most popular of all the African cichlids, with the possible exception of some of the Rift Lake species. It is a colorful, though variable, species in which the females always appear to be full of eggs and exhibit a particularly striking, reddish belly patch (not so pronounced in males). A well-matched pair make excellent parents. A large morph (possibly a separate species), usually referred to as *Pelvicachromis cf. pulcher* (Giant), is also available.

Peten Cichlid

Petenia splendida

Other common names:
Giant Cichlid, Bay/Red Snook

Distribution: Belize, Guatemala, Nicaragua, and southern Mexico.

Size: Up to 20in (50cm) reported, usually smaller; females smaller than males.

Behavior: Adults territorial and aggressive; should be kept only with similar species.

Diet: Large commercial formulations accepted, but livefoods preferred.

Aquarium: Spacious, with robust, well-bedded decor, caves, and large rocks. Well-filtered, medium-hard, slightly alkaline water advisable. Temperature range: 71–77°F (22–25°C); slightly higher for breeding.

Breeding: Large numbers of eggs are laid on a precleaned site, and both they and the fry are protected by the parents.

Juveniles of this species, which is one of the larger cichlids, are occasionally available in the hobby. While these specimens may appear attractive, the real beauty of the Peten Cichlid is fully appreciated only in mature fish. As well as the more usual silver-gray morph, an orange morph occurs. Peten Cichlids were first introduced to the United States in 1975.

Deepwater Hap

Placidochromis electra

Synonyms: *Haplochromis electra, H. jahni*

Distribution: Eastern coast of Lake Malawi, from Hai Reef southward to Makanjila Point, taking in Likoma Island.

Size: Around 6³/₄in (17cm).

Behavior: More peaceful and less territorial than many of its closest relatives.

Diet: Wide range of commercial formulations.

Aquarium: Properly constructed backgrounds with plenty of boltholes and sandy areas. Must be well lit and well filtered. Medium-hard, alkaline water important. Temperature range: 75–79°F (24–26°C).

Breeding: Spawning tubes, i.e. lengths of plastic piping, placed either on sand or on a rock, with female subsequently picking up eggs and incubating them orally.

This species is relatively easy to distinguish from other blue Rift Lake cichlid species by its two dark patches, one extending from the eye down to the throat area, and the other located on the "shoulder." The males, which grow considerably larger than the females, are much more colorful, exhibiting a more intense blue coloration.

Fenestratus

Protomelas fenestratus

Synonym: *Haplochromis fenestratus*

Distribution: Throughout Lake Malawi.

Size: Around 6in (15cm).

Behavior: Territorial but not overaggressive.

Diet: Wide range of foods accepted, but livefoods preferred.

Aquarium: Properly constructed backgrounds with plenty of boltholes and sandy areas. Must be well lit. Well-filtered, medium-hard, alkaline water important. Temperature range: 75–79°F (24–26°C).

Breeding: Males construct sand nests to which they attract females; female incubates eggs orally.

Also known in the trade as *Haplochromis steveni* "Thick Bars," this is one of several *Protomelas* species available, some of which are still awaiting scientific description. Male Fenestratus are the more brightly colored of the sexes, with the females having a more inconspicuous gray to silver coloration.

Egyptian Mouthbrooder

Pseudocrenilabrus multicolor

Synonyms:
Haplochromis multicolor,
Hemihaplochromis
multicolor

Distribution: From Lower
Nile basin southward to
Uganda and Tanzania (as
far as Lake Victoria).

Size: Up to 3in (8cm);
females smaller than males.

Behavior: Generally (but not
invariably) peaceful and
tolerant; territorial during
breeding.

Diet: All foods accepted.

Aquarium: Well planted,
with sandy bottom,
swimming areas, and
adequate shelter (caves).
Turbulent water conditions
should be avoided. Floating
plants recommended to
provide subdued lighting
conditions underwater.
Water chemistry not critical
as long as extremes are
avoided. Temperature range:
68–79°F (20–26°C).

Breeding: Eggs are laid
either in a depression dug
by male or on a rock, and
are picked up by female;
female incubates eggs orally
and subsequently protects
the fry.

This interesting species was first imported into Europe as far back as 1902.
It once enjoyed enormous popularity owing to its breeding habits—the
female not only broods the eggs in her mouth, but offers the fry protection
by signaling for them to take shelter in her gaping mouth in case of
danger. However, the popularity of the Egyptain Mouthbrooder has since
been overtaken by more colorful species, particularly from the African
Rift Lakes.

South African Mouthbrooder

Pseudocrenilabrus philander

Other common name:
Dwarf Copper
Mouthbrooder

Synonym:
Hemihaplochromis philander

Distribution: From southern
Africa northward to
Mozambique.

Size: Up to 4¼in (11cm).

Behavior: Territorial and
aggressive, particularly
toward its own kind during
breeding, when burrowing
activities increase.

Diet: All foods accepted.

Aquarium: Well planted,
with sandy bottom,
swimming areas, and
adequate shelter (caves).
Turbulent water conditions
should be avoided. Floating
plants recommended to
provide subdued lighting
conditions underwater.
Water chemistry not critical
as long as extremes are
avoided. Temperature range:
68–79°F (20–26°C).

Breeding: Eggs are laid
either in a depression dug
by male or on a rock, and
are picked up by female;
female incubates eggs orally
and subsequently protects
the fry.

Three subspecies of *P. philander* are generally recognized, with two—
P. p. dispersus and *P. p. philander*—being more regularly available than
the third, *P. p. luebberti*. All require the same aquarium conditions, and
all are well worth keeping. However, to avoid crossbreeding, the three
subspecies should not be kept together.

Aurora Cichlid

Maylandia aurora (previously Pseudotropheus aurora)

Synonyms: *Maylandia aurora, Metriaclima aurora*

Distribution: Lake Malawi: originally around Likoma Island and a short stretch of the eastern coast (between Mara Point and Tumbi Point). Subsequently introduced around Thumbi West Island and Otter Point.

Size: Around 4¹/₄in (11cm).

Behavior: Territorial and aggressive.

Diet: Wide range of foods accepted.

Aquarium: Properly constructed backgrounds that reach almost to the water surface, with plenty of boltholes. Must be well lit and well filtered. Medium-hard, alkaline water important. Temperature range: 75–79°F (24–26°C).

Breeding: Maternal mouthbrooder.

At the present time, all three scientific names above are in use for species that, like the impressive Aurora Cichlid, form part of the so-called zebra complex, which includes the Zebra Cichlid (*Metriaclima zebra*) and Kennyi Mbuna (*Pseudotropheus lombardoi*). Until the matter is resolved, and for some time to come, both the Aurora Cichlid and the other members of the complex will therefore continue to appear under a variety of names in aquarium literature.

Bumblebee Cichlid

Pseudotropheus crabro

Other common name:
Hornet Cichlid

Distribution: Most of Lake Malawi.

Size: Wild specimens reported up to 4³/₄in (12cm); aquarium specimens may be larger.

Behavior: In the wild, this species is usually associated with the large catfish *Bagrus meridionalis*, which it "serves" as a cleaner. *P. crabro* also feeds on catfish eggs and fry. In the aquarium, males are territorial but not overaggressive.

Diet: Wide range of foods accepted.

Aquarium: Properly constructed backgrounds that reach almost to the water surface, with plenty of boltholes. Must be well lit and well filtered. Medium-hard, alkaline water important. Temperature range: 75–79°F (24–26°C).

Breeding: Maternal mouthbrooder.

This species, beautifully marked in brown and yellow, is not a member of the zebra complex and is thus not included in the *Pseudotropheus/ Maylandia/Metriaclima* debate. This relatively large fish is well named, because its vertical black-and-yellow bands resemble a bumblebee or a hornet—although adult dominant males of the species often appear virtually black.

Kennyi Mbuna

Maylandia lombardoi (previously Pseudotropheus lombardoi)

Synonyms: *Maylandia lombardoi, Metriaclima lombardoi*

Distribution: Mbenji Island and Nkhomo Reef in Lake Malawi.

Size: Around 4¼in (11cm).

Behavior: Territorial and aggressive.

Diet: Wide range of foods accepted.

Aquarium: Properly constructed backgrounds that reach almost to the water surface, with plenty of boltholes. Must be well lit and well filtered. Medium-hard, alkaline water important. Temperature range: 75–79°F (24–26°C).

Breeding: Maternal mouthbrooder.

In this zebra complex species, males, while varying in coloration, are orange/yellow, with or without vertical dark bands. They also have a yellow egg-shaped spot on the anal fin. Females are pale metallic blue with dark vertical bands, and brood their eggs in their mouths.

Eduard's Mbuna

Chindongo socolofi (previously Pseudotropheus socolofi)

This is one of a number of species that are named after someone, in this case Ross Socolof. However, some writers believe that the species itself is not valid and that the specimens collected from the wild are crosses between an undescribed species from Mozambique, which was introduced into the area where "*socolofi*" is now found, and one or more of the resident species.

Distribution: Central eastern coast of Lake Malawi from Tumbi Point to Cobue; fish reported from elsewhere, e.g. Thumbi West Island in the extreme southwest of the lake, are likely to be the result of the introductions that give rise to the doubt regarding the validity of the species.

Size: Aquarium specimens up to 4³/₄in (12cm); wild-caught fish usually smaller.

Behavior: Territorial, but one of the more peaceful mbunas.

Diet: Wide range of foods accepted.

Aquarium: Properly constructed backgrounds that reach almost to the water surface, with plenty of boltholes. Must be well lit and well filtered. Medium-hard, alkaline water important. Temperature range: 75–79°F (24–26°C).

Breeding: Maternal mouthbrooder.

Altum Angel

Pterophyllum altum

Other common names:
Deep-finned Angel, Long-finned Angel

Distribution: Central Río Orinoco, partly in Colombia and partly in Venezuela.

Size: Up to c.10in (25cm) reported, but usually smaller.

Behavior: Territorial, but generally peaceful; will nevertheless consume very small fishes.

Diet: A wide selection of foods accepted, but livefoods preferred; vegetable supplement recommended.

Aquarium: Deep, with tall plants and noncalcareous rock decorations or, preferably, bogwood; subdued lighting advisable. Excellent water quality essential, but filtration should not cause excessive turbulence. Soft, acid water important. Temperature range: 75–84°F (24–29°C).

Breeding: Challenging and only occasionally achieved in aquaria. Eggs are usually laid on a vertical service, e.g. on Amazon Swordplant (*Echinodorus* sp.), and both they and the fry are cared for by the pair.

While the Angel (*Pterophyllum scalare*) has been known for well over 100 years, the Altum Angel was imported into Europe for the first time only in 1950. Despite its overall similarity to its better-known relative, the Altum is easily distinguished by its much deeper (taller) size, especially when its dorsal and anal fins are extended. A further difference is that while *P. scalare* breeds with great ease in aquaria, *P. altum* is extremely challenging in this respect.

Angel

Pterophyllum scalare

Other common name:
Scalare

Distribution: Widely distributed in the Amazon basin, from Peru to the mouth of the Amazon River at Belém. Also found in many tributaries and in northeast South America.

Size: Around 6in (15cm); occasionally larger.

Behavior: Territorial but not aggressive, though very small fish may be regarded as food.

Diet: Wide range of foods accepted, but livefoods preferred; vegetable supplement recommended.

Aquarium: As for Altum Angel (*P. altum*), but temperature range: 75–82°F (24–28°C).

Breeding: Easy. Eggs are usually laid on a vertical surface, e.g. on an Amazon Swordplant (*Echinodorus* sp.) and are protected, as are fry, by both parents. After hatching, the fry feed on body mucus ("milk") secreted by the parents.

This is by far the best known of the angel species. It is also one of the most popular of all aquarium fish. It was first imported into Europe in 1909 and, since then has been bred extensively in captivity. Captive breeding has led to the development of numerous fin and color varieties. The vast majority of specimens available in shops come from this source, with wild-caught specimens catering primarily for the specialist market.

Left: Bright Veiltail.
Right: Bicolor Marble.

Above left, from top: Black Normal Fin; Bicolor Goldenhead Red Wedge; Golden Spotted Koi Angel. **Above:** Leopard.

Three-spot Geophagus

Satanoperca daemon

Other common name:
Three-spot Demonfish

Synonym: *Geophagus daemon*

Distribution: Río Negro (Brazil), Orinoco (Venezuela), and extending into Colombia.

Size: Around 10in (25cm) or even slightly larger.

Behavior: Generally tolerant of other fish despite its size. Constantly digs, so plants need protection.

Diet: Wide range of foods accepted.

Aquarium: Large, with adequate shelter and fine substratum. Protect plants (by making base of stems inaccessible) and use only robust types. Water chemistry not critical, but well-filtered, soft to medium-hard, slightly acid to neutral water recommended. Temperature range: 72–79°F (22–26°C).

Breeding: Very rare in aquaria; believed to be a substrate spawner.

This is a challenging species to rear from young, and even more challenging to breed. As in other members of the genus, the sexes are difficult to tell apart. The male is slightly slimmer and the genital papilla (a tiny projection from the genital aperture during breeding) is pointed, whereas in the female it is rounded.

Jurupari

Satanoperca jurupari

This is the most widely available species in the genus. One of the reasons may be its interesting breeding habits. Although it lacks the distinct body spots of the Three-spot Geophagus (*S. daemon*), *S. jurupari* makes up for it with its beautifully reflective scales. Males and females have similar coloration, but the body of the male is slimmer.

Other common name: Demonfish

Synonym: *Geophagus jurupari*

Distribution: Brazil and Guyana.

Size: Around 10in (25cm).

Behavior: Perhaps the most peaceful in the genus, except during breeding; active burrower.

Diet: Wide range of foods accepted.

Aquarium: Large, with adequate shelter and fine substratum. Plants should be protected by making base of stems inaccessible, and only robust types should be used. Water chemistry not critical, but well-filtered, soft to medium-hard, slightly acid to neutral water recommended. Temperature range: 72–79°F (22–26°C).

Breeding: A "delayed mouthbrooder," the eggs being picked up by the female about one day after laying. From then on, mouthbrooding duties may be shared by both parents.

African Buffalohead

Steatocranus casuarius

Other common names:
African Blockhead, African Bumphead, African Lumphead

Synonym: *Steatocranus elongatus*

Distribution: Lower and central Democratic Republic of the Congo (Zaire).

Size: Fully mature males reported up to 6½in (16.5cm), but usually much smaller; females smaller.

Behavior: Intolerant, particularly of its own kind and other bottom dwellers. Pairs form very strong bond that may last for life.

Diet: Most foods accepted, particularly sinking types.

Aquarium: Numerous caves and other shelters but with no sharp edges (the species tends to rest on rocks or "hop" between them). Well-filtered, slightly acid to neutral, medium-hard water recommended. Temperature range: 75–82°F (24–28°C).

Breeding: Eggs are laid in caves, and they and the fry are guarded by both parents.

All the common names of this species—which is the only *Steatocranus* frequently seen in the hobby—accurately describe the head shape of fully mature males. Females also possess the nuchal (head) hump, but it is much less pronounced than in males. *Steatocranus* is a bottom dweller with limited swimming ability.

Green Discus and Blue Discus

Symphysodon aequifasciatus

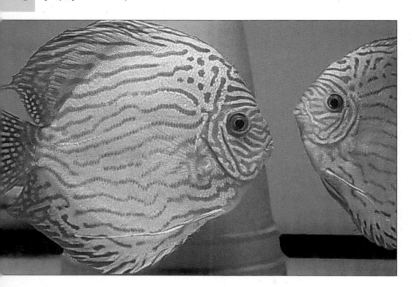

Synonym: *Symphysodon aequifasciata*

Distribution: Widely distributed in tributaries of the Amazon basin.

Size: Reported up to 6in (15cm), but many cultivated varieties can exceed this.

Behavior: Territorial during breeding; generally sedate and peaceful at other times.

Diet: Livefoods preferred, but deep-frozen, freeze-dried, and meat-based formulations, and some dry foods (e.g. flakes) accepted. Commercially produced Discus preparations are available.

The common name for this species derives from its disklike body shape. Traditionally *S. aequifasciatus* has been divided into three subspecies: *S. a. aequifasciatus* (Green Discus), *S. a. axelrodi* (Brown Discus), and *S. a. haraldi* (Blue Discus). This division still applies in most aquarium literature.

In the wild there are four main color forms of *S. aequifasciatus*: green, blue, brown, and a reddish color. Captive breeding over many years—including countless crosses between the naturally occurring forms as well as between

them and the cultivated types—has resulted in a wide range of Discus varieties. More new varieties are created every year, particularly in the Far East.

The tall body shape of these fish means that a tall tank is essential, and they are best kept as a single-species group. During breeding, pairs should be isolated in a tank that includes rocks on which the females can lay their eggs.

Aquarium: Large tall tank thickly planted around the sides and back, with open swimming area at front. If rocks are present, they should be noncalcareous. Water soft and acid—preferably tannin-stained (bogwood will achieve this, as will a peat component in the filter and/or a proprietary "blackwater" preparation). Temperature range: 79–86°F (26–30°C); even slightly higher for breeding.

Breeding: Adhesive eggs are laid on precleaned site—usually vertical or nearly so: broadleaved plants, slates, tall rocks, special Discus-spawning earthenware cones, or even the aquarium panes. Both parents protect eggs, which take about 2–3 days to hatch. The fry then feed for a time on body mucus ("Discus milk") secreted by the parents. Some commercially produced Discus milk preparations are available.

Above right: Blood Pearl.
Below right: Red Turquoise with red background.
Opposite: Red Turquoise with blue background.

Clockwise from bottom left: Turquoise; Green; Brown; Solid Turquoise; Pigeon Blood.

Heckel Discus

Symphysodon discus

Other common name:
Pompadour

Distribution: Río Negro tributaries, Brazil.

Size: Up to 8in (20cm).

Behavior: Territorial during breeding; generally sedate and peaceful at other times.

Diet: Livefoods preferred, but deep-frozen, freeze-dried, and meat-based formulations, and some dry foods (e.g. flakes) accepted. Special, commercially produced Discus preparations are available.

Aquarium: Large, thickly planted around sides and back, with open swimming area at front. Any rocks should be noncalcareous. Water soft and acid— preferably tannin-stained (bogwood will achieve this, as will a peat component in the filter and/or a proprietary "blackwater" preparation). Temperature range: 79–86°F (26–30°C); even slightly higher for breeding.

Breeding: As for *S. aequifasciatus,* but successful spawning is more difficult to achieve in aquaria.

Heckel Discus—whatever their place of origin and body coloration or patterning—can generally be distinguished from *S. aequifasciatus* by the central (fifth) vertical body band that extends from the base of the dorsal fin to the anal fin. In *S. discus* the band is nearly always wider than the other bands and much more prominent, while in *S. aequifasciatus* all the body bands tend to be more-or-less equally wide and prominent. Some breeders have found the prominent band of *S. discus* "distracting," and as a result it has not been as widely bred or developed in captivity as *S. aequifasciatus*. A subspecies, the so-called Pineapple Discus (*S. d. willischwartzi*), is sometimes cited. Most authorities, however, believe it to be a form of *S. discus* and not a valid subspecies.

Aureum Cichlid

Thorichthys aureus

Other common name:
Guatemala Gold Cichlid

Synonym: *Herichthys aureus*

Distribution: Belize, Guatemala, and Honduras.

Size: Fully mature males over 6³/₄in (16cm); females smaller.

Behavior: Territorial, particularly during breeding —but not overaggressive toward other similar-sized species.

Diet: Wide range of foods accepted.

Aquarium: Roomy, well planted, with ample shelter, open swimming area, and fine-grained substratum. A flat or rounded rock should be provided. Neutral or alkaline, medium-hard water recommended. Temperature range: 70–77°F (21–25°C); slightly higher for breeding.

Breeding: Eggs are laid on precleaned site, and both they and the fry are defended by the parents.

When fully colored, mature males of this species are perhaps the most beautiful of all *Thorichthys*, though they lack the brilliant red of *T. meeki*. The body coloration is generally white or silvery gray, and males have a long hairlike extension at the end of their dorsal fins.

Firemouth

Thorichthys meeki

Synonym: *Herichthys meeki*

Distribution: Guatemala and Yucatán region in Mexico.

Size: Males up to 6in (15cm); females smaller.

Behavior: Territorial, particularly during breeding —but not overaggressive toward other similar-sized species.

Diet: Wide range of foods accepted.

Aquarium: Roomy, well planted, with ample shelter, open swimming area, and fine-grained substratum. A flat or rounded rock should be provided. Neutral or alkaline, medium-hard water recommended. Temperature range: 70–77°F (21–25°C); slightly higher for breeding.

Breeding: Eggs are laid on precleaned site, and both they and the fry are defended by the parents.

The Firemouth is by far the best-known *Thorichthys* species in the hobby, having been first imported into Europe in 1937. The "fire" from which the common name derives is not restricted to the mouth, but extends to the throat, cheeks, and all along the lower area of the body, as far as the caudal fin, making it a most impressive species indeed.

Five-spot Tilapia

Coptodon mariae (previously Tilapia mariae)

Other common name:
Tiger Tilapia

Distribution: Benin, Cameroon, Ghana, and Ivory Coast.

Size: Up to 13³/₄in (35cm) reported.

Behavior: Juveniles are relatively peaceful shoalers. Adults highly territorial and aggressive; may be kept only with similar-sized, robust tankmates.

Diet: All substantial foods accepted.

Aquarium: Spacious, with large shelters, open swimming space, and at least one large flat or smooth rock. Use only unpalatable or artificial plants. Well-filtered water important, but water chemistry not critical. Temperature range: 72–77°F (22–25°C); slightly higher for breeding.

Breeding: Eggs are laid on precleaned site and transferred to predug pits. Both parents guard eggs and fry.

Juvenile *T. mariae* are strikingly marked with vertical dark and light bands; they also shoal. As they grow, though, the bands become reduced to blotches, which end up running as a horizontal line from behind the gill cover to the base of the caudal fin. Specimens also become progressively more aggressive as they mature.

Elongatus Mbuna

Chindongo elongatus (previously Tropheops elongatus)

Other common name:
Slender Mbuna

Synonym: *Pseudotropheus "elongatus"*

Distribution: Probably Mbamba Bay in the Tanzanian section of Lake Malawi. Various "elongatus" occur elsewhere in the lake.

Size: Around 4³/₄in (12cm).

Behavior: Generally aggressive and territorial but not always so.

Diet: Wide range of foods accepted; vegetable component advisable.

Aquarium: Properly constructed backgrounds that reach almost to the water surface, with plenty of boltholes. Must be well lit and well filtered. Medium-hard, alkaline water important. Temperature range: 73–79°F (23–26°C).

Breeding: Maternal mouthbrooder.

There are so many different types of naturally occurring "elongatus" that it is difficult to identify any particular one as being the true "elongatus." Perhaps the specimens from around Mbamba Bay will eventually fill this niche. Similar "fluidity" applies to the generic name, with *Tropheops* becoming more widely accepted as a full genus (following the recommendation of Ethelwyn Trewavas in 1984), rather than as a subgenus of *Pseudotropheus*. However, both names appear widely in aquarium literature.

Above: Mbenji Blue.
Left: Luhuchi.
Below left: Mpanga.

Duboisi

Tropheus duboisi

Other common name:
White-spotted Cichlid

Distribution: Discontinuous in the northern half of Lake Tanganyika.

Size: Around 5in (13cm).

Behavior: Regarded as the most peaceful member of its genus, but can be territorial and sometimes aggressive toward rivals.

Diet: Predominantly vegetable diet.

Aquarium: Properly constructed backgrounds with plenty of boltholes and sandy areas. Must be well filtered and have good illumination to encourage growth of encrusting green algae. Medium-hard, alkaline water important. Temperature range: 73–81°F (23–27°C).

Breeding: Maternal mouthbrooder, with eggs being laid in the open and immediately picked up by female.

The white spots referred to in the alternative common name of this popular species occur in juveniles, which carry the numerous spots on an almost black background body color. Adults—which are very differently colored to the juveniles—occur in a number of color forms, a reflection of the discontinuous distribution of the species in its natural habitat.

Moorii

Tropheus moorii

Distribution: Southern half of Lake Tanganyika.

Size: Up to 6in (15cm) reported.

Behavior: Relatively peaceful member of its genus, but can be territorial and sometimes aggressive toward rivals.

Diet: Predominantly vegetable diet.

Aquarium: Properly constructed backgrounds with plenty of boltholes and sandy areas. Must be well filtered and have good illumination to encourage growth of encrusting green algae. Medium-hard, alkaline water important. Temperature range: 73–81°F (23–27°C).

Breeding: Maternal mouthbrooder, with eggs being laid in the open and immediately picked up by female.

This species is very similar in overall body shape to the Duboisi (*T. duboisi*). It is, however, even more variable—with many different color morphs, ranging from yellow to brown to blue to deep purple—and occurs in a different part of Lake Tanganyika.

Uaru Cichlid

Uaru amphiacanthoides

Other common names:
Waroo Cichlid, Triangle Cichlid

Distribution: Northern Amazon and Guyana.

Size: Up to 12in (30cm), but usually smaller.

Behavior: Quite peaceful despite its size; likes to shoal.

Diet: Some commercial dry foods accepted, but prefers livefoods and deep-frozen or freeze-dried diets; juveniles welcome a vegetable component.

Aquarium: Roomy, with ample cover around sides and back, large, open swimming area at front, subdued lighting, and large shelters. Use only robust aquarium plants. Soft, acid, tannin-stained water (bogwood, peat filtration, or commercial "blackwater" preparation will achieve this) recommended. Temperature range: 77–82°F (25–28°C); even slightly higher for breeding.

Breeding: Challenging to achieve in aquaria. Eggs are laid on precleaned site and are protected, as are the fry, by both parents. Both produce "body milk" on which the fry feed during the early stages of their development.

The last of the common names derives from the shape of this species' body patch, which is dark and roughly triangular, with the triangle's apex pointing toward the tail. The sharpness of the shape, as well as its "triangularity," varies among individuals. In its native waters, the Uaru is generally regarded as a food fish. Juveniles look quite different than adults, exhibiting numerous light body spots.

Black-belt Cichlid

Vieja maculicauda

Synonyms: *Cichlasoma maculicauda, Herichthys maculicauda, Heros maculicauda*

Distribution: Widely distributed in Central America.

Size: Fully mature males reported up to 16in (40cm), but usually smaller; females smaller.

Behavior: Not overaggressive given its territorial instincts and large size. Shows a distinct liking for succulent vegetation.

Diet: Wide range of large aquarium foods accepted; vegetable component recommended.

Aquarium: Large, with sizable shelters (caves, bogwood, etc.) and at least one flat or smooth rock. Well-filtered water important, but water chemistry not critical as long as extremes are avoided. Use only unpalatable or artificial plants. Temperature range: 72–79°F (22–26°C).

Breeding: Eggs are laid on precleaned site and are protected, as are the fry, by both parents.

The Black-belt Cichlid is an old favorite. It is easily distinguished by its prominent vertical central-body band, from which the common name derives. This band runs from the center of the dorsal fin right down to the belly, although its breadth and sharpness vary from specimen to specimen and according to the individual's mood.

Quetzal

Vieja melanura (previously Vieja synspilum)

Other common name:
Firehead Cichlid

Synonyms: *Cichlasoma synspilum, Herichthys synspilus, Heros synspilus, Paratheraps synspilum*

Distribution: Widely distributed in Central America.

Size: Fully mature males up to 16in (40cm), but usually smaller; females smaller.

Behavior: Relatively peaceful toward other similar-sized fish but not its own kind. Territorial, particularly during breeding.

Diet: Wide range of large aquarium foods accepted; vegetable component recommended.

Aquarium: Large, with sizable shelters (caves, bogwood, etc.) and at least one flat or smooth rock. Well-filtered water important, but water chemistry not critical as long as extremes are avoided. Use only unpalatable or artificial plants. Temperature range: 72–79°F (22–26°C).

Breeding: Eggs are laid on precleaned site and are protected, as are the fry, by both parents.

This is a large multicolored cichlid in which mature males develop a pronounced head (nuchal) hump; females possess a more modestly sized version. Spawning this species is not particularly difficult; obtaining a compatible pair is difficult. The usual advice given is to obtain about six juveniles and grow them on, allowing a natural pair to select themselves. Suitable alternative accommodations must, however, be found for the remaining unpaired fish as they are unlikely to be tolerated within the chosen pair's territory.

Yellow-finned Xenotilapia

Xenotilapia flavipinnis

Distribution: Throughout Lake Tanganyika.

Size: Around 3¹/₂in (9cm).

Behavior: Peaceful, though males will defend spawning site; may be kept as a shoal in a roomy aquarium.

Diet: Range of commercial diets, particularly sinking formulations, accepted, but livefood and deep-frozen/freeze-dried foods preferred.

Aquarium: Properly constructed backgrounds with plenty of boltholes and sandy areas. Well-filtered, well-oxygenated, medium-hard, alkaline water important. Temperature range: 73–81°F (23–27°C).

Breeding: Mouthbrooding is shared by both parents, with female incubating eggs and fry for around 9 days. Male then takes over mouthbrooding duties for a further 5–6 days. While the fry are in the open, both parents share protective duties.

This species is often available under the trade name Xenotilapia Boulengeri. Members of the genus prefer life close to the bottom, especially over sandy or muddy areas. They are active diggers, particularly at breeding time, and may be harassed by some of the more aggressive African Rift Lake cichlid species.

CATFISH

Family Cichlidae

Despite the diversity of size, body shape, and habit that they exhibit, catfish are one of the easiest groups of fish to identify since they all have catlike "whiskers" (known as barbels). Usually there are four pairs of these sensory structures: one on the head, one on the upper jaw, and two on the chin. Some types of catfish have reduced barbels, while others may lack one or more pairs (but never all four).

It is a combination of features rather than a single one that identifies a species as a catfish. However, most of the features are skeletal and not directly observable in living specimens. Among them is the "Weberian apparatus," a remarkable bony structure that links the swimbladder with the inner ear. The Weberian apparatus helps catfish pick up sounds from the surrounding environment by accentuating sound waves. This is particularly important for species that live in turbid water, which characterizes many catfish habitats. By combining the benefits rendered by the Weberian apparatus with sensory information given by the barbels, many catfish actually thrive in low-visibility, silt-laden conditions that other fish would find difficult or intolerable.

In some catfish the swimbladder has an extra function: sound production. Some types of catfish use this or other sound-producing mechanisms to such an extent that they have become known in the hobby as talking, squeaking, or croaking catfish, e.g. *Amblydoras hancocki*.

Another characteristic of many catfish is a two-spine locking mechanism on the dorsal fin. The first spine is sometimes so small as to be barely visible to the naked eye, but the second—irrespective of the size of the first one—is always prominent. When a catfish is disturbed, it instinctively extends

Right: *Hypostomus* sp.

Left: *Corydoras sterbai.*

toxicity produced by venomous glands adds to the dangers of being stung. The Asian Stinging Catfish (*Heteropneustes fossilis*) is more aggressive and will actively seek out victims. Its sting is extremely painful and may have serious consequences. Even more potent is the venom of the marine catfish in the genus *Plotosus* whose sting can be fatal.

the dorsal fin, causing the first spine to lock the second one into its upright position. Combined with extended spines on other fins and the tough scales (scutes) or body armor that many species possess, this acts as an effective defensive strategy and makes many catfish difficult prey for predators. In a number of species fin spines are not just physical defensive structures, but chemical (venomous) ones as well. In these species it is the pectoral fin spines that are usually important. Catfish species that can inflict injury via their spines are known as passive stingers—they do not actively seek out a vitcim but they extend their protective spines if they are threatened in any way Careful handling of aquarium specimens is therefore absolutely essential.

In some of the madtoms (*Noturus* spp.), generally regarded as passive stingers,

In terms of size, catfish probably vary more widely than any other major group of fishes known to aquarists. At one extreme, there are giants such as the Wels Catfish (*Silurus glanis*), which can often attain a length of about 10ft (3m)—and has reportedly been recorded at $16\frac{1}{2}$ft (5m)—and the Giant or Mekong Catfish (*Pangasianodon gigas*), which can grow to over $6\frac{1}{2}$ft (2m). At the other end of the scale, there are tiny species such as the Pygmy Catfish (*Corydoras pygmaeus*), which is fully mature at a mere $1\frac{1}{2}$in (3.5cm).

According to some authorities, there are 34 families of catfish, forming the order Siluriformes. More than 410 genera and 2,400 species are known.

Red Whiptail Catfish

Phractura ansorgii

Other common name:
African Whiptail Catfish

Family: Amphiliidae

Distribution: Nigeria and Togo.

Size: Usually reported as around 2in (5cm), but occasionally larger.

Behavior: Will spend much time resting on plants or aquarium decor.

Diet: A range of foods accepted, including flakes and tablets.

Aquarium: Well planted, with some broadleaved species and pieces of bogwood recommended. Well-oxygenated water and a current (as produced by a power filter or powerhead) should be provided. Water chemistry not critical, but extreme pH and hardness should be avoided. Temperature range: 72–77°F (22–25°C).

Breeding: No documented accounts currently available.

Few Amphiliidae (African hillstream catfishes) are ever found in aquaria. Their natural habitat is fast-flowing vegetated water, and this is reflected in their long, slim body shape. In this species the females are the more strikingly patterned of the sexes, with dark brown bands on the body. These bands are absent in the males, which tend to be pale. However, when ready to breed, the males take on an overall reddish body color.

Silver Shark

Sciades seemanni (previously Arius jordani)

Other common names: Colombian Shark Catfish, High-fin/Black-fin/Silver Shark Catfish

Family: Ariidae

Distribution: Coastal regions of (mainly) Colombia and Peru.

Size: Around 13in (33cm).

Behavior: Not over-aggressive, but will eat small fish.

Diet: Wide range of foods accepted.

Aquarium: Spacious, with ample swimming areas and water current. A small amount of sea salt (about 1 teaspoonful per gallon/4.5 liters) recommended. This can be reduced gradually over time, if desired. Water chemistry not critical. Temperature range: 72–82°F (22–28°C).

Breeding: No documented accounts currently available. All members of the genus are believed to be mouthbrooders.

This is predominantly an estuarine species, but one that can adapt to freshwater conditions if the change is made gradually. Juveniles are more attractive than adults, which, owing to their relatively large size, are unsuitable for community aquaria.

Banjo Catfish
Amaralia hypsiura

Family: Aspredinidae

Subfamily: Bunocephalinae

Distribution: Río Branco (Brazil).

Size: Around 4in (10cm).

Behavior: A peaceful, sedentary species that spends most of the day resting on or buried in the substratum; becomes relatively active as night approaches.

Diet: All sinking formulations, including bottom-dwelling livefoods, accepted.

Aquarium: Numerous shelters (pieces of bogwood are ideal) and fine-grained substratum should be provided. Dry (as opposed to fresh), well-browned oak leaves—presoaked to allow them to sink—should cover at least past of the substratum (retailers may be able to supply some of the leaves that are usually placed in transportation bags by suppliers of these fish). Water chemistry not critical. Temperature range: 70–79°F (21–26°C).

Breeding: No documented accounts currently available.

Species of the genus *Amaralia* are generally so similar that they can be difficult to differentiate from each other. In addition, some are now regarded as *Bunocephalus* and *Disichthys*, creating further confusion. Their main claim to fame is their unusual shape.

Zamora Woodcat

Auchenipterichthys thoracatus

Other common name:
Midnight Catfish

Synonyms: *Auchenipterus thoracatus, Zamora cunchi*

Family: Auchenipteridae

Distribution: Upper Amazon.

Size: Up to 5¼in (13.5cm).

Behavior: Nocturnal; not overaggressive, but predatory on small fish.

Diet: Livefoods preferred, but will accept other diets.

Aquarium: Numerous shelters are required as daytime hiding places. Water chemistry not critical, but extremes of pH and hardness should be avoided. Temperature range: 70–77°F (21–25°C).

Breeding: Challenging in aquaria. Fertilization is internal and the sperm "plug" can remain potent for several months in, at least, some species of the family. Egg deposition can therefore occur some time after mating.

There are only two species in the genus *Auchenipterichthys*, with the Zamora Woodcat being the one seen more frequently in aquaria. It is able to produce a buzzing sound by rotating its pectoral-fin spines in their sockets. The noise is amplified by the swimbladder, which has an elastic spring mechanism that can make it vibrate and emit sounds.

Snowflake Woodcat

Tatia aulopygia

Other common name: Driftwood Catfish

Family: Auchenipteridae

Distribution: Mainly Guaporé River, bordering Brazil.

Size: Around 4in (10cm).

Behavior: Generally sedentary during the day.

Diet: Livefoods preferred, but may accept other diets.

Aquarium: Well planted, with numerous shelters. The water should be well-oxygenated. Water chemistry not critical but extremes should be avoided. Temperature range: 72–79°F (22–26°C).

Breeding: No documented accounts currently available. In a closely related species, *T. galaxias* (Starry Woodcat), fertilization is internal, with the eggs being subsequently released by female, and hatching taking 3–4 days at 72°F (22°C).

There are some 14 species in this genus, all of which are relatively small and easy to distinguish from each other. The Snowflake Woodcat is dark bodied with numerous small creamy-white flecks on its body (hence the "snowflake" part of its common name). In some mature specimens, which may be particularly dark, the "flakes" may almost disappear. In contrast, the belly is white.

Giraffe Catfish

Auchenoglanis occidentalis

Other common names: African Eyespot, Dusky Vacuum-mouthed Catfish

Family: Bagridae

Distribution: Widely distributed in tropical regions of Africa.

Size: Up to 24in (60cm).

Behavior: Peaceful despite its size.

Diet: Wide range of chunky foods taken.

Aquarium: Large, deep, and efficiently filtered, with sandy substratum and large pieces of bogwood. Water chemistry not critical. Temperature range: 72–77°F (22–25°C).

Breeding: No documented accounts currently available.

The Giraffe Catfish—so-called because of the patchworklike body patterning found in many specimens—was first imported into the hobby in 1909. Despite this long history, it has never been kept in large numbers, no doubt because of its large size. Modern aquarium technology and advances in husbandry techniques, however, bring the successful upkeep of this species within the reach of any aquarist who can provide adequate accommodations for this gentle giant.

Mottled Catfish

Chrysichthys ornatus

Other common name:
African Woodcat

Family: Bagridae

Distribution: Widely distributed in tropical regions of West Africa.

Size: Up to c.8in (20cm).

Behavior: Lively; increasingly predatory on small fishes as full size is attained.

Diet: Livefoods preferred; may be weaned on to chunky commercial preparations.

Aquarium: Should be spacious, with suitable cover (bogwood or equivalent) and efficient filtration. Protect plants against uprooting (by making base of stems inaccessible). Water chemistry not critical. Temperature range: 68–79°F (20–26°C).

Breeding: No documented accounts currently available.

While there are around 40 species in the genus *Chrysichthys*, few are ever seen in aquaria—*C. ornatus* being one of the exceptions. It is an attractively marked species with sharp dorsal and pectoral fin spines. Careful handling is therefore essential. It is ranked as one of the smaller members of the genus, with some of its larger relatives, such as *C. grandis*, attaining a size of c.6½ft (2m) and a weight of c.420lb (190kg).

Asian Bumblebee Catfish

Pseudomystus siamensis (previously Leiocassis siamensis)

Other common name:
Barred Siamese Catfish

Family: Bagridae

Distribution: Widely distributed in Thailand, sometimes even occurring near estuaries and hence in brackish conditions.

Size: Around 7in (18cm).

Behavior: Largely nocturnal. Not excessively predatory, but may take small fishes; progressively intolerant of its own species.

Diet: Livefoods preferred, but may become accustomed to deep-frozen, freeze-dried, and other commercial preparations.

Aquarium: Adequate bogwood or rock shelters and subdued lighting required. Efficient filtration recommended but water chemistry not critical. Temperature range: 72–77°F (22–25°C).

Breeding: No documented accounts currently available.

This is the most popular and widely available species in the genus— all the members of which are very attractive. Its striking body patterning consists of irregular vertical bars on a yellowish to dark gray background (or occasionally a plain dark body). The markings contrast sharply with its white caudal fin, which bears two rather faint black blotches—one on each lobe.

Bar-tailed Bagrid

Mystus nigriceps (previously Mystus micracanthus)

Other common name:
Two-spot Pink Bagrid

Family: Bagridae

Distribution: Borneo, Java, Sumatra, and Thailand.

Size: Around 6in (15cm).

Behavior: Does well with similar-sized tankmates, but may prey on small fish.

Diet: Some commercial formulations accepted, but livefoods preferred.

Aquarium: Spacious, well filtered, with open swimming areas and hiding places. Water chemistry not critical. Temperature range: 68–79°F (20–26°C).

Breeding: No documented accounts currently available.

Both common names apply equally well to this attractive, modest-sized catfish. Owing to a golden anterior border, the black body spot, in particular, stands out beautifully against the pink body color. When kept under correct aquaria conditions, this fish can turn a beautiful deep red-brown color.

Banded Mystus

Mystus vittatus

Other common name:
Striped Catfish

Family: Bagridae

Distribution: Myanmar (Burma), India, Sri Lanka, Nepal, Malaysia, and Thailand.

Size: Around 8in (20cm).

Behavior: Does well with similar-sized tankmates, but may prey on small fish.

Diet: Some commercial formulations accepted, but livefoods preferred.

Aquarium: Spacious and well filtered, with open swimming areas and hiding places. Water chemistry not critical. Temperature range: 72–82°F (22–28°C).

Breeding: Although it is known that an active courtship, accompanied by "tweeting" noises, culminates in eggs being released among roots or plants, there are no known breeding successes in aquaria.

This species has a similar body color to *M. micracanthus,* but it is overlaid with two distinct darker bands that run from behind a body spot (similar in color to that possessed by *M. micracanthus* but smaller) to the base of the caudal fin. A fainter band is also discernible above the main one.

False Corydoras

Aspidoras pauciradiatus

Other common name:
Blotch-fin Aspidoras

Synonym: *Corydoras pauciradiatus*

Family: Callichthyidae

Subfamily: Corydoradinae

Distribution: Mainly Araguaia River (Brazil), but also reported from the Río Negro.

Size: Up to 1 1/2in (4cm) reported, but usually no larger than 1 1/4in (3cm).

Behavior: A (sometimes) retiring shoaler that should not be kept with boisterous tankmates.

Diet: Wide range of foods accepted.

Aquarium: Well planted, with numerous shelters and fine-grained substratum. Avoid excessive water turbulence but use efficient filtration and well-oxygenated water. Slightly acid to neutral, softish water preferred. Temperature range: 72–79°F (22–26°C).

Breeding: No documented accounts currently available.

Both the first common name and the synonym for this species indicate just how closely *Aspidoras* and *Corydoras* species catfish are related to each other. The main distinguishing skeletal feature between the two—but one that cannot be observed in living specimens—is the number of cranial fontanels (skull pores, openings, or "holes"): *Aspidoras* sp. has two, while *Corydoras* sp. and *Brochis* sp. have one. The False Corydoras is a delightful species, liberally speckled in black and with a distinctive black blotch on the dorsal fin.

Giant Brochis

Corydoras britskii (previously Brochis britskii)

Other common name:
Britski's Catfish

Family: Callichthyidae

Subfamily: Corydoradinae

Distribution: Mainly Mato Grosso, Brazil.

Size: Up to 5in (13cm) reported, but usually a little smaller.

Behavior: Peaceful shoaler that, despite its size, can be kept with small tankmates.

Diet: Wide range of foods accepted.

Aquarium: Roomy, well planted, with open areas as well as hiding places. Substratum fine grained, with no sharp edges on which the fish could damage their mouths and/or barbels. Water chemistry not critical but quality must be good. Temperature range: 72–77°F (22–25°C).

Breeding: No documented accounts currently available.

Brochis species are very similar overall to *Corydoras* species. However, they can be easily distinguished by their much higher number of dorsal fin rays. *Brochis* sp. have 11 or more rays (Giant Brochis possesses 15–18), while in *Corydoras* sp. the number rarely exceeds seven. The Giant Brochis is a relatively new addition to the hobby, first making its appearance in significant numbers during the last decade and a half of the 20th century.

Hog-nosed Brochis

Corydoras multiradiatus (previously Brochis multiradiatus)

Other common name:
Long-finned Brochis

Family: Callichthyidae

Subfamily: Corydoradinae

Distribution: Madeira River region (Brazil); Río Lagarto/ Upper Napo (Ecuador); Ucayali and Nanay (Peru).

Size: Up to 4in (10cm).

Behavior: Peaceful shoaler that, despite its size, can be kept with small tankmates.

Diet: Wide range of foods accepted.

Aquarium: Roomy, well planted, with open areas as well as hiding places. Substratum fine grained, with no sharp edges on which the fish could damage their mouths and/or barbels. Water chemistry not critical but quality must be good. Temperature range: 72–77°F (22–25°C).

Breeding: No documented accounts currently available.

As its scientific name implies, Hog-nosed Brochis has many dorsal fin rays (around 17). Although it is slightly outdone in this department by *B. britskii*, the latter had not yet been discovered when Hog-nosed Brochis was first described. Both species are similar-looking overall, but this one lacks the bony plate that covers the underside of the head in its close relative. It also possesses a much longer snout and is a little smaller.

Common Brochis

Corydoras splendens (previously Brochis splendens)

Other common names: Emerald, Short-bodied, or Sailfin Brochis/ Corydoras/Catfish

Synonym: *Brochis coeruleus*

Family: Callichthyidae

Subfamily: Corydoradinae

Distribution: Brazil, Ecuador, and Peru.

Size: Up to 3in (8cm).

Behavior: Peaceful shoaler that, despite its size, can be kept with small tankmates.

Diet: Wide range of foods accepted.

Aquarium: Roomy, well planted, with open areas as well as hiding places. Substratum fine grained, with no sharp edges on which the fish could damage their mouths and/ or barbels. Water chemistry not critical, but quality must be good. Temperature range: 70–82°F (21–28°C).

Breeding: Challenging in aquaria. Eggs deposited on the undersides of broadleaved plants (egg deposition among floating plants has also been reported). No parental care is exhibited, and hatching takes about 4 days.

Of all its common names, the one that fits this species best is Emerald Brochis. It is a truly beautiful species that can be found in at least two (named) naturally occurring color forms—spotted and black—in addition to the more usual emerald one. Of the three *Brochis* species, this is the one that has been in the hobby longest, having first been imported in the late 1930s.

Armored Catfish

Callichthys callichthys

Family: Callichthyidae

Subfamily: Callichthyinae

Distribution: Widely distributed in tropical regions of South America.

Size: Up to 8in (20cm) reported, but usually smaller.

Behavior: Relatively inactive during daylight. May consume very small tankmates, but generally peaceful.

Diet: Wide range of chunky foods accepted, particularly sinking formulations such as granules and tablets. Food should be administered during the evening, shortly before tank lights are switched off.

Aquarium: Thickly planted, with numerous shelters. Water chemistry not critical. Temperature range: 64–82°F (18–28°C).

Breeding: A cover of floating plants must be provided. The male will build a nest of mucus-covered bubbles among the floating plants. Spawning takes place beneath this raft, and the eggs are deposited among the bubbles. The male will then vigorously defend the nest against all comers.

The feature that best distinguishes this subfamily from that containing *Corydoras* species and their relatives (Corydoradinae) is the snout. In the Callichthyinae, it is depressed, i.e. "flattened," to a certain extent, while in the Corydoradinae it is considerably more rounded. The Armored Catfish surfaces periodically to gulp in air, which it passes down into its hindgut, where oxygen is absorbed into the bloodsteam. The family Callichthyidae was named for the Armored Catfish, which has been known in the hobby for over a century, having first been imported into Europe in 1897.

Skunk Corydoras

Corydoras arcuatus

Other common name:
Arched Corydoras

Family: Callichthyidae

Subfamily: Corydoradinae

Distribution: Brazil, Ecuador, and Peru.

Size: Up to 3in (8cm) reported for the "Super Arcuatus" morph, but usually around 2in (5cm).

Behavior: Peaceful shoaler that looks impressive in a group.

Diet: Wide range of foods accepted, particularly bottom-dwelling livefoods and sinking commercial formulations.

Aquarium: Well planted, with open swimming areas, and fine-grained substratum. Water chemistry not critical, but excessively acid conditions must be avoided. Temperature range: 72–79°F (22–26°C).

Breeding: The female swallows the male's sperm and releases them from her gut onto her cupped pelvic fins, into which she has already released a few eggs. She deposits these adhesive eggs on a surface, where they will hatch 5–6 days later, depending on temperature.

This is a predominantly pink-bodied species with an elegant black "arch" that extends from the snout backward and upward through the eye to the front of the dorsal fin, and then along the back (but just below the top edge), all the way to the lower edge of the caudal-fin base. The Skunk Corydoras is one of several similarly patterned species that can easily be confused with each other.

Bronze Corydoras

Corydoras aeneus

Other common name:
Bronze Catfish

Family: Callichthyidae

Subfamily: Corydoradinae

Distribution: Bolivia, Brazil, Colombia, Ecuador, Peru, Suriname, Trinidad, and Venezuela.

Size: Around 2³/₄in (7cm); occasionally a little larger.

Behavior: Peaceful shoaler that looks impressive in a group.

Diet: Wide range of foods accepted, particularly bottom-dwelling livefoods and sinking commercial formulations.

Aquarium: Well planted, with open swimming areas, and fine-grained substratum. Water chemistry not critical but excessively acid conditions must be avoided. Temperature range: 64–79°F (18–26°C); avoid prolonged exposure to lower temperatures.

Breeding: The female swallows the male's sperm and releases them from her gut onto her cupped pelvic fins, into which she has released a few eggs. She deposits the eggs on a surface, where they hatch 5–6 days later.

Corydoras species are by far the most popular of all the catfish kept in aquaria. Most are hardy, adaptable, peaceful shoalers, and they have an appealing habit of seeming to "wink" at their owners. The effect is, in fact, created by rotating the eyes quickly. As the eye is rotated downward, the pupil and iris disappear briefly from view, and the surrounding reflective tissues become momentarily visible. As the eye rotates back into its more normal orientation, the illusion of a wink is created. Of all the *Corydoras* species, Bronze Corydoras is the best known and one of the most popular. Several naturally occurring color forms include Belem, Peru Gold Shoulder Red, Gold Shoulder Green, Peru Green Stripe, Peru Gold Stripe, and even Aeneus Black. There is also a cultivated albino form.

Above, below, and opposite: Wild color variants. **Below right:** Albino.

Banded Corydoras

Corydoras barbatus

Other common names: Filigree Cory, Barbatus Catfish

Family: Callichthyidae

Subfamily: Corydoradinae

Distribution: Regions around Rio de Janeiro and São Paulo, Brazil.

Size: Up to 5in (13cm), but usually considerably smaller.

Behavior: Peaceful shoaler; looks impressive in a group.

Diet: Wide range of foods accepted, particularly bottom-dwelling livefoods and sinking commercial formulations.

Aquarium: Well planted, with open swimming areas, and fine-grained substratum. Water chemistry not critical, but excessively acid conditions must be avoided. Temperature range: 68–77°F (20–25°C). Water chemistry should be slightly on the acid side.

Breeding: Challenging. Female swallows male's sperm and releases them from her gut onto her cupped pelvic fins, into which she has already released a few eggs. She deposits the eggs on a surface, where they will hatch 5–6 days later, depending on temperature.

The Banded Corydoras—the largest of the corydoras—is a slender-looking species often found in flowing waters in its natural habitat. It is a very distinctly marked corydoras that, despite its relatively restricted geographical distribution, occurs in at least two forms, the one from around Rio being darker and containing more yellow in the body pattern.

Delphax Corydoras

Corydoras delphax

Other common name:
False Blochi Catfish

Family: Callichthyidae

Subfamily: Corydoradinae

Distribution: Mainly Inírida River system (Colombia).

Size: Up to 3in (7.5cm) reported, but usually smaller.

Behavior: Peaceful shoaler that looks impressive in a group.

Diet: Wide range of foods accepted, particularly bottom-dwelling livefoods and sinking commercial formulations.

Aquarium: Well planted, with open swimming areas, and fine-grained substratum. Water chemistry not critical, but excessively acid conditions must be avoided. Temperature range: 70–79°F (21–26°C), but exposure to lower temperatures should not be prolonged.

Breeding: Female swallows the male's sperm and releases them from her gut onto her cupped pelvic fins, into which she has already released a few eggs. She deposits these adhesive eggs on a surface, where they will hatch 5–6 days later, depending on temperature.

This is a boldly spotted species with a black blotch in the anterior half of the dorsal fin and another over and above the eye. The space between these black areas (known as the "saddle") is light in color, but variably so, ranging from golden to pinkish hues.

Elegant Corydoras

Corydoras elegans

Family: Callichthyidae

Subfamily: Corydoradinae

Distribution: Tefé River region (Brazil), Aguarico system (Ecuador), and Napo River system (Peru).

Size: Around 2in (5cm).

Behavior: One of relatively few *Corydoras* species that frequently swim in midwater.

Diet: Wide range of foods accepted, particularly bottom-dwelling livefoods and sinking commercial formulations.

Aquarium: Well planted, with open swimming areas, and fine-grained substratum. Water chemistry not critical, but excessively acid conditions must be avoided. Temperature range: 70–79°F (21–26°C); avoid prolonged exposure to lower temperatures.

Breeding: Female swallows the male's sperm and releases them from her gut onto her cupped pelvic fins, into which she has already released a few eggs. She deposits these adhesive eggs on a surface, where they will hatch 5–6 days later, depending on temperature.

While undoubtedly a beautiful species, the claim made by this species' common name seems somewhat excessive since there are numerous *Corydoras* species that could embody the label of "elegant" every bit as well as—or better than—this one. Several naturally occurring morphs of this widely distributed species are known.

Salt-and-pepper Corydoras

Corydoras habrosus

Other common name:
Rio Salinas Cory

Family: Callichthyidae

Subfamily: Corydoradinae

Distribution: Originally reported from the Salinas River, Venezuela; also known from rivers in Suriname.

Size: Up to 1¹/₂in (4cm), but usually a little smaller.

Behavior: A peaceful species that likes to swim in midwater.

Diet: Wide range of foods accepted, particularly bottom-dwelling livefoods and sinking commercial formulations.

Aquarium: Well planted, with open swimming areas, and fine-grained substratum. Water chemistry not critical, but excessively acid conditions must be avoided. Temperature range: 70–77°F (21–25°C).

Breeding: Female swallows the male's sperm and releases them from her gut onto her cupped pelvic fins, into which she has already released a few eggs. She deposits these adhesive eggs on a surface, where they will hatch 5–6 days later, depending on temperature.

This is one of the so-called "dwarf" corydoras. It is a distinctly patterned species that must be kept in a sizable shoal for best effect. Owing to its small size, it should not be housed with larger or aggressive species. It is not totally defenseless, however, as its strong dorsal and pectoral spines will prove to any would-be predator. This species is sometimes confused with the even smaller *C. cochui* from the Araguaia River in Brazil.

Dwarf Corydoras

Corydoras hastatus

Other common name:
Spotlight Mini Cory

Family: Callichthyidae

Subfamily: Corydoradinae

Distribution: Mato Grosso (Brazil) and Paraguay.

Size: Around 1 1/4in (3cm).

Behavior: This peaceful species likes to swim in midwater.

Diet: Wide range of foods accepted, particularly bottom-dwelling livefoods and sinking commercial formulations.

Aquarium: Well planted, with open swimming areas, and fine-grained substratum. Water chemistry not critical, but excessively acid conditions must be avoided. Temperature range: 70–77°F (21–25°C); avoid prolonged exposure to lower temperatures.

Breeding: Female swallows the male's sperm and releases them from her gut onto her cupped pelvic fins, into which she has already released a few eggs. She deposits these adhesive eggs on a surface, where they will hatch 5–6 days later, depending on temperature.

The Dwarf Corydoras and *C. cochui* are the smallest members of the genus. They are closely followed by *C. habrosus* (Salt-and-pepper Corydoras) and *C. pygmaeus* (Pygmy Corydoras)—from Guyana, Suriname, and possibly Peru—with which they are sometimes confused. However, Dwarf Corydoras has a black spot on the caudal peduncle, while *C. pygmaeus* has a black longitudinal line that runs from the snout to the tail.

Bandit Corydoras

Corydoras metae

Other common name:
Rio Meta Corydoras

Family: Callichthyidae

Subfamily: Corydoradinae

Distribution: Meta River (Colombia).

Size: Around 2$\frac{1}{2}$in (6cm), but usually a little smaller.

Behavior: Peaceful shoaler that looks impressive in a group.

Diet: Wide range of foods accepted, particularly bottom-dwelling livefoods and sinking commercial formulations.

Aquarium: Well planted, with open swimming areas, and fine-grained substratum. Water chemistry not critical, but excessively acid conditions must be avoided. Temperature range: 70–79°F (21–26°C); avoid prolonged exposure to lower temperatures.

Breeding: Female swallows the male's sperm and releases them from her gut onto her cupped pelvic fins, into which she has already released a few eggs. She deposits these adhesive eggs on a surface, where they will hatch 5–6 days later, depending on temperature.

This pink and black corydoras has a black "mask" that extends from the top of the head, through the eye, to the bottom edge of the gill covers—hence the "Bandit" part of the name. The front of the dorsal fin is also black, this pigmentation running in a single central band along the back to the top front edge of the caudal fin and then down to the bottom front edge of the fin. From the side it can easily be confused with *C. melini* (Diagonal Stripe, or False Bandit, Corydoras) from the state of Amazonas in Brazil. However, from above the single black dorsal band of the Bandit Corydoras splits into two separate narrower bands in *C. melini*; they extend diagonally toward the caudal peduncle (the base of the tail fin).

CATFISH

Peppered Corydoras

Corydoras paleatus

Family: Callichthyidae

Subfamily: Corydoradinae

Distribution: Argentina, Southern Brazil, (possibly) Paraguay, Suriname, and around Montevideo in Uruguay.

Size: Around 3in (7.5cm).

Behavior: Peaceful shoaler; looks impressive in a group.

Diet: Wide range of foods accepted, particularly bottom-dwelling livefoods and sinking commercial formulations.

Aquarium: Well planted, with open swimming areas, and fine-grained substratum. Water chemistry not critical, but excessively acid conditions must be avoided. Temperature range: 64–79°F (18–26°C), but lower end best avoided for albino and golden varieties; top end should be avoided.

Breeding: Female swallows the male's sperm and releases them from her gut onto her cupped pelvic fins, into which she has already released a few eggs. She deposits these adhesive eggs on a surface, where they will hatch 5–6 days later, depending on temperature.

Discovered by Charles Darwin over 150 years ago, the Peppered Corydoras —along with Bronze Corydoras (*C. aeneus*)—is the most frequently available and popular member of its genus in the hobby. It is widely distributed and consequently exhibits considerable variation, with some populations having larger irregular body spots and others possessing an exceptionally long dorsal fin. There are also at least two cultivated varieties: an albino and one (Golden Paleatus) with a golden/pinkish base color and a liberal "dusting" of fine black dots.

Panda Corydoras

Corydoras panda

Family: Callichthyidae

Subfamily: Corydoradinae

Distribution: Ucayali River system (Peru).

Size: Up to 2in (5cm) reported, but usually smaller.

Behavior: Peaceful shoaler; looks impressive in a group.

Diet: Wide range of foods accepted, particularly bottom-dwelling livefoods and sinking commercial formulations.

Aquarium: Well planted, with open swimming areas, and fine-grained substratum. Water chemistry not critical, but excessively acid conditions must be avoided. Temperature range: 72–79°F (22–26°C); avoid prolonged exposure to lower temperatures.

Breeding: More challenging than *C. aneus*. Female swallows the male's sperm and releases them from her gut onto her cupped pelvic fins, into which she has already released a few eggs. She deposits these adhesive eggs on a surface, where they will hatch 5–6 days later, depending on temperature.

The Panda Corydoras is a pink-bodied fish with three black blotches: one extends from the top of the head through the eye and onto the cheek, the second occupies most of the dorsal fin, and the third is located on the caudal peduncle. Two naturally occurring morphs are recognized, depending on the size of this last blotch: Big-spot and Small-spot.

Sterba's Corydoras

Corydoras sterbai

Family: Callichthyidae

Subfamily: Corydoradinae

Distribution: Upper Guaporé River system (Bolivia/Brazil), Ucayali River system (Peru).

Size: Up to 3in (8cm) reported, but usually considerably smaller.

Behavior: Peaceful shoaler; looks impressive in a group.

Diet: Wide range of foods accepted, particularly bottom-dwelling livefoods and sinking commercial formulations.

Aquarium: Well planted, with open swimming areas, and fine-grained substratum. Water chemistry not critical, but excessively acid conditions must be avoided. Temperature range: 70–79°F (21–26°C), but avoid prolonged exposure to lower temperatures.

Breeding: Female swallows the male's sperm and releases them from her gut onto her cupped pelvic fins, into which she has already released a few eggs. She deposits these adhesive eggs on a surface, where they will hatch 5–6 days later, depending on temperature.

This is a particularly beautiful species in which the rich speckling of the anterior half of the body merges into a number of thin, irregular dark bands that run onto the caudal peduncle. The lower cheek area and, particularly, the pectoral fin spine can be a rich golden yellow. Some of these golden hues extend into the pelvic fins. The anal, caudal, and dorsal fins are also liberally speckled.

Porthole Catfish

Dianema longibarbis

Family: Callichthyidae

Subfamily: Callichthyinae

Distribution: Ambyiac and Pacaya Rivers (Peru).

Size: Up to 4in (10cm).

Behavior: Peaceful shoaler; can be kept with smaller tankmates except perhaps very small fry. Becomes progressively more active as evening falls.

Diet: Wide range of foods accepted.

Aquarium: Spacious, containing clumps of vegetation, open swimming areas, and resting and hiding places (e.g. pieces of bogwood). Water chemistry not critical but softish, slightly acid conditions preferred. Temperature range: 72–79°F (22–26°C).

Breeding: Challenging in aquaria. Males build bubble nests into which the eggs are deposited. Shallow water and raised temperature (82°F/28°C) recommended.

As the scientific name for this species indicates, the mouth is adorned with long barbels, the two longest of which (the top ones) are generally held out horizontally and pointing forward. The relatively light body armor helps distinguish the two *Dianema* species from their closest relatives in the subfamily, *Callichthys* and *Hoplosternum*.

Flag-tailed Catfish

Dianema urostriata

Other common name:
Stripe-tailed Catfish

Family: Callichthyidae

Subfamily: Callichthyinae

Distribution: Manáus area of the Río Negro (Brazil).

Size: Females reported up to 4³/₄in (12cm); males about ³/₄in (2cm) shorter.

Behavior: Peaceful shoaler; can be kept with smaller tankmates except perhaps very small fry. Becomes progressively more active as evening falls.

Diet: Wide range of foods accepted.

Aquarium: Spacious, containing clumps of vegetation, open swimming areas, and resting and hiding places (e.g. pieces of bogwood). Water chemistry not critical but softish, slightly acid conditions preferred. Temperature range: 72–79°F (22–26°C).

Breeding: Challenging in aquaria. Males build bubble nests into which the eggs are deposited. Shallow water and raised temperature (82°F/28°C) recommended.

This species is very similar to the *D. longibarbis* (Porthole Catfish). However, it can be immediately distinguished by its boldly striped caudal fin (in *D. longibarbis* the tail is plain). Occasionally specimens without any body speckling appear in shipments of this attractive species.

Cascudo Hoplo

Hoplosternum littorale

Family: Callichthyidae

Subfamily: Callichthyinae

Distribution: Widely distributed in tropical South America.

Size: Up to 8³⁄₄in (22cm).

Behavior: Generally peaceful except at spawning time.

Diet: Wide range of foods accepted.

Aquarium: Roomy, well covered, with plenty of resting and hiding places and subdued lighting. Water chemistry not critical. Temperature range: 70–79°F (21–26°C); slightly higher for breeding.

Breeding: Male builds bubble nest at the water surface. Eggs are deposited among the bubbles and are guarded by male. Hatching takes 3–4 days.

This is one of three similar-looking species that have traditionally been regarded as members of the genus *Hoplosternum*. In 1997 a review resulted in their being split into three distinct genera: *Hoplosternum*, *Lethoplosternum,* and *Megalechis*. Of the three, Cascudo Hoplo was the only species left within its original genus. It is the largest of the three species and may also be distinguished by its lightly forked caudal fin. Owing to its wide distribution, a number of variants are known, but whether they are morphs or separate species remains to be decided.

Port Hoplo

Megalechis thoracata

Synonym: *Hoplosternum thoracatum*

Family: Callichthyidae

Subfamily: Callichthyinae

Distribution: Widely distributed in northern South America.

Size: Up to 7in (18cm).

Behavior: Generally peaceful except at spawning time.

Diet: Wide range of foods accepted.

Aquarium: Roomy, well covered, with plenty of resting and hiding places and subdued lighting. Water chemistry not critical. Temperature range: 64–82°F (18–28°C); slightly higher for breeding.

Breeding: Male builds bubble nest at the water surface. Eggs are deposited among the bubbles and are guarded by male. Hatching takes 3–4 days. Port Hoplo is perhaps the easiest of the three hoplos to breed in aquaria.

This is the most variable of the three hoplos, so much so that some of the naturally occurring morphs may eventually turn out to be valid species in their own right. The one easily discernible feature that they all possess (and that distinguishes them from the other hoplos) is the sharply truncated caudal fin. Port Hoplo males can also be distinguished from their *H. littorale* counterparts in that Port Hoplo's main pectoral fin spine does not turn up at the tip with advancing age (as it does in *H. littorale*). In addition, during the breeding season this ray turns orange in Port Hoplo and deep red to maroon in *H. littorale*.

Frogmouth Catfish

Chaca chaca

Other common name:
Angler Catfish

Family: Chacidae

Distribution: Reported from Bangladesh, India, Myanmar (Burma), Borneo, and Sumatra.

Size: Up to 8in (20cm).

Behavior: Lone, predominantly nocturnal predator; should not be housed with tankmates that may be small enough to be swallowed.

Diet: Live fish and crustacea preferred (a factor that needs to be considered prior to purchase). May be weaned off these and onto chunky foods, such as tablets.

Aquarium: Appropriate hiding places (e.g. bogwood or rocks) and subdued lighting recommended. Water chemistry not critical. Temperature range: 72–75°F (22–24°C).

Breeding: No documented accounts currently available.

The Frogmouth Catfish is inactive during the day, lying perfectly camouflaged among the leaf litter that accumulates on the bottom of its native streams. In this position, it both rests and waits for suitable prey to come its way. When this happens, it wiggles its short upper jaw barbels to lure the potential victim into range of its cavernous mouth. Most feeding and higher levels of activity are, however, reserved for the hours of darkness. A very similar species, *C. bankanensis* (Chocolate Frogmouth Catfish), from peninsular Malaysia and Indonesia, is also available.

Walking Catfish

Clarias batrachus

Other common name:
Clarias Catfish

Family: Clariidae

Distribution: Widespread in tropical regions of Asia.

Size: Up to c.20in (50cm) reported.

Behavior: Predatory species; must not be kept with tankmates that are small enough to be swallowed.

Diet: Wide range of live and chunky commercial foods accepted.

Aquarium: Large, well covered, and well filtered. Decoration and shelters should consist of large pieces of bogwood, smooth rocks, or equivalent. Large, robust (or artificial) plants may be provided. Water chemistry not critical. Temperature range: 68–77°F (20–25°C) adequate, but wider range tolerated.

Breeding: Not reported in aquaria. In the wild (or commercial farms), eggs are laid in burrows excavated in the banks of rivers and ponds.

So called because of its reported ability to "walk" out of water (e.g. during storms or humid weather), the Walking Catfish is, first and foremost, a food fish. The main reason that it has become known in the hobby is that albinos, which are produced primarily for human consumption, are particularly attractive and are therefore of interest to some aquarists. However, owing to the large size that specimens can attain, the species is suitable only for the specialist who can cater adequately for its needs. This species may be illegal or restricted in some U. S. states and in parts of Canada; it is best to seek advice locally before purchase.

Painted Talking Catfish

Acanthodoras cataphractus

Family: Doradidae

Distribution:
Lower Amazon River, Brazil.

Size: 4in (10cm).

Behavior: Peaceful species that becomes more active during the night and likes to rest partly buried or in hollows during the day. Avoid keeping with small tankmates.

Diet: Wide range of foods accepted. Feed just before aquarium lights are switched off in the evening.

Aquarium: Adequate shelters, ample planting, and soft substratum required. Water chemistry not critical. Temperature range: 72–80°F (22–27°C).

Breeding: Challenging in aquaria. Eggs are laid in a depression and guarded by both parents. Hatching takes 4–5 days.

Of the three species in the genus, two—Painted Talking Catfish and Talking Catfish (*A. spinosissimus*) from Ecuador or eastern Peru—are frequently encountered in the hobby, while the third, *A. calderonensis*, is only rarely available. Both talking catfish species are often confused. However, the "granules" on the skull are much sharper in *A. spinosissimus*; and the gill cover in Painted Talking Catfish has fine grooves, while in *A. spinosissimus* it is granular in texture.

Spotted Doradid

Agamyxis pectinifrons

Other common names:
White-spotted Doradid, Spotted Talking Catfish

Family: Doradidae

Distribution: Ecuador.

Size: Up to 5½in (14cm) reported.

Behavior: Peaceful species that becomes more active during the night and likes to rest partly buried or in hollows during the day. Avoid keeping with small tankmates.

Diet: Wide range of foods accepted. Feed just before aquarium lights are switched off in the evening.

Aquarium: Adequate shelters, ample planting, and soft substratum required. Water chemistry not critical. Temperature range: 70–79°F (21–26°C).

Breeding: No documented accounts currently available.

As in the other talking catfishes, Spotted Doradid is able to produce sounds by rotating its pectoral fin spines and amplifying this via its swimbladder. The overall color is almost black, overlaid with numerous white or cream spots.

Hancock's Catfish

Platydoras hancockii (previously Amblydoras hancocki)

Other common name:
Talking Catfish

Family: Doradidae

Distribution: Widely
distributed from Brazil and
Colombia to Guyana.

Size: Up to 6in (15cm)
reported, but usually
smaller.

Behavior: May be more
active than some of its
relatives during the day.

Diet: Wide range of foods
accepted. Feed just before
aquarium lights are
switched off in the evening.

Aquarium: Adequate
shelters, ample planting,
and soft substratum
required. Water chemistry
not critical. Temperature
range: 70–82°F (21–28°C).

Breeding: No accounts
of aquarium spawnings
available. In the wild, it is
reported that eggs are laid
on the bottom, covered up
with leaves, and guarded
by both parents.

This is perhaps the most widely available of all the talking catfishes. It is
an attractively marked species that tends to "talk" more than most other
members of the family (producing sounds by rotating its pectoral fin
spines and amplifying the noise by means of its swimbladder).

Star-gazing Doradid

Astrodoras asterifrons

Other common name: Starry Growler

Family: Doradidae

Distribution: Reported from Bolivia and the Brazilian Amazon.

Size: Up to 4³/₄in (12cm), but usually smaller.

Behavior: Peaceful species that becomes more active during the night and likes to rest partly buried or in hollows during the day. Avoid keeping with small tankmates.

Diet: Wide range of foods accepted. Feed just before aquarium lights are switched off in the evening.

Aquarium: Adequate shelters, ample planting, and soft substratum required. Water chemistry not critical. Temperature range: 70–77°F (21–25°C).

Breeding: No documented accounts currently available.

Similarly colored to *Amblydoras hancocki* (Hancock's Catfish), Star-gazing Doradid is the only species in its genus. It can be distinguished from its closest relatives, such as *Acanthodoras* and *Amblydoras* species, in that its dorsal fin spine is serrated only along the front edge and not along the sides and back as well.

Striped Raphael Catfish

Platydoras costatus

Other common names: Chocolate Doradid, Humbug Catfish

Family: Doradidae

Distribution: Widespread in the Brazilian Amazon and Peru.

Size: Up to 8³⁄₄in (22cm).

Behavior: Sedentary and peaceful toward other species, but territorial toward its own. Likes to burrow.

Diet: Wide range of foods accepted.

Aquarium: Spacious, with adequate shelter and fine substratum. Protect plants against burrowing (by making base of stems inaccessible). Water chemistry not critical, but extremes must be avoided. Temperature range: 74–86°F (24–30°C).

Breeding: No documented accounts currently available.

This is a beautifully marked species in which the base chocolate (or almost black) color of the body contrasts sharply with the white or creamy bands. Its only significant drawback for many aquaria is its eventual size. The Striped Raphael Catfish has tiny curved spines running along the length of its body for protection, so it is best handled with care.

Black Doradid

Oxydoras niger (previously Pseudodoras niger)

Family: Doradidae

Distribution: Widely distributed in the Amazon basin.

Size: Up to 39in (100cm) reported.

Behavior: Peaceful despite its size. Likes the company of its own species.

Diet: Wide range of chunky foods accepted.

Aquarium: Large, well filtered, with fine- or medium-grained substratum. Water chemistry not critical. Temperature range: 70–75°F (21–24°C).

Breeding: No documented accounts currently available.

This is a very large species that should be purchased only by aquarists who can provide it with appropriate accommodation. The strong thorny spines on its body plates and powerful fin spines also mean that it must be handled with care. However, although the Black Doradid is extremely large, it is not aggressive toward other fish of a similar size.

Black Bullhead

Ameiurus melas (previously Ictalurus melas)

Synonym: *Ameiurus melas*

Family: Ictaluridae

Distribution: Widely distributed in North America and introduced into many locations outside its range.

Size: Up to 24½in (62cm), but usually much smaller.

Behavior: Predatory; must not be housed with tankmates that are small enough to be swallowed.

Diet: Live fish preferred (a factor that requires consideration prior to purchase), but other chunky livefoods and commercial diets may be accepted.

Aquarium: Large, well filtered. Substantial decor, e.g. bogwood, must be provided. Water chemistry not critical. Temperature range: from 50–86°F (10–30°C).

Breeding: Challenging. Eggs are laid in a depression and guarded by the spawners, which also care for the fry for a short time after hatching.

Many of the bullhead catfishes, including this one, are considered primarily as food or bait fishes, although several species—again, including the Black Bullhead—are also popular in the hobby among catfish specialists. Small- or moderate-sized specimens may be housed in unheated aquaria, although its wide temperature tolerance also makes it suitable for appropriately large tropical setups.

Channel Catfish

Ictalurus punctatus

Other common names: Graceful Catfish, Stinging Catfish, Spotted Catfish

Family: Ictaluridae

Distribution: Widely distributed in North America and introduced elsewhere.

Size: Up to 47¼in (120cm), but usually considerably smaller.

Behavior: Predatory; must not be housed with tankmates that are small enough to be swallowed.

Diet: Live fish preferred (a factor that requires consideration prior to purchase), but other chunky livefoods and commercial diets may be accepted.

Aquarium: Large, well filtered. Substantial decor, e.g. bogwood, must be provided. Water chemistry not critical. Temperature range: from 50–86°F (10–30°C).

Breeding: Challenging. Eggs are laid in a depression and guarded by the spawners, which also care for the fry for a short time after hatching; eggs may also be laid in caves or under rocks and be guarded by male.

This is the most commonly seen species of its genus, probably as a result of the production of albino specimens (primarily for the food fish industry). The species' name *punctatus* comes from the Latin, meaning "little spots," and refers to the dark spots scattered along the sides of the Channel Catfish. The adult coloration is pale gray to olive on the back and white to yellowish on the underside.

Adonis Catfish

Acanthicus adonis

Family: Loricariidae

Subfamily: Ancistrinae

Distribution: Tocantins River (Brazil).

Size: Up to 15³/₄in (40cm) reported, but usually smaller.

Behavior: Generally sedentary, although territorial toward its own species and with a distinct appetite for plants.

Diet: Almost exclusively vegetarian. Slices of potato or cucumber plus lettuce leaves may be provided on a regular basis.

Aquarium: Spacious, well filtered, with shelters and unpalatable/robust plants. A water current (created by, e.g., the outflow from a powerhead) recommended. Softish, slightly acid to neutral water preferred. Temperature range: 70–75°F (21–24°C).

Breeding: No documented accounts available.

This species is a relative newcomer to the hobby, having been described as recently as 1988. In most features, it is very similar to *A. hystrix* (Black Adonis Catfish). However, the Adonis Catfish has large white or cream-colored spots on a velvety black body. It has a long lyre-shaped tail. The spots reduce in number and size with age, while the tail grows longer.

Spotted Bristlenose

Ancistrus dolichopterus

Other common names:
Big-finned Bristlenose, Blue Chin Ancistrus

Family: Loricariidae

Subfamily: Ancistrinae

Distribution: Widespread in tropical South America.

Size: Around 5in (13cm).

Behavior: Peaceful toward other tankmates, but males territorial and aggressive toward other *Ancistrus* sp. Exhibits distinct appetite for succulent plants.

Diet: Predominantly vegetarian, but commercial formulations accepted. A slice of potato or cucumber or lettuce leaves will be appreciated.

Aquarium: Spacious, with ample bogwood shelters. Water well filtered and flowing (such as produced by powerhead outlet). Water chemistry not critical. Temperature range: 73–81°F (23–27°C).

Breeding: Eggs are laid in hollows in bogwood or roots, and they and the fry are guarded by male. Soft, acid water appears to enhance chances of success. Hatching takes about 5 days.

There are around 50 described species of *Ancistrus* and an almost equal number of undescribed ones referred to by their "L" number, which is their "Loricariid number," e.g. *Ancistrus* sp. Orange Spot (L110). For detailed information on this genus, it is therefore advisable to consult specialist literature. In all species, mature males exhibit the characteristic filament-like outgrowths of the snout—the "bristlenose"—from which one of its common names is derived.

Stick Catfish

Farlowella acus

Other common name:
Twig Catfish

Family: Loricariidae

Subfamily: Loricariinae

Distribution: Venezuela and southern tributaries of the Amazon.

Size: Around 6in (15cm).

Behavior: Peaceful, generally retiring; should not be kept with boisterous tankmates.

Diet: Largely herbivorous; vegetable dietary component, such as peas, lettuce, vegetable flake, etc., is therefore essential.

Aquarium: Well planted, with hiding places, and clean, well-oxygenated, flowing, soft, slightly acid water recommended. Temperature range: 70–79°F (21–26°C).

Breeding: Adhesive eggs are laid, often in flowing water, and are guarded by male or by both parents.

This slender species looks like a stick or twig in shape and coloration. Owing to its vegetarian habits, it is not the easiest of loricariids to keep and is better suited to experienced aquarists than to newcomers to the hobby. *Farlowella gracilis* (also known as Twig Catfish) from Colombia has long, slender extensions to the caudal fin and is also regularly available.

Sailfin Pleco

Pterygoplichthys gibbiceps (previously Glyptoperichthys gibbiceps)

Other common names:
Spotted Pleco, Sailfin
Suckermouth Catfish

Synonym: *Pterygoplichthys gibbiceps*

Family: Loricariidae

Subfamily: Hypostominae

Distribution: Peru.

Size: Up to 24in (60cm), but usually smaller.

Behavior: Predominantly nocturnal and peaceful, even toward smaller tankmates.

Diet: Almost exclusively vegetarian; offer plant-based sinking formulations, slices of potato or cucumber, lettuce, spinach, or peas.

Aquarium: Large, well planted, well filtered, with numerous shelters. Water chemistry not critical. A "moonlight" fluorescent tube to facilitate night viewing is advisable. Temperature range: 68–81°F (22–27°C).

Breeding: No documented accounts of aquarium breeding currently available.

This species still appears under its former scientific name in many aquarium books. However, the genus *Pterygoplichthys* is no longer valid, having been replaced by two genera, *Glyptoperichthys* and *Liposarcus*. The common name of pleco is also applied to species of the genus *Hypostomus*, from which *Glyptoperichthys* is easily distinguished by its dorsal fin, which has more than ten rays; *Hypostomus* has only seven.

Zebra Pleco

Hypancistrus zebra

Other common name:
Zebra Peckoltia

Family: Loricariidae

Subfamily: Ancistrinae

Distribution: Reported upriver of Altamira on the Xingu River (Brazil).

Size: Up to 4³/₄in (12cm) reported, but usually smaller.

Behavior: Peaceful and sometimes retiring.

Diet: Considerably less herbivorous than many of its relatives; will accept a range of (primarily) sinking formulations.

Aquarium: Well planted, with hiding places and subdued lighting recommended. Softish, slightly acid water preferred. Temperature range: 72–77°F (22–25°C).

Breeding: Breeding in aquaria has been documented, but conditions are unclear.

The Zebra Pleco, spectacularly patterned in black and white (as its name suggests), is a relatively recent introduction into the hobby. For a time it was known only by its "L" number (L46) until it was officially described and named in 1991. Although once rare, it is now readily available.

Pleco

Hypostomus plecostomus

Other common name:
Plec

Synonym: *Plecostomus plecostomus*

Family: Loricariidae

Subfamily: Hypostominae

Distribution: Suriname.

Size: Up to 24in (60cm) reported.

Behavior: Peaceful despite its large size; most active at dusk and during the night.

Diet: Herbivorous (vegetable flakes, pellets, or tablets, algae, lettuce, spinach, peas, potato, cucumber slices, etc.).

Aquarium: Large, well planted, with numerous sizable shelters. Water chemistry not critical but quality must be good. Temperature range: 72–82°F (22–28°C).

Breeding: No documented accounts of aquarium breeding currently available. In the wild and in commercial ornamental fisheries, the species breeds in deep burrows excavated in riverbanks. The male guards the eggs, and the fry feed off the body mucus.

Even today, over 240 years after this species was first described (as *Plecostomus* rather than *Hypostomus*), confusion still exists about its name, or even the correct identity of plecos available to aquarists under the name *Hypostomus plecostomus*. The generic name *Hypostomus* did not appear until 1803, yet—for reasons that are unclear—it replaced *Plecostomus*. Despite this, aquarists around the world have traditionally referred to *H. plecostomus* and the other *Hypostomus* species as plecos or plecs, thus heightening the confusion. *Hypostomus* species, of which there are more than 100, are distinguished from their closest relatives in the genera *Glyptoperichthys* and *Liposarcus* in several ways. The most distinguishable feature is the small number of dorsal-fin rays (seven) possessed by *Hypostomus*. Of the numerous species in the genus, very few are ever available within the hobby; *H. plecostomus* is one of them. At least two commercially produced varieties—an albino and a piebald— are occasionally available.

Spotted Hypostomus

Hypostomus punctatus

Other common name:
Spotted Pleco

Synonym: *Plecostomus punctatus*

Family: Loricariidae

Subfamily: Hypostominae

Distribution: Southern and southeastern Brazil.

Size: Around 12in (30cm).

Behavior: Peaceful despite its large size; most active at dusk and during the night.

Diet: Herbivorous (vegetable flakes, pellets, or tablets, algae, lettuce, spinach, peas, potato, cucumber slices, etc.).

Aquarium: Large, well planted, with numerous sizable shelters. Water chemistry not critical but quality must be good. Temperature range: 72–82°F (22–28°C).

Breeding: No documented accounts of aquarium breeding currently available. In the wild and in commercial ornamental fisheries, the species breeds in deep burrows excavated in riverbanks. The male guards the eggs, and the fry feed off the body mucus.

This beautifully spotted species is one of the few species of *Hypostomus* (other than *H. plecostomus*) regularly available in shops. It is somewhat smaller than *H. plecostomus,* making it a little easier to accommodate. Its body coloration is generally brown or gray with darker brown spots.

Snow King Plec

Pterygoplichthys anisitsi (previously Liposarcus anisitsi)

Other common name:
Snow King Pleco

Synonyms:
*Pterygoplichthys anisitsi,
Glyptoperichthys anisitsi*

Family: Loricariidae

Subfamily: Hypostominae

Distribution: Brazil and
Paraguay.

Size: Over 15³/₄in (40cm).

Behavior: Peaceful despite its
large size; most active at
dusk and during the night.

Diet: Herbivorous (vegetable
flakes, pellets, or tablets,
algae, lettuce, spinach,
peas, potato, cucumber
slices, etc.).

Aquarium: Large, well
planted, with numerous
sizable shelters. Water
chemistry not critical but
quality must be good.
Temperature range:
72–82°F (22–28°C).

Breeding: No documented
accounts of aquarium
breeding available. In the
wild and in commercial
ornamental fisheries, the
species breeds in deep
burrows excavated in
riverbanks. The male guards
the eggs, and the fry feed
off the body mucus.

Along with the black-spotted *Liposarcus multiradiatus* from the Amazon
basin, Bolivia, Paraguay, and Peru, the white-spotted Snow King Plec is the
most widely available species in the genus. This is largely as a result of
large-scale breeding of the species (predominantly in Floridian ornamental
fish farms).

Emperor Panaque

Panaque nigrolineatus

Other common names:
Pin-striped Panaque,
Royal Panaque

Family: Loricariidae

Subfamily: Ancistrinae

Distribution: Southern Colombia.

Size: Up to 12in (30cm) reported, but usually smaller.

Behavior: Generally peaceful toward other tankmates, but strongly territorial toward its own species.

Diet: Predominantly herbivorous: sinking plant-based formulations (e.g. vegetable tablets, granules, or flakes), lettuce or spinach leaves, peas, etc.

Aquarium: Spacious, well filtered, with flowing water (as produced by powerhead outlet), along with adequate plant and bogwood or rock cover. Softish, slightly acid water preferred, though some deviation tolerated. Temperature range: 72–79°F (22–26°C).

Breeding: No documented accounts currently available.

There are only some half a dozen species in the genus *Panaque*, of which two—Emperor Panaque and the black-bodied *P. suttoni* (Blue-eyed Plec, Pleco, or Panaque) from northern South America—are regularly available. Distinguished by their large heads, sloping foreheads, and beautiful eyes, panaques make interesting additions to appropriately furnished and maintained aquaria.

Redfin Otocinclus

Parotocinclus maculicauda

Family: Loricariidae

Subfamily: Hypoptopomatinae

Distribution: Southern Brazil.

Size: Around 1³/₄in (4.5cm).

Behavior: Peaceful; should not be housed with boisterous tankmates.

Diet: Predominantly herbivorous: algae and vegetable flakes, plus lettuce or spinach leaves, peas, etc.

Aquarium: Well planted, with numerous hiding and resting places. Good filtration and fine-grained substratum recommended. At first, the water should be soft and acid; both values can be raised gradually once fish are acclimatized. Temperature range: 72–77°F (22–25°C).

Breeding: No documented accounts currently available.

This liberally spotted species has red edges on its dorsal, pectoral, and caudal fins. The genus itself can be distinguished from its close relative, *Otocinclus*, by the adipose fin (absent in *Otocinclus*). Of the 13 or so other species, only *P. amazonensis* (False Sucker), from coastal areas of southern Brazil, is seen with any regularity.

Spiny Plec

Pseudacanthicus spinosus

Other common name:
Spiny Pleco

Family: Loricariidae

Subfamily: Ancistrinae

Distribution: Brazilian Amazon basin.

Size: Around 9³/₄in (25cm).

Behavior: Highly territorial, particularly toward its own species.

Diet: Wide range of sinking foods accepted.

Aquarium: Large, well filtered, with flowing water (as produced by powerhead outlet), recommended. Provide large bogwood or rock shelters. Softish, slightly acid to slightly alkaline water advisable. Temperature range: 72–79°F (22–26°C).

Breeding: No documented accounts currently available.

As the name implies, this is a spiny fish, but it also possesses serrations on the scales. All members of this genus are spiny by nature, making them difficult to handle. There are probably about 12 species in the genus (the number is unclear, as some have not been described and are currently referred to only by their "L" numbers). Of the described species, *P. leopardus* (Leopard Plec), from the Rio Negro area in Brazil, is one of the few other *Pseudacanthicus* that are fairly regularly available.

Electric Catfish

Malapterurus electricus

Family: Malapteruridae

Distribution: Widely distributed in central Africa.

Size: Up to 39in (1m) reported, but usually much smaller.

Behavior: Lone nocturnal predator that stuns its prey.

Diet: Chunks of meat, large livefoods, e.g. earthworms and live fish (a factor that demands consideration prior to purchase).

Aquarium: Large, well filtered, with large shelters. Use only robust plants. Water chemistry not critical. Temperature range: 72–86°F (22–30°C).

Breeding: No documented accounts of aquarium breeding currently available.

A fish that can generate an electrical current of up to 400 volts is most certainly one for the specialist who knows and respects its amazing qualities. High-voltage discharges are emitted only by the largest specimens, but even modest-sized individuals pack quite a punch. In addition to this species, one other electric catfish is known: *M. microstoma* (Smallmouth Electric Catfish) from the Congo basin. Of the two, Electric Catfish is the one more commonly encountered, and it is seen both in its wild type and in its mottled or albino form.

Moustache Synodontis

Hemisynodontis membranacea (previously Hemisynodontis membranaceus)

Family: Mochokidae

Distribution: Widely distributed from west Africa to the Nile basin.

Size: Up to approximately 20in (50cm), but usually smaller.

Behavior: Relatively peaceful despite its size; prefers to be kept in groups. Tends to feed in an upside-down position, as the common name for the family (upside-down catfish) implies (although few species actually exhibit this behavior).

Diet: Floating livefoods and other formulations (including pellets) preferred.

Aquarium: Large, with substantial shelters. Use only robust, well-protected plants. Water chemistry not critical. Temperature range: 72–77°F (22–25°C).

Breeding: No documented accounts currently available.

The Moustache Synodontis—the only species in its genus—has the typical Mochokidae pointed head and bony headshield (bony plate) sloping up to a dorsal fin with a prominent front spine and a large, well-developed adipose fin. Its mouth barbels are also well developed, with one pair carrying the characteristic membrane responsible for its common name. Some authors believe this genus to be synonymous with *Synodontis*.

Payne's Synodontis

Mochokiella paynei

Family: Mochokidae

Distribution: Sierra Leone.

Size: Around 2in (5cm), but often smaller.

Behavior: A peaceful species; most active at dusk and during the night.

Diet: Livefoods preferred, but other formulations also accepted.

Aquarium: Well planted, with adequate shelter and some open swimming areas. Softish, slightly acid to slightly alkaline water preferred. Temperature range: 72–77°F (22–25°C).

Breeding: No documented accounts currently available.

Payne's Synodontis is one of the smaller species and the only representative of its genus. Atypically for a mochokid catfish, it has a somewhat blunt snout. Its attractive mottled patterning and its small size make it more suitable for community aquaria than the majority of its relatives.

Angel Catfish

Synodontis angelicus

Other common names:
Angel Synodontis, Polka Dot Synodontis

Family: Mochokidae

Distribution: Stanley Pool (D. R. Congo) and Cameroon.

Size: Up to 7in (20cm) reported, but usually smaller.

Behavior: Territorial toward its own species, with open aggression sometimes displayed in confined spaces. Swims upside-down only occasionally; most activity occurs at dusk and during the night.

Diet: Livefoods are preferred, but some commercial formulations also accepted.

Aquarium: Spacious, well planted, with adequate shelter, fine-grained substratum, and subdued lighting. A "moonlight" fluorescent tube will make nighttime activity of the species easily observable. Soft to moderately hard, slightly acid to slightly alkaline water preferred. Temperature range: 72–82°F (22–28°C).

Breeding: No documented accounts currently available.

This is a dark chocolate-brown fish with numerous cream-colored spots. The intensity of the dark coloration, as well as the number, color, and size of the spots, can vary considerably from individual to individual, but all variants are impressively patterned.

Featherfin Synodontis

Synodontis eupterus

Family: Mochokidae

Distribution: Widely distributed from west Africa to the White Nile.

Size: Around 6in (15cm).

Behavior: Peaceful, even toward smaller tankmates. Swims upside-down only occasionally.

Diet: Livefoods are preferred, but some commercial formulations also accepted.

Aquarium: Spacious, well planted, with adequate shelter, fine-grained substratum, and subdued lighting. A "moonlight" fluorescent tube will make nighttime activity of the species easily observable. Soft to moderately hard, slightly acid to slightly alkaline water preferred. Temperature range: 72–79°F (22–26°C).

Breeding: No documented accounts currently available.

As its common name suggests, this species develops a dorsal-fin extension. When raised and with all its filaments extended, it looks like a moving fan. This, together with its numerous small, dark body spots, make it a much sought-after *Synodontis* species. There is a marked difference in patterning between Featherfin juveniles and adults. Juvenile Featherfins have a "zebra" appearance, with lines of black and white and irregular spots. As they mature, they develop a duller gray-brownish color, while keeping the lined appearance at the tail.

Black-spotted Upside-down Catfish

Synodontis nigriventris

Other common name:
Common Upside-Down Catfish

Family: Mochokidae

Distribution: Congo basin.

Size: Up to 4in (10cm) reported, but often smaller.

Behavior: A peaceful fish that can be kept in groups; spends most of its time in an upside-down position; most activity occurs at dusk and during the night.

Diet: Floating livefoods and freeze-dried or deep-frozen diets are preferred.

Aquarium: Spacious, well planted, with adequate shelter, fine-grained substratum, and subdued lighting. A "moonlight" fluorescent tube will make nighttime activity easily observable. Soft to moderately hard, slightly acid to slightly alkaline water preferred. Temperature range: 72–82°F (22–28°C).

Breeding: Challenging, but achievable, in aquaria. Eggs laid in a depression, hollow, or on the roof of a cave. There may be some degree of parental care. Hatching takes about 7 days.

Of all the *Synodontis* species known in the hobby, this is the one that spends the most time in an inverted swimming position. The habit is so highly developed in this fish that it has actually evolved reversed body shading, i.e. in some species the belly is darker than the back— the complete opposite to the shading pattern exhibited by other fishes, including other members of the Mochokidae. Despite its upside-down habit, the Black-spotted Upside-down Catfish is perfectly capable of swimming the "right way up," and occasionally does so. Interestingly, young fish do not adopt the upside-down orientation until they are about two months old.

One-spot Synodontis

Synodontis notatus

Family: Mochokidae

Distribution: D. R. Congo.

Size: Up to 8in (20cm) reported, but usually smaller.

Behavior: Peaceful toward tankmates, but adults can be boisterous.

Diet: Livefoods are preferred, but some commercial formulations also accepted.

Aquarium: Spacious, well planted, with adequate shelter, fine-grained substratum, and subdued lighting. A "moonlight" fluorescent tube will make nighttime activity of the species easily observable. Soft to moderately hard, slightly acid to slightly alkaline water preferred. Temperature range: 72–79°F (22–26°C).

Breeding: No documented accounts currently available.

This is one of the most frequently seen and distinctive species of *Synodontis*. It can be easily identified by its single central body spot (although some specimens may exhibit more than one) on a pinkish, grayish, or silvery background.

Iridescent Shark

Pangasianodon hypophthalmus (previously Pangasius hypophthalmus)

Other common names:
Asian Shark Catfish, Siamese Shark

Family: Pangasiidae

Distribution: Around Bangkok, Thailand.

Size: Up to 39in (1m) reported, but usually smaller.

Behavior: Large shoals are encountered in the wild; in aquaria, however, only single specimens should be kept, except during the juvenile phase; a nervous, predatory species that can disrupt aquarium decor.

Diet: Substantial, chunky livefoods and commercial preparations accepted.

Aquarium: Spacious, well covered, with ample swimming space, efficient filtration, and water current (as produced by power filter or powerhead outlet). Neutral, soft to medium-hard water preferred. Temperature range: 72–79°F (22–26°C).

Breeding: No documented accounts currently available.

The Pangasiidae contains *Pangasianodon gigas* (Giant Catfish), which can grow to over 6½ft (2m) and weigh over 240lb (110kg). The genus *Pangasius* is the only one of the pangasiids encountered with any frequency in the hobby, with the Iridescent Shark being the species most often seen, either in its wild type or albino forms. Most specimens offered are juveniles, but they will soon grow into large fish. This is therefore a species that is suitable only for aquarists who can provide appropriate accommodations. It is widely bred commercially as a food fish as well as an ornamental one.

Spotted Shovelnosed Catfish

Hemisorubim platyrhynchos

Other common names:
Porthole Shovelnose Catfish, Flat-nosed Antenna Catfish

Family: Pimelodidae

Distribution: Northern and eastern South America.

Size: Up to 20in (50cm), but usually smaller.

Behavior: Predatory.

Diet: Chunky livefoods and meat-based diets accepted, as well as tablets and granules.

Aquarium: Large, well covered, well filtered, with water current (as produced by power filter or power-head outlet) essential. Provide large shelters. Water chemistry not critical, but extremes must be avoided. Subdued lighting and soft substratum also recommended. Temperature range: 72–81°F (22–27°C).

Breeding: Unknown in aquaria.

This large, attractively spotted catfish is reasonably easy to manage in home aquaria. The Spotted Shovelnosed Catfish is easy to distinguish from other members of the family. Firstly, it has large spots along the side of the body, and secondly, it has a protruding lower jaw. (All other shovelnosed catfishes have a longer upper jaw.)

Sailfin Marbled Catfish

Leiarius pictus

Other common name:
Sailfin Pim

Family: Pimelodidae

Distribution: Amazon basin.

Size: Up to 24in (60cm).

Behavior: Highly predatory.

Diet: Large livefoods—including fish—accepted (a factor that demands consideration prior to purchase).

Aquarium: Large, well covered, well filtered, with water current (as produced by power filter or power-head outlet) essential. Provide large shelters. Water chemistry not critical, but extremes must be avoided. Temperature range: 72–81°F (22–27°C).

Breeding: No documented accounts currently available.

This spectacular species is distinguished by its large, sail-like dorsal fin and bold chocolate-brown and creamy-pink body patterning. Its most obvious disadvantages as an aquarium fish are its large size and feeding habit, which make it suitable only for those specialist hobbyists who can cater for its needs. A mottled species, *L. marmoratus* (False Perrunichthys), from the Brazilian and Peruvian Amazon, is also occasionally available.

Red-tailed Catfish

Phractocephalus hemioliopterus

Family: Pimelodidae

Distribution: Widely distributed in the Amazon basin.

Size: Up to 4ft (1.2m).

Behavior: Highly predatory.

Diet: Large livefoods, including fish, preferred (a factor that requires consideration prior to purchase). Chunky meat- or fish-based foods and commercial formulations may be accepted.

Aquarium: Large, well covered, well filtered, with some large pieces of decor. Water chemistry not critical but quality must be good. Temperature range: 70–81°F (21–27°C).

Breeding: No documented accounts of aquarium breeding currently available, although the species has been bred commercially.

This catfish is exceptional in that its coloration remains bright and distinct, even in large specimens. It is undoubtedly one of the most attractive of all large catfish, and offers the extra advantage that it can become very tame. On the downside is its eventual large size—an important factor that needs careful consideration. The small, commercially bred juveniles that are generally available will, in appropriate conditions, grow into giants in a relatively short period of time.

Angelicus Pim

Pimelodus pictus

Synonym: *Pimelodella pictus*

Family: Pimelodidae

Distribution: Colombia and Peru.

Size: Up to 6in (15cm) reported, but usually smaller.

Behavior: May prey on small tankmates, but generally peaceful toward similarly sized fish; most active in the evening and during the night.

Diet: Livefoods preferred, but will accept some commercial formulations.

Aquarium: Sufficiently large to accommodate a group, and with open swimming spaces and adequate shelter. Well-filtered, soft, slightly acid water preferred. Temperature range: 72–77°F (22–25°C).

Breeding: No documented accounts available.

This striking fish is one of the most frequently seen pims in the hobby. It is also one of the most peaceful, although care must be taken not to house it with small tankmates. There are two subspecies of *P. pictus* available—the more commonly seen Peruvian pictus has large black spots, while the Columbian has many smaller spots and is usually smaller.

Sturgeon Catfish

Platystomatichthys sturio

Family: Pimelodidae

Distribution: Amazon basin.

Size: Up to 24in (60cm) reported.

Behavior: Highly predatory.

Diet: Large livefoods, including fish, accepted (a factor that demands consideration prior to purchase).

Aquarium: Large, well covered, well filtered, with water current (as produced by power filter or power-head outlet) essential. Provide large shelters. Water chemistry not critical but extremes must be avoided. May be difficult to acclimatize to aquarium conditions. Temperature range: 72–81°F (22–27°C).

Breeding: No documented accounts currently available.

The common name of this species derives from the long snout, which may be upturned at the tip and thus look very similar to the snout possessed by many *Acipenser* (sturgeon) species. Another notable feature of the species is the extremely long maxillary barbels, which can extend beyond the tip of the caudal fin.

Glass Catfish

Kryptopterus bicirrhis

Family: Siluridae

Distribution: Eastern India and southeast Asia.

Size: Up to 6in (15cm), but usually smaller.

Behavior: Peaceful, midwater shoaler; must be kept in a group.

Diet: Swimming livefoods preferred, but deep-frozen, freeze-dried, and other formulations may be accepted, especially if distributed via a current (as produced by a powerhead).

Aquarium: Well planted, with ample open swimming areas. Water chemistry not critical, but soft, slightly acid water preferred. Temperature range: 70–79°F (21–26°C).

Breeding: No documented accounts currently available.

The Glass Catfish belongs to the same family as the gigantic *Silurus glanis* (Wels Catfish), which can attain lengths of around 10ft (3m), and *Wallago attu*, which can grow to over 6½ft (2m); both are most unsuitable aquarium fish despite being occasionally available. Unusually for a catfish, the Glass Catfish is a midwater swimmer that looks absolutely stunning when kept—as it should be—in a shoal. A second, less transparent species from the same general area—*K. macrocephalus* (the so-called Poor Man's Glass Catfish)—is also available, along with a smaller, highly transparent species, *K. minor*, and a species from Borneo, *K. cryptopterus*. All have the same basic requirements.

CATFISH

Clown Catfish
Gagata cenia

Family: Sisoridae

Distribution: Mainly from north and northeast India.

Size: Around 6in (15cm).

Behavior: Generally peaceful, active shoaler.

Diet: Livefoods preferred, but other foods also accepted.

Aquarium: Plants not vital, but well-lit, well-planted aquarium with gravelly bottom and some flat or smoothly rounded resting places recommended. Provide a water current (as produced by power filter or powerhead outlet). Hard alkaline water preferred. Temperature range: 64–72°F (18–22°C).

Breeding: No documented accounts available.

So called (like many other similarly patterned species) because of its black spots on a light background, the Clown Catfish has been known since 1822—although it did not begin to appear with much frequency until the 1990s. An albino form is occasionally available.

Butterfly Catfish

Erethistes hara (previously Hara hara)

Family: Sisoridae

Distribution: Indian subcontinent.

Size: Up to 1 ½in (4cm).

Behavior: Peaceful, retiring; may be kept in groups.

Diet: Sinking livefoods preferred, but commercial formulations also accepted.

Aquarium: Well filtered, with numerous shelters and subdued lighting recommended. Soft, acid water preferred. Temperature range: 64–72°F (18–22°C).

Breeding: No documented accounts available.

Two species of *Hara* are occasionally available—the Butterfly Catfish and its smaller relative, *H. jerdoni* (Dwarf Anchor Catfish). The two other species in the genus are only rarely seen in aquaria. All species have the same basic requirements.

CYPRINIDS

Family Cyprinidae

The family Cyprinidae is the largest of the exclusively freshwater families of fishes. With the possible exception of the freshwater/brackish/marine family, the Gobiidae, it is also the largest family of vertebrates. The family as we currently recognize it is deemed by some authorities to be artificially large. Not surprisingly, therefore, opinions vary as to how it should be subdivided. The following listing of subfamilies follows that of Nelson (1994).

Below: *Danio rerio.*

Cyprininae (about 700 species). These fish usually (but not invariably) possess anterior and posterior barbels. For instance, while the three *Carassius* species (including the Goldfish, *C. auratus*) do not possess barbels, the Common Carp and, therefore, Koi (*Cyprinus carpio*), *Barbus* and relatives, as well as *Labeo* and *Epalzeorhynchus* ("Sharks" and Flying Foxes), and numerous other species do have barbels.

Gobioninae, which includes the European Gudgeon (*Gobio gobio*).

Rasborinae (= Danioninae), which—as the name implies—includes all the popular tropical aquarium rasboras and danios.

Acheilognathinae, which includes the amazing bitterlings (*Rhodeus* and *Tanakia*).

Leuciscinae, the intra-subfamilial relationships of which are, perhaps, debatable, but that—as things stand—includes the minnows (*Phoxinus*), the Ide or Orfe (*Leuciscus*), the Roach (*Rutilus*), the Rudd (*Scardinius*), and the Tench (*Tinca*).

Cultrinae, consisting of Eastern Asian genera like *Parabramis*.

Alburninae, including the Bleak (*Alburnus*).

Psilorhynchinae, with two genera from Nepal, India, and parts of Myanmar (Burma): *Psilorhynchoides* and *Psilorhynchus*.

There are about 2,010 species in the family spread among some 210–220 genera in Eurasia, North America, and Africa. With such a high number of species and such wide distribution, it is to be expected that cyprinids will exhibit great diversity of shape, size, and characteristics.

There are giant species, such as *Catlocarpio siamensis* from Thailand and *Tor putitora*, the Large-scaled Barb or Mahseer, from the Bhramaputra, in Eastern India, both of which are known to grow to lengths

in excess of 8ft (2.5m). In contrast, the largest specimen of *Danionella translucida* (from Burma) so far found is a mere   in (1.2cm) in length. Cyprinids have a protrusile, or extendible, mouth and jaws without teeth. However, they possess pharyngeal ("throat") bones with teeth. They also exhibit a number of skull bone and muscle modifications, along with two pairs of mouth barbels (but not in all species) and a scaleless head. They lack an adipose (second dorsal) fin.

Above: *Rasbora rasbora* "Burma."

The difficulty with using these features to identify a fish as belonging to the family Cyprinidae is that none of them is unique to cyprinids. Furthermore, all of them, and others, are shared with the other families that together constitute the order Cypriniformes. The selection of species that follows can be safely regarded as consisting of noncontroversial, universally accepted members of the family Cyprinidae.

Bala Shark

Balantiocheilos melanopterus

Other common names:
Tri-color Shark, Silver Shark, Malaysian Shark

Synonym: *Balantiocheilus melanopterus*

Subfamily: Cyprininae

Distribution: Southeast Asia; Kalimantan (Borneo), Thailand, Sumatra, and peninsular Malaysia.

Size: Usually sold as juveniles measuring 4in (10cm) or less, but can grow to around 14in (35cm) in roomy aquaria with good water quality and an appropriate diet.

Behavior: Nonaggressive; active shoaler.

Diet: Will accept a wide range of livefoods and commercial diets, which should include vegetable matter. Likely to damage delicate plants.

Aquarium: Roomy with ample swimming space and a well-fitting cover. Will tolerate a wide range of hardness and pH (but ideally keep between slightly acid and neutral). Temperature range: 72–82°F (22–28°C).

Breeding: Not reported in home aquaria. However, it is commercially bred in large numbers.

Shark in name and, superficially, in shape (but not in demeanor), the Bala Shark is a predominantly herbivorous species that can attain a substantial size. With the improvements in aquarium technology, and as the keeping of larger setups becomes more feasible, the Bala Shark is likely to remain popular among aquarists. It may even be possible to breed this attractive and active fish in aquaria before long.

The Bala Shark is a shoaling species and should be kept in groups. However, the average home aquarium will only be able to house a shoal of juveniles, which will soon outgrow their quarters. This species is bred commercially in the Far East, and it is these captive-bred stocks that meet most of the demand within the hobby.

Arulius Barb

Dawkinsia arulius (previously Barbus arulius)

Other common names:
Four-spot Barb, Longfin Barb

Synonyms: *Puntius arulius,*
Capoeta arulius

Subfamily: Cyprininae

Distribution: Southern and
southeast India.

Size: Up to 4³/₄in (12cm).

Behavior: Sociable fish
that is tolerant of other
species and should be
kept in a shoal.

Diet: Wide range of foods
accepted; vegetable matter
should be included.

Aquarium: Roomy with
plenty of swimming space
and clumps of vegetation.
Although tolerant of a
range of conditions, soft,
slightly acid water is
recommended. Temperature
range: 66–77°F (19–25°C).

Breeding: This is an egg-
scattering species which
releases its spawn among
vegetation. Relatively few
eggs are laid.

The Arulius Barb is an active shoaler in which males are slow to develop
their full adult characteristics, consisting of extended dorsal fin rays. This
relative slowness (it can take over a year) is one of the main reasons why
the species has not become more popular. Although mature males can
grow fairly large for a community fish, this barb is relatively peaceful
and can be kept with tankmates smaller than itself. In reflected light the
white/silvery areas between the black body bands have an iridescent
sheen —particularly attractive in mature males.

Rosy Barb

Pethia conchonius (previously Barbus conchonius)

Synonym: *Puntius conchonius*

Subfamily: Cyprininae

Distribution: Northern India.

Size: Up to 6in (15cm), but usually much smaller.

Behavior: Active shoaler; tolerant of others.

Diet: All livefoods and commercial diets are accepted.

Aquarium: Open swimming areas along with plant thickets should be provided. Although a wide range of water chemistry conditions are tolerated, extremes of pH and hardness should be avoided. Temperature range: as low as 59°F (15°C) can be tolerated during the winter season without trouble. At other times of the year, 64–77°F (18–25°C).

Breeding: A typical egg scatterer among fine-leaved vegetation. As with all other scatterers, the parents will consume their eggs given the opportunity. Hatching takes about 30 hours at the higher end of the temperature range.

This is one of the most famous and popular species in the aquarium hobby. As the name implies, the basic body color is rosy—but only really pronounced in males, particularly during the breeding season. Over the years, many varieties of this attractive fish have been produced by commercial breeders, most notably long-finned, red, and copper/bronze types in which the females are also more deeply pigmented than their wild or basic counterparts. The Rosy Barb can tolerate relatively low temperatures, making it suitable for some coldwater aquaria, but not in areas that experience severe winter weather.

Above left: Wild. **Above right:** Gold. **Below:** Neon Gold. **Opposite:** Gold.

Cuming's Barb

Pethia cumingii (previously Barbus cumingii)

Synonym: *Puntius cumingii*

Subfamily: Cyprininae

Distribution: Mountain streams in southwest Sri Lanka.

Size: Up to 2in (5cm).

Behavior: Peaceful shoaling species.

Diet: Wide range of natural and commercial foods accepted.

Aquarium: Medium-sized aquarium with open swimming spaces and shaded areas. Neutral, slightly soft water suits this species best. Temperature range: 72–81°F (22–27°C).

Breeding: Typical egg-scattering barb. Not one of the easiest species to breed. Hatching takes just over 1 day at the higher end of the temperature range.

Cuming's Barb is a delightful little fish that does well in aquaria. Two different color variants are found in the species' native waters in Sri Lanka: a red-finned variety from the Kelani River catchment and northward from there, and a yellow-finned variety from the Kalu River and the areas to the south. Speckled red and speckled yellow specimens are also encountered in the wild.

While in the past all the Cuming's Barbs available were caught in the wild, recent years have seen the development of very successful captive breeding programs. Today, all Cuming's Barbs exported from Sri Lanka are bred in farms.

Clown Barb

Barbodes everetti (previously Barbus everetti)

Synonym: *Puntius everetti*

Subfamily: Cyprininae

Distribution: Southeast Asia; Singapore, Kalimantan (Indonesia), Sarawak (Malaysia).

Size: Up to 5in (13cm), but generally smaller.

Behavior: Peaceful shoaler, but older (and larger) specimens may be aggressive toward small fish. Prefers the lower reaches of the aquarium and has a tendency to nibble tender plants.

Diet: A wide range of livefoods and commercial diets is accepted; a vegetable supplement should be provided.

Aquarium: Roomy with open swimming spaces and heavily planted areas. Soft, slightly acid water preferred, with regular partial water changes. Temperature range: 75–86°F (24–30°C).

Breeding: Not an easy egg-scattering species to breed. Chances of success improve if potential fully mature breeders are kept apart for several weeks and conditioned well with livefoods and vegetable matter.

Fish that have either black bands or spots separated by golden or orange patches are often given the name "Clown," and this species is no exception. When fully colored, it is a truly beautiful fish. It is not always as widely available as some other species, but when it is—and when it is displayed as a sizable shoal of fully mature fish—it almost sells itself. Unfortunately, males can take up to 18 months to mature and show their full colors, so the majority of specimens that are offered for sale are not as attractive as they will eventually become. It is therefore worth bearing this in mind when on the lookout for fish to buy and investing in the future by obtaining a small shoal of specimens, whatever their size.

Black-spot Barb

Puntius filamentosus (previously Barbus filamentosus)

Other common name:
Filament Barb

Synonym: *Puntius filamentosus*

Subfamily: Cyprininae

Distribution: Sri Lanka and southern India.

Size: Up to 6in (15cm) reported, but usually remains considerably smaller, rarely exceeding 4–4¾in (10–12cm).

Behavior: A lively, sociable species that should be kept in a shoal.

Diet: Wide range of foods accepted; vegetable supplement recommended.

Aquarium: Owing to its relatively large size, a spacious aquarium is required, with ample swimming space. Subdued lighting shows off its iridescence to good effect. Soft, slightly acid water is recommended. Temperature range: 68–75°F (20–24°C); slightly higher for breeding purposes.

Breeding: Large numbers of eggs (up to 1,000) are laid by this egg-scattering, egg-eating species. Hatching takes 36 hours at the top end of the temperature range.

The Black-spot Barb is another species that only exhibits its full characteristics once it matures fully. Even then, it is only the males that develop the extended dorsal fin rays responsible for one of the common names, the Filament Barb. Immature specimens, which account for the majority of those offered for sale, are very attractive in their own right but do not give a true indication of the full beauty and elegance of this fish. This, allied to the fact that some specimens can reportedly grow to a substantial size, means that the Black-spot Barb is not always widely available.

Golden Dwarf Barb

Pethia gelius (previously Barbus gelius)

Synonym: *Puntius gelius*

Subfamily: Cyprininae

Distribution: Widely reported as from central India, but also known from eastern and northeastern India.

Size: Up to 1½in (4cm), but often smaller.

Behavior: A sociable shoaling species that should never be kept either as single specimens or pairs.

Diet: Large selection of small livefoods and commercial diets accepted; vegetable supplement recommended.

Aquarium: May be kept in smaller aquaria, but does well in larger ones; both open swimming areas and plant thickets are recommended. Softish, slightly acid to neutral water is recommended. Temperature range: as low as 61°F (16°C) during winter, up to 72°F (22°C) at other times, and slightly higher for breeding.

Breeding: This species lays its eggs on the underside of a broad leaf (when such plants are available). Hatching takes about 1 day.

Despite its small size and apparently delicate appearance, the Golden Dwarf Barb is relatively hardy and easy to keep. It should, however, only be kept with other small species. Markings vary among individuals, but all specimens are attractive, particularly under lighting conditions that allow the golden body sheen to glisten. Males of the species are slimmer than the females.

T-barb

Barbodes lateristriga (previously Barbus lateristriga)

Other common name:
Spanner Barb

Synonym:
Puntius lateristriga

Subfamily: Cyprininae

Distribution: Widely
distributed in Southeast
Asia.

Size: Up to 7in (18cm)
reported for some wild
specimens; usually up
to 4in (10cm) in aquaria.

Behavior: Juveniles shoal
while adults tend to be
more solitary.

Diet: All foods accepted;
vegetable supplement
recommended.

Aquarium: Roomy with
open swimming spaces
and plant thickets. Water
chemistry is not critical,
but softish, slightly acid
to neutral conditions are
preferred. Temperature
range: as low as 66°F (19°C)
in winter, but generally
72–79°F (22–26°C).

Breeding: A prolific egg
scatterer. Hatching takes
about 1 day.

The T-barb is one of the larger species of barb available, at least in theory.
In practice, most specimens remain well below their maximum potential
size, making it possible to keep this unusually marked species in medium-
sized aquaria. Owing to its wide distribution in the wild, the T-barb occurs
in a number of forms.

Ruby Barb

Pethia nigrofasciata (previously Barbus nigrofasciatus)

Other common names:
Black Ruby, Purple-headed Barb

Synonym: *Puntius nigrofasciatus*

Subfamily: Cyprininae

Distribution: Southwest Sri Lanka.

Size: Up to 2½in (6.5cm), but often a little smaller.

Behavior: A sociable shoaling species that looks best when kept in groups of 6 or more individuals.

Diet: All livefoods and commercial diets accepted; vegetable supplement recommended.

Aquarium: As with many other Sri Lankan barbs, this species looks at its best in subdued lighting in an aquarium that provides swimming space and plant thickets. Soft, slightly acid water is preferred. Temperature range: 72–79°F (22–26°C); slightly higher for breeding.

Breeding: A typical egg-scattering, egg-eating species. Hatching takes about 1 day.

Once widely regarded as Sri Lanka's most popular freshwater fish, the Ruby Barb is now bred commercially in large numbers, both in its native country as well as in all other aquarium fish breeding regions. As a result, several cultivated varieties have been produced over the years—some consisting of color variations on the basic wild type, and some of them have fin modifications as well. Ruby Barbs can be susceptible to shock if transfer from one type of water to another or introduction into a new aquarium is undertaken without due care.

Tinfoil Barb

Barbonymus schwanefeldii (previously Barbus schwanenfeldi)

Other common names:
Goldfoil Barb,
Schwanenfeld's Barb

Synonyms: *Barbus schwanefeldi, Puntius schwanenfeldi*

Subfamily: Cyprininae

Distribution: Widely distributed in Southeast Asia.

Size: Up to 14in (35cm) for fully mature wild specimens; smaller than this in aquaria.

Behavior: An active shoaler that should only be kept with similarly sized fish.

Diet: All foods accepted; vegetable component, e.g. lettuce leaves, essential.

Aquarium: Spacious aquarium with well-fitting cover, lots of swimming space and robust or unpalatable plants. Water chemistry is not critical, but raw water should be avoided. Temperature range: 72–77°F (22–25°C).

Breeding: Widely bred commercially, but not in home aquaria. Eggs are scattered over the substratum or among plants. Hatching takes about 1 day.

This is the largest barb species usually kept in home aquaria, most commonly as juveniles, since adults will outgrow the average setup. As specimens grow, they can become aggressive, particularly toward small fish. This, added to the species' plant-eating habits, makes the Tinfoil less suitable than many other barb species. A very attractive gold-bodied, red-finned variety is now available.

Golden Barb

Puntius semifasciolatus (previously Barbus semifasciolatus)

Other common names:
Schubert's/Half-striped/Green Barb

Synonyms:
Puntius semifasciolatus,
Capoeta semifasciolatus,
Barbus schuberti,
"Barbus schuberti,"
Barbus "schuberti"

Subfamily: Cyprininae

Distribution: Southern China.

Size: Up to 4in (10cm) reported, but usually smaller.

Behavior: Peaceful shoaler.

Diet: All types of food accepted; vegetable supplement recommended.

Aquarium: Swimming space with planted areas recommended. Water chemistry is not critical, but raw water should be avoided. Temperature range: 64–75°F (18–24°C); slightly higher for breeding.

Breeding: Typical egg-scattering, egg-eating species. Hatching takes about 36 hours.

The burnished yellow body coloration of mature wild males has been developed by specialist breeders over the years into the widely available and very popular Golden or Schubert's Barb, to such an extent that the true wild type of this species is now rarely found in shops. As this fish matures, the back can darken into a deep orange-red in some specimens, particularly in males. None of the names incorporating *"schuberti"* is a valid scientific name.

Tiger Barb

Puntigrus tetrazona (previously Barbus tetrazona)

Other common name:
Sumatra Barb

Synonyms:
Puntius tetrazona,
Capoeta tetrazona

Subfamily: Cyprininae

Distribution: Indonesia (particularly Sumatra) and Borneo, including Kalimantan.

Size: Up to 2³/₄in (7cm), but usually a little smaller.

Behavior: Extremely active shoaler that will nip fins of other fish if kept singly or in pairs. A minimum of 6 specimens should be kept.

Diet: All foods accepted; vegetable component recommended.

Aquarium: Provide ample open swimming area surrounded by plant thickets. Will accept a wide range of water chemistry conditions (as long as the quality is good), but will not breed successfully unless conditions are soft and slightly acid. Temperature range: 68–79°F (20–26°C); a little higher for breeding.

Breeding: Typical egg scatterer and egg eater. Hatching takes about 36 hours. Mated pairs are recommended for best results.

This is the most widely available and popular of the barbs kept in home aquaria. It has a long aquarium history, having been introduced in the mid-1930s and has been bred in vast numbers by both aquarists and commercial breeders. Many color varieties are currently available, with new ones continuing to appear from time to time.

Cherry Barb

Puntius titteya (previously Barbus titteya)

Synonym: *Puntius titteya*

Subfamily: Cyprininae

Distribution: Southwest Sri Lanka.

Size: Up to 2in (5cm) widely reported; usually smaller.

Behavior: Not as active or as prone to shoaling as many other barb species. It is nevertheless a peaceful fish that should be kept in groups.

Diet: Most small foods are accepted; vegetable component recommended.

Aquarium: This species is a little more retiring than most other barbs. Large open areas should be avoided, but some swimming space should be provided, with ample shelter around. Soft, slightly acid water is best. Temperature range: 72–75°F (22–24°C) is adequate for normal maintenance, but should be raised to around 79°F (26°C) for breeding.

Breeding: Typical egg-scattering, egg-eating species. Hatching takes about 1 day.

This is a stunningly beautiful fish when in peak condition. In particular, fully mature males exhibit the cherry coloration to perfection. Wild-caught specimens are variable in their coloration, with at least three varieties known from different localities. Virtually all aquarium specimens are now commercially bred, in Sri Lanka or elsewhere. An albino variety is occasionally available.

Pearl Danio

Danio albolineatus (previously Brachydanio albolineatus)

Subfamily: Rasborinae (Danioninae)

Distribution: Southeast Asia.

Size: Up to 2½in (6cm); usually smaller.

Behavior: Very active shoaler that prefers the upper layers of the water column, but will swim at all levels.

Diet: Most livefoods and commercial diets are accepted.

Aquarium: A well-covered aquarium with ample swimming areas should be provided, with no tall plants obstructing this space (tall plants are best arranged around the sides and back of the aquarium). Water chemistry is not critical, but overall quality must be good. Temperature range: 68–77°F (20–25°C); a little higher for breeding.

Breeding: Chances of success are enhanced if two males and a female are introduced into a breeding tank placed in a sunny position. This is an egg-scattering, egg-eating species. Hatching takes about 36–48 hours.

The danios (*Brachydanio* and *Danio* species) are all active shoalers and have been part of the hobby for many years. The Pearl Danio was first imported into Europe in 1911 and is still very popular today. This is despite the fact that it is not often displayed to maximum effect and therefore does not always show off its best colors. Two forms of the Pearl Danio are generally available (although several more exist): the wild type and, less frequently, a yellow morph usually referred to as the Yellow Danio.

Kerr's Danio

Danio kerri (previously Brachydanio kerri)

Other common name:
Blue Danio

Subfamily: Rasborinae
(Danioninae)

Distribution: Restricted to
2 islands in Thailand.

Size: Up to 2in (5cm).

Behavior: Active shoaler;
excellent jumper.

Diet: Most foods accepted.

Aquarium: A well-covered
aquarium with ample
swimming areas should be
provided, with no tall plants
obstructing this space (tall
plants are best arranged
around the sides and back
of the aquarium). Water
chemistry is not critical, but
overall quality must be
good. Temperature range:
72–77°F (22–25°C); a little
higher for breeding.

Breeding: Eggs are
scattered, primarily, over
the substratum. Hatching
can take up to 4 days. Will
hybridize with its closest
relatives.

This is a much more recent introduction than the Pearl Danio
(*B. albolineatus*), first making its appearance in the mid-1950s.
Although quite widely available, this danio is not kept as often as
some of its nearest relatives. Like them, it is a beautiful, active jumper.

Spotted Danio

Danio nigrofasciatus (previously Brachydanio nigrofasciatus)

Subfamily: Rasborinae (Danioninae)

Distribution: Myanmar (Burma).

Size: Around 1 1/2in (4cm).

Behavior: A peaceful shoaler; not quite as active as some of its closest relatives.

Diet: Most foods accepted.

Aquarium: A well-covered aquarium with ample swimming areas should be provided, with no tall plants obstructing this space. Water chemistry is not critical, but overall quality must be good. Temperature range: 74–82°F (24–28°C); a little higher for breeding.

Breeding: Chances of success are enhanced if two males and a female are introduced into a breeding tank placed in a sunny position. An egg-scattering, egg-eating species. Hatching takes about 36–48 hours at around 77–82°F (25–28°C). It can hybridize with *B. albolineatus* and possibly other danios.

Like *B. albolineatus* (the Pearl Danio), the Spotted Danio has been around since 1911. Although it is not nowadays kept by as many aquarists as it once was, it remains a firm favorite, especially among experienced hobbyists who appreciate its beauty despite its small size.

Zebra Danio

Danio rerio (previously Brachydanio rerio)

Other common name:
Leopard Danio

Synonyms: *Brachydanio frankei, B. "frankei"*

Distribution: Zebra from Eastern India; Leopard not encountered in the wild.

Size: 2¹/₂in (6cm) including extended fins; short-finned varieties generally only attain around 1³/₄in (4.5cm).

Behavior: Extremely active shoaler that may nip fin extensions of fancy varieties of guppies, swordtails, angels, etc.

Diet: Most foods accepted.

Aquarium: Open spaces surrounded by plant thickets. Water chemistry is not critical, but soft, slightly acid water is preferred. Temperature range: 64–75°F (18–24°C); short-finned wild-type specimens can tolerate slightly lower temperatures in winter.

Breeding: Egg-scattering, egg-eating species. Eggs may be released over the substratum as well as among plants. Best results are obtained with pairs that select themselves from a shoal; they will tend to stay together. Hatching takes about 2 days.

This is by far the most popular of all the danios. It is widely available in several forms, including wild, golden, and long-finned types in different combinations. Of these, the wild type is the most robust. The Leopard Danio—also available as a long-finned variant—has traditionally been regarded as a separate species, *B. frankei*. However, genetic analysis of crosses between Leopard Danios and Zebra Danios have now confirmed that the Leopard is a Zebra morph and therefore belongs to the same species.

Goldfish

Carassius auratus

Synonym: *Carassius auratus auratus*

Subfamily: Cyprininae

Distribution: China and parts of Siberia. However, widely introduced in numerous tropical, subtropical, and temperate regions worldwide.

Size: Up to around 12in (30cm) for slim-bodied types; round-bodied varieties tend to be considerably smaller, but some types of Orandas, for example, can also grow to substantial sizes.

Behavior: Generally peaceful, although some specimens—in particular mature males during the breeding season—can harass other fish. All varieties will eat soft succulent plants and will constantly root around the bottom of the tank.

Diet: All foods accepted; vegetable component important.

The Goldfish is believed to be not just the most widely kept ornamental fish in the world, but the most popular of all pets. Virtually every aquarist and pondkeeper has kept a Goldfish at one time or another. Although there is documentary evidence of the Goldfish having been kept as a pet in ponds in China as far back as the Sung Dynasty (960–1279 A.D.), there are indications that its history could stretch back to the Western Jin Dynasty (262–315 A.D.), which would make the Goldfish–human association at least 1,700 years old. Over the centuries countless varieties of the Goldfish have been developed in numerous countries. Today there are over 100 officially recognized varieties and an unknown number of "unofficial" ones.

Aquarium: It should be roomy with wide open areas that allow full view of the fish. Robust and/or unpalatable plants should be used, perhaps supplemented with artificial types. Roots should be protected. Water chemistry is not critical but quality must be good. Efficient filtration and aeration are essential. Temperature range: from well below 50°F (10°C) to above 86°F (30°C); higher temperatures should not be maintained on a long-term basis.

Breeding: Persistent chasing (driving) by the male—which develops white pimplelike tubercles on its snout and gill covers during the breeding season—will eventually result in the pair (or a shoal) spawning among any fine-leaved vegetation. Goldfish are egg scatterers/eaters, so either they or the eggs should be removed after spawning, which tends to occur at temperatures above 68°F (20°C). Hatching can take up to 1 week, but generally takes less.

Above: (1) Common Goldfish; (2) Bristol Shubunkin; (3) Veiltail; (4) Ranchu; (5) Pom Pom; (6) Bubble-eye. **Opposite:** Normal Gold.

A few of the best-known varieties are shown here. However, as variants are continually combined to select color or fin features, the rate at which new Goldfish varieties become available shows no sign of slowing down.

The alternative scientific name given above, *Carassius auratus auratus*, indicates that the Goldfish was until quite recently regarded as a subspecies of *C. auratus*, the other one being *C. auratus gibelius*, the Gibel or Prussian Carp. Today, however, both are regarded as valid species in their own right.

Left: Calico Wakin.
Below left: Orange-and-black Oranda.
Below center: Red-and-white Telescope-eye.
Below right: Calico Oranda.
Right, clockwise from top: Red-and-white Hua (Hong Bai Ji); Red-and-white (Shi-er Hong Ji); White-red; White Eggfish.

Above: Red-and-white Veiltail.
Inset: Golden Black.

Indian Glass Barb

Laubuka laubuca (previously Chela laubuca)

Other common names: Indian Glass Hatchet, Blue Laubuca

Subfamily: Rasborinae (Danioninae)

Distribution: Southeast Asia (widely distributed).

Size: Up to 2¹/₂in (6cm).

Behavior: A peaceful shoaler rgar has a strong preference for the surface layers of the aquarium.

Diet: Wide range of (predominantly) floating foods accepted; will not feed off the bottom.

Aquarium: Open swimming areas surrounded by vegetation. Frequent partial water changes recommended, as well as soft, slightly acid water. Temperature range: 75–79°F (24–26°C).

Breeding: Eggs laid among fine-leaved vegetation. Hatching takes about 1 day.

There are several species of *Chela* occasionally available: *C. laubuca* (the most common), *C. cachuis* (Neon Hatchet), *C. dadyburjori* (Burjor's Brilliance or Orange Chela), *C. fasciata* (Striped Chela), and—perhaps the most colorful of all—*C. auropurpurens* (Orange False Barilius).

All are small with the exception of the last species, which is reported to attain 4in (10cm) in length. Despite two of its common names, *C. laubuca* is neither a barb nor a hatchetfish. Chelas can prove delicate during the initial phases of acclimatization.

Siamese Flying Fox

Crossocheilus oblongus (previously Crossocheilus siamensis)

Other common name:
Siamese Algae Eater

Synonym: *Notropis siamensis*

Subfamily: Cyprininae (classified as Garrinae by some authors)

Distribution: Thailand, peninsular Malaysia.

Size: Up to 6in (15cm) reported, but usually smaller.

Behavior: Tolerant of other species, but less so of its own.

Diet: Wide range of foods accepted; vegetable component essential. Reported to eat planarian worms (flatworms), which are sometimes introduced accidentally with livefoods.

Aquarium: Roomy tank with thickets of vegetation (Siamese Flying Foxes will eat algae, but do not generally harm other plants). Hiding places should be provided. Well-oxygenated, soft, slightly acid water is recommended, though harder, more alkaline conditions are also tolerated. Temperature range: 73–79°F (23–26°C).

Breeding: No details are available.

What the Siamese Flying Fox may lack in brilliant coloration it more than makes up for with its other attributes. In particular, it is one of the few aquarium fish that actually eats thread algae. Its only potential drawback for many home aquaria is that it can grow to a substantial size.

Koi

Cyprinus carpio

Other common name:
Brocaded Carp

Subfamily: Cyprininae

Distribution: Originally from the Danube and other freshwaters of the Black Sea basin. Now found throughout Europe (except the extreme north) and numerous other regions.

Size: Up to 40in (1m) for fully grown wild *C. carpio*; usually a little smaller for Koi, even "jumbo" specimens.

Behavior: Generally peaceful, even toward smaller fish, but some males may become a little aggressive during the breeding season. All types will eat soft succulent plants and will spend much of the time rooting around the bottom of the aquarium.

Diet: All foods accepted; vegetable component important. Treats can include items like shrimp, peas, lettuce, and brown bread, but not as major components of the diet.

In the past these highly developed varieties of the Common Carp have only been kept in ponds, but improvements in aquarium technology, along with the rise in interest in "companion pets," have led to some types of Koi being introduced into large aquaria. Fairy or Butterfly (long-finned) Koi are the most popular of the "aquarium" varieties, but even the more traditional pond varieties are now being sought by aquarists, many of whom also keep Koi in ponds.

The history of the Koi, although considerably shorter than that of the Goldfish (the first recognized Koi being associated with developments during the early 19th century in Niigata Prefecture on the Japanese island of Honshu), is long enough to have produced numerous color and scale modifications. The result is a bewildering array of fish bred in vast quantities in Japan, Israel, Italy, the UK, the United States, the Far East, and virtually every other region with an interest in coldwater fishkeeping. However, Japan still leads the way in terms of pedigree fish production.

Aquarium: Only large and deep aquaria that are efficiently filtered can be considered suitable. Use robust and unpalatable plants, perhaps combined with artificial types. Protect plant roots. Water chemistry not critical. Temperature range: from well below 50°F (10°C) to above 86°F (30°C); higher temperatures should not be maintained for long periods.

Breeding: Difficult to achieve in most aquaria owing to lack of space. Eggs are scattered among vegetation when the temperature rises above 63°F (17°C). Injuries may result during the vigorous chasing (driving) that occurs. Spawning brushes or mats are recommended, to be subsequently removed to another aquarium for hatching, which takes 3–4 days at 68–72°F (20–22°C).

Top: Yamabuki Hariwake; **Center:** Kumonryo; **Below:** Kin Ki Utsuri. **Opposite:** Kohaku.

Above: Boke Showa.
Left: Tancho Sanke.
Above right: Ki Bekko.
Right: Kage Showa.

Red Shiner

Cyprinella lutrensis

Other common names: Sandpaper Shiner, Red Horse Minnow, Rainbow Dace

Synonym: *Notropis lutrensis*

Subfamily: Leuciscinae

Distribution: Mississippi River basin (United States) and Gulf drainages west of the Mississippi. Widely introduced elsewhere in the United States; also in northern Mexico.

Size: 3½in (9cm).

Behavior: A very active shoaler.

Diet: All foods accepted.

Aquarium: Roomy with ample swimming space; well-filtered, well-oxygenated water and frequent partial water changes recommended. Water chemistry not critical. Temperature range: 50–77°F (10–25°C).

Breeding: Eggs laid in a depression on a sandy/silty bottom. Hatching takes several days.

Two of the common names refer to the red patches that mature males develop on top of and behind the head, as well as on all the fins. This contrasts beautifully with the grayish blue of the rest of the body, making the Red Shiner a most attractive choice for the coldwater aquarium. While the Red Shiner (wild type or albino) is by far the most common shiner, other *Cyprinella* and *Notropis* species are beginning to appear with greater regularity.

Giant Danio

Devario aequipinnatus (previously Danio aequipinnatus)

Synonym:
Danio malabaricus

Subfamily: Rasborinae
(Danioninae)

Distribution: Southwest
India and Sri Lanka.

Size: Up to 6in (15cm)
reported, but usually
considerably smaller.

Behavior: Very active
peaceful shoaler that
prefers the upper layers
of the water column.

Diet: Wide range of foods
accepted.

Aquarium: Roomy with
well-fitting cover, open
swimming spaces, and plant
thickets. Water chemistry
not critical but quality must
be good. Temperature
range: 72–75°F (22–24°C);
slightly higher for breeding.

Breeding: Female scatters
eggs among fine-leaved
vegetation. Hatching
takes about 1 day.

The genus *Danio* is very similar to *Brachydanio*, differing only in details
relating to fin-ray and lateral-line features. More obvious is the larger size
attained by *Danio* species.

There is still considerable debate as to whether *D. aequipinnatus* and
D. malabaricus are one and the same species or whether, at least in Sri
Lanka, they constitute two very closely related species. Most authorities
believe them to be the same fish. Several color varieties, including a
golden one, are available.

Bengal Danio

Devario devario (previously Danio devario)

Other common name:
Turquoise Danio

Subfamily: Rasborinae
(Danioninae)

Distribution: Northern and
eastern India, Bangladesh,
and Pakistan.

Size: Up to 6in (15cm)
reported, but generally
significantly smaller.

Behavior: An active shoaling
species that can be a little
timid. It prefers to frequent
the top layers.

Diet: Wide range of foods
accepted.

Aquarium: A dark
substratum helps show
off this species to good
effect. Provide ample
spaces surrounded by
plant thickets. Water
chemistry not critical.
Temperature range:
59–79°F (15–26°C)
considered adequate,
but 68–79°F (20–26°C)
is recommended.

Breeding: This is a typical
egg scatterer. Hatching
takes about 1 day.

This species is the least streamlined of the danios. The females, in
particular, have a relatively deep body. Bengal Danio is also the most
subtly colored member of the genus, being golden brown on the back
and belly, and blue with transverse yellow stripes on the flanks. Its colors
are best exhibited in reflected light and when kept as a shoal. The Bengal
Danio's dorsal fins are longer than those of other danios.

Barred Danio

Devario pathirana (previously Danio pathirana)

Subfamily: Rasborinae (Danioninae)

Distribution: Southwest Sri Lanka.

Size: About 2$\frac{1}{2}$in (6cm).

Behavior: Not as active as some of its closest relatives. Tends to form small groups rather than large shoals in the wild and exhibits fin-nipping behavior at times.

Diet: Wide range of foods accepted.

Aquarium: Roomy with well-fitting cover, open swimming spaces, and plant thickets. Water chemistry not critical but quality must be good. Temperature range: 72–75°F (22–24°C); slightly higher for breeding.

Breeding: Egg-scattering species but details are unavailable.

This is the most recently discovered and kept of the *Danio* species (officially described in 1990) and, in the opinion of some, the most beautiful. Within its restricted range it has been found in both still and flowing waters. Although bred in captivity, this species is not yet available in large numbers. It is, however, an adaptable fish that is likely to become progressively more popular.

Red-tailed Black Shark

Epalzeorhynchos bicolor (previously Epalzeorhynchus bicolor)

Other common name:
Red-tailed Labeo

Synonym: *Labeo bicolor*

Subfamily: Cyprininae (classified as Garrinae by some authors)

Distribution: Thailand.

Size: Up to 4³/₄in (12cm).

Behavior: A loner that stakes out its own territory and will become aggressive toward other members of its species. This intolerance can be extended to other species as well, particularly by older specimens.

Diet: Wide range of foods accepted; sinking formulations and a vegetable component are recommended.

Aquarium: Spacious, with shelters or caves provided. A fine-grained substratum is recommended, as is soft to medium-hard water. Temperature range: 72–79°F (22–26°C); higher for breeding.

Breeding: Infrequent in aquaria. Eggs are reported to be laid in a depression in the substratum. Hatching takes about 2 days.

This is by far the most strikingly colored of all the aquarium "sharks"—which are only sharklike in their overall body shape, and even then only superficially. Unless water conditions are to its liking, this species will not show off its best colors, becoming darkish gray and faint red rather than jet black and bright red. Due attention must therefore be paid to aquarium layout and conditions.

Rainbow Shark

Epalzeorhynchos frenatum (previously Epalzeorhynchus frenatus)

Other common names:
Ruby Shark, Red-finned
Shark

Synonyms: *Labeo frenatus,*
Labeo erythrurus

Subfamily: Cyprininae
(classified as Garrinae by
some authors)

Distribution: Thailand.

Size: Up to 6in (15cm), but
usually quite a bit smaller.

Behavior: A loner that stakes
out its own territory and will
become aggressive toward
other members of its
species. This intolerance can
be extended to other species
as well, particularly by older
specimens.

Diet: Wide range of
foods accepted; sinking
formulations and a
vegetable component
are recommended.

Aquarium: Spacious, with
shelters or caves provided.
A fine-grained substratum
is recommended, as is soft
to medium-hard water.
Temperature range:
72–79°F (22–26°C);
higher for breeding.

Breeding: Infrequent in
aquaria; no documented
accounts appear to be
available.

This is a slimmer species than *E. bicolor*. Its body color is overall grayish
brown to black, with an occasional violet iridescence. The fins are orange-
red or red. In males the rear portion of the anal fin is black. A short dark
band extends from the gill cover through the eye. Specimens offered as
Labeo erythrurus are generally believed to be either mature *E. frenatus* or
a local variety. A commercially produced albino morph is widely available.

Flying Barb

Esomus thermoicos

Synonym: *Esomus danrica*

Subfamily: Rasborinae (Danioninae)

Distribution: India, Sri Lanka, and Thailand.

Size: Up to 6in (15cm) reported, but usually much smaller. About 2½in (6cm) common in wild-caught specimens.

Behavior: Very active fish with a tendency to leap out of the water. Prefers the top layers of the aquarium.

Diet: Wide range of foods accepted.

Aquarium: Roomy, well-covered tank with ample surface swimming space surrounded by plants. Water chemistry not critical but quality must be good. Temperature range: 72–75°F (22–24°C); higher—around 81°F (27°C)—for breeding.

Breeding: Eggs are scattered among plants. Hatching takes 1–2 days, depending on temperature.

Most books will refer to the Flying Barb as *Esomus danrica* rather than *E. thermoicos*. However, comparative work carried out on Indian and Sri Lankan collections indicates that both nominal species are more closely related than first thought; they may be subspecies or even just normally varying populations. Further work is awaited. The most unusual feature of this attractive species is its very long, filamentlike barbels that are responsible for its common name (even though it is not a barb). It does, however, jump ("fly").

Siamese Stone-lapping Sucker

Garra cambodgiensis (previously Garra taeniatia)

Subfamily: Cyprininae

Distribution: Thailand.

Size: Up to 6in (15cm).

Behavior: Generally tolerant of other species, but may disrupt the substratum, particularly when kept in groups.

Diet: Most foods accepted, especially sinking formulations.

Aquarium: Roomy, with ample resting/hiding places and robust plants, with roots protected. Water should be well aerated and filtered. Temperature range: 75–79°F (24–26°C).

Breeding: No details are available.

Over recent years a number of *Garra* species have begun appearing in the hobby with increasing regularity. All are, basically, bottom-dwelling species from flowing-water habitats and are not difficult to keep. The Siamese Stone-lapping Sucker is the most commonly encountered species.

Gudgeon

Gobio gobio

Subfamily: Gobioninae

Distribution: Europe, except most of Italy, northern Finland, Sweden, and the Adriatic coast. Spanish, Scottish, and Northern Irish populations are introduced rather than native.

Size: Up to 8in (20cm), but usually smaller.

Behavior: Peaceful bottom dweller that will learn to take food from the surface.

Diet: Most foods accepted, particularly sinking formulations and livefoods.

Aquarium: Well-filtered, well-oxygenated water essential (this species is sensitive to pollution). Substratum should be fine-grained and shelters should be provided. Neutral to slightly alkaline, medium-hard water is preferred. Temperature range: 50–68°F (10–20°C).

Breeding: Infrequent in aquaria. Adhesive eggs laid on substratum in flowing water. Hatching takes 10–30 days, depending on temperature.

The Gudgeon is predominantly a bottom-dwelling species that has traditionally been regarded as a pondfish by (mostly) European hobbyists. However, as coldwater aquarium keeping has expanded, the species has gained greater popularity. One of the Gudgeon's distinguishing features is the pair of barbels either side of its mouth.

Black Shark

Labeo chrysophekadion

Other common name:
Black Labeo

Subfamily: Cyprininae

Distribution: Southwest Asia (widely distributed).

Size: Up to 24in (60cm) reported.

Behavior: A loner that is aggressive toward members of its own species.

Diet: All foods accepted; vegetable component important.

Aquarium: Roomy, well-filtered, well-aerated aquarium with large shelters, e.g. caves or bogwood. Water chemistry not critical. Temperature range: 75–81°F (24–27°C).

Breeding: No reports available.

This is the largest "shark" species kept in aquaria. Most specimens offered are around 4in (10cm) or smaller. They will grow quickly and are therefore not suitable for the average aquaria. However, if sufficiently spacious accommodation is available, a lone large specimen will prove a long-lived and impressive companion. Two other *Labeo* species (both smaller, but still substantial) are also available: *L. forskalii* (Plain Shark) and *L. variegatus* (Harlequin or Variegated Shark).

Golden Orfe

Leuciscus idus

Other common name:
Ide

Synonym: *Idus idus*

Subfamily: Leuciscinae

Distribution: Most of Europe.

Size: Up to 39in (1m) in the wild; cultivated varieties do not normally exceed 24in (60cm), even in large ponds.

Behavior: Active shoaler that prefers the upper layers.

Diet: All foods accepted, but livefoods preferred.

Aquarium: Very spacious aquarium with open swimming areas and well-fitting cover. Well-oxygenated, well-filtered water is very important. Water chemistry not critical. Temperature range: from near-freezing to over 86°F (30°C), but higher temperatures should be short-lived.

Breeding: Infrequent in aquaria. Egg-scattering species. Hatching may take up to 20 days at cool temperatures.

Leuciscus idus is usually available as a gold morph—known as the Golden Orfe—and is one of the most popular pondfish kept in Europe. However, growing numbers are now also kept in aquaria, either temporarily (for subsequent release into a garden pond) or on a permanent basis. In addition to the gold morph, there is the wild type (silver) morph and a blue variety that looks particularly attractive in aquaria.

European Minnow

Phoxinus phoxinus

Subfamily: Leuciscinae

Distribution: British Isles and eastern Spain to eastern Siberia.

Size: Rarely exceeds 4in (10cm).

Behavior: An agile shoaler; prefers the upper layers.

Diet: All foods accepted, including algae and livefoods such as small mollusks, crustaceans, and insects.

Aquarium: Spacious aquarium with open swimming areas. Well-oxygenated, well-filtered water is important. Water should be medium hard; pH 6.5–7 recommended. Temperature range: 73–77°F (23–25°C) preferred.

Breeding: Water should be clear and shallow—about 6in (15cm) deep—with gravel on the bottom and a few stones. Eggs are laid on the stones and hatching takes about 6 days.

The European Minnow is a small cyprinid, rarely growing to more than 4 inches (10cm) in length. Its body color is greenish-brown on the back with dark spots, creating an attractive, almost banded appearance. During the spawning season the males change color dramatically. Their back darkens, the belly and lower fins become red, while the sides turn a golden color.

Fathead Minnow

Pimephales promelas

Other common names:
Golden Minnow, Rosy Red

Subfamily: Leuciscinae

Distribution: Most of North America; introduced into many exotic locations as far south as Mexico.

Size: Up to 4in (10cm); usually considerably smaller.

Behavior: Active shoaler; males become territorial during breeding.

Diet: All foods accepted.

Aquarium: Caves and broad-leaved floating plants should be provided. Water chemistry not critical. Temperature range: 50–77°F (10–25°C).

Breeding: Eggs are attached to the undersurface of floating plants or the roof of a cave and are guarded by the male. Hatching takes around 1 week.

The Fathead Minnow was originally cultivated commercially in the United States as a bait fish. However, the attractive coloration of the golden morph, added to its interesting breeding habits, soon created a demand among aquarists. Today, virtually all the Fathead Minnows in the hobby are of the golden variety.

Red-tailed Rasbora

Rasbora borapetensis

Subfamily: Rasborinae (Danioninae)

Distribution: Thailand and western Malaysia.

Size: 2in (5cm).

Behavior: A peaceful shoaler.

Diet: Most small foods accepted, but livefoods preferred.

Aquarium: For best effect, lighting should not be too bright (floating plants will help diffuse it). Open swimming spaces and abundant vegetation should be provided. Soft, slightly acid water (perhaps filtered through peat) recommended. Temperature range: 72–79°F (22–26°C).

Breeding: Egg-scattering and egg-eating species. Shallow water is therefore recommended. Hatching takes about 1½ days.

This is a slender fish that only looks its best when water and tank conditions are right. At other times the red coloration responsible for the common name, and which makes a shoal of these rasboras an absolute delight, fades significantly.

Greater Scissortail

Rasbora caudimaculata

Other common names:
Giant Scissortail, Spot-tailed Scissortail

Subfamily: Rasborinae (Danioninae)

Distribution: Southeast Asia.

Size: Up to 4³/₄in (12cm) reported, but usually smaller.

Behavior: An active shoaler with excellent jumping ability.

Diet: All foods accepted, particularly livefoods.

Aquarium: Roomy, well-covered tank with ample swimming areas and plant thickets. Water chemistry not critical. Temperature range: 68–77°F (20–25°C); slightly higher for breeding.

Breeding: Egg-scattering species; breeding infrequent in aquaria.

Despite two of its common names, *R. caudimaculata* is no larger than its more widely available close relative *R. trilineata* (the Scissortail). Both are very attractive fish when conditions are to their liking. The Greater Scissortail is a long, slender fish with a dark green shiny body. The tail fins have black markings at the tip. Males are more slender than females and have additional yellow coloration in the tail fins.

Elegant Rasbora

Rasbora elegans

Other common name:
Two-spot Rasbora

Subfamily: Rasborinae
(Danioninae)

Distribution: Southeast
Asia.

Size: Up to 8in (20cm)
reported, but usually much
smaller.

Behavior: A peaceful shoaler
despite its size.

Diet: All foods accepted.

Aquarium: Roomy with a
well-fitting cover, ample
swimming areas and plant
thickets; a dark substratum
is recommended. Soft,
slightly acid water and
regular partial changes
preferred. Temperature
range: 72–77°F (22–25°C).

Breeding: Low water level
recommended for this egg-
scattering/eating species.
Introducing the female a
day or so before the male
may help. Hatching takes
about 1½ days.

While the Elegant Rasbora is, undoubtedly, an "elegant" fish, it is no more
so than its close relatives. The most striking features of this attractive fish
are its body spots. They can vary in shape, the posterior one sometimes
being almost diamond shaped. The black line that runs along the base
of the anal fin is also very distinctive.

Slim Harlequin

Trigonostigma espei (previously Rasbora espei)

Other common names:
Narrow-wedged/Glowlight/
Espe's Rasbora

Synonyms: *Rasbora
heteromorpha espei,
Trigonostigma espei*

Subfamily: Rasboriniae
(Danioninae)

Distribution: Thailand.

Size: Up to 2in (5cm)
reported, but usually
smaller.

Behavior: A peaceful shoaler.

Diet: All small commercial
and live foods.

Aquarium: Subdued lighting
and a dark substratum show
this species off to best
effect. Soft, slightly acid
water is recommended.
Temperature range:
73–82°F (22–28°C).

Breeding: Infrequent in
aquaria. Shallow, mature
water and trio (one female/
two males) recommended.
Eggs laid on underside
of broad-leaved plants.
Hatching takes about 1 day.

As of 1999 this species, along with *R. heteromorpha* (the Harlequin) and
R. hengeli, was transferred to a new genus, *Trigonostigma*. While accepting
this revision, the former two are included in this book under *Rasbora* until
the new name becomes more widely used in aquarium literature.

The Slim Harlequin can be easily distinguished from its better-known
relative the Harlequin: the most distinctive feature of both—the dark
body-cone pattern—is much narrower in the Slim Harlequin. In this,
it resembles the other closely related species, *R. hengeli* (the Glass or
Hengel's Harlequin) from Sumatra, which is rarely kept (most "*hengeli*"
are probably, in fact, *espei*). Further work is required to establish
differences between the two.

Harlequin

Trigonostigma heteromorpha (previously Rasbora heteromorpha)

Other common name:
Red Rasbora

Synonyms: *Trigonostigma heteromorpha*

Subfamily: Rasborinae (Danioninae)

Distribution: Peninsular Malaysia, Singapore, Sumatra, and probably Thailand.

Size: Up to 1³/₄in (4.5cm).

Behavior: A peaceful shoaler.

Diet: Most foods accepted.

Aquarium: Subdued lighting and a dark substratum show this species off to best effect. Soft, slightly acid water is recommended. Temperature range: 73–79°F (22–26°C).

Breeding: Infrequent in aquaria. Shallow, mature water and trio (one female/two males) recommended. Eggs laid on underside of broad-leaved plants. Hatching takes about 1 day.

The Harlequin is one of the old aquarium favorites, having first been imported into Europe way back in 1906. It is still very popular today, largely owing to its striking coloration and dark body cone. Of the three "harlequins," this species possesses the widest body cone, making it immediately identifiable. A dark or blue variety is now also widely available.

Glowlight Rasbora

Trigonopoma pauciperforatum (previously Rasbora pauciperforata)

Under appropriate conditions the Glowlight Rasbora really lives up to its name. Unlike other rasboras, however, this species can tolerate relatively low temperatures during the winter, something that may improve the chances of achieving breeding success, particularly if pairs are allowed to select themselves from a shoal.

Other common names: Red-striped Rasbora, Red-line Rasbora

Subfamily: Rasborinae (Danioninae)

Distribution: Western Malaysia, Sumatra.

Size: Up to 2³/₄in (7cm) reported; usually smaller.

Behavior: A rather timid species that prefers the lower reaches of the aquarium, especially among vegetation.

Diet: Will take a range of commercial formulations, but prefers livefoods.

Aquarium: Subdued illumination and ample vegetation recommended. Soft, slightly acid water with regular partial water changes and filtration through peat is preferred. Temperature range: 66–70°F (19–21°C) during winter, rising to 73–77°F (23–25°C) at other times, and slightly higher for breeding.

Breeding: A challenging species that scatters eggs among fine-leaved vegetation. Hatching takes about 1–1¹/₂ days.

Scissortail

Rasboroides vaterifloris (previously Rasbora trilineata)

Other common name:
Three-lined Rasbora

Subfamily: Rasborinae
(Danioninae)

Distribution: Malaysia,
Borneo, and Sumatra.

Size: Up to 6in (15cm)
reported; almost always
considerably smaller.

Behavior: An active shoaling
species.

Diet: Wide range accepted,
but livefoods preferred.

Aquarium: Ample swimming
areas surrounded by plant
thickets. Dark substratum
and soft, slightly acid water
with regular partial changes
recommended. Temperature
range: 72–77°F (22–25°C);
slightly higher for breeding.

Breeding: Shallow water
required with plenty of
fine-leaved vegetation.
Challenging egg-scattering
and egg-eating species.
Hatching takes about 1 day.

This is another of the larger rasboras (although the maximum size is rarely
attained, either in aquaria or in the wild). It is a species that only looks at
its best when kept in a shoal. It prefers the middle and upper reaches of
the aquarium but will also venture farther down.

Fire Rasbora

Rasbora vaterifloris

Other common names:
Golden/Pearly Rasbora, Fire Barb, Orange-finned Barb

Subfamily: Rasborinae (Danioninae)

Distribution: Sri Lanka.

Size: Up to 1½in (4cm); usually a little smaller.

Behavior: A shy, peaceful shoaler that avoids bright lights.

Diet: Wide range of foods accepted, particularly livefoods; will not generally feed off the bottom.

Aquarium: Subdued lighting and a dark substratum recommended. Sensitive to water conditions, which should be mature, soft, slightly acid, and well filtered. Some swimming areas with ample planting should be provided. Temperature range: 75–82°F (24–28°C).

Breeding: Challenging. Prolific in the wild but not in aquaria. Shallow, mature, well-planted conditions recommended. Egg-scattering species. Hatching takes about 1½ days.

Without being one of the most colorful of the rasboras, this species is one of the most beautiful when in peak condition and under appropriate lighting. It has a dark pink arched body. The fins have dark orange streaks, and its eyes are metallic orange in color. It is a challenging fish best avoided by less experienced aquarists.

Bitterling
Rhodeus sericeus

Synonyms: *Rhodeus amarus, R. amarus sericeus, R. sericeus amarus*

Subfamily: Acheilognathinae (sometimes Rhodeinae)

Distribution: Most of Europe north of the Alps, excluding Scandinavia and most of the British Isles (although there are introduced populations).

Size: 4in (10cm).

Behavior: An active fish; may be kept in pairs or small groups.

Diet: All foods, particularly livefoods; vegetable component recommended.

Aquarium: Roomy and well planted. At least part of the substratum should be fine-grained to accommodate freshwater mussels if breeding is required. Water chemistry not critical but quality must be good. Temperature range: 64–70°F (18–21°C); cold spell at around 50°F (10°C) during winter improves chances of breeding success.

Breeding: Eggs are laid and fertilized inside breathing tube (inhalant siphon) of mussel. Hatching can take up to 3 weeks.

Despite it being a long-established aquarium fish, there is still debate regarding the correct scientific name of this species, with the weight of opinion tending toward *R. sericeus*. Males look particularly attractive during the breeding season (April to August) and when they are subjected to side lighting.

Rudd

Scardinius erythrophthalmus

Other common name:
Red-eye

Subfamily: Leuciscinae

Distribution: Europe north of the Pyrenees, but absent in the extreme north; introduced into numerous exotic locations.

Size: Up to 18in (45cm); usually considerably smaller.

Behavior: An active, peaceful shoaler that prefers the upper layers of the water column.

Diet: Wide range of foods accepted.

Aquarium: Roomy, well oxygenated and well filtered. Water chemistry not critical. Temperature range: from close to freezing up to tropical temperatures, but 50–68°F (10–20°C) recommended.

Breeding: Only feasible in large aquaria. Up to 200,000 eggs may be released by a large female. Hatching takes 8–15 days.

The Rudd is a stocky, deep-bodied fish. It has an olive-colored back, silvery-green sides, and a silvery-white belly. The species is available in the hobby in two color forms: the silvery wild type and a cultivated golden form. It is the latter that is kept, primarily by European pondkeepers, but to an increasing extent by aquarists as well.

White Cloud Mountain Minnow

Tanichthys albonubes

Subfamily: Rasborinae (Danioninae)

Distribution: The type with light-colored fin edges found in the White Cloud Mountain region near Canton, China; "red" type found around Hong Kong, probably from aquarium-bred escapees.

Size: 1³/₄in (4.5cm).

Behavior: A peaceful shoaler.

Diet: All foods accepted.

Aquarium: A dark substratum in a well-planted tank that offers some swimming spaces is recommended. Water chemistry not critical. Temperature range: 50°F (15°C) during winter to 64–77°F (18–25°C) at other times.

Breeding: Eggs are scattered among fine-leaved vegetation. Hatching takes about 1½ days.

Two color types of this popular fish are available: one with light-colored anal and dorsal fin edges and one with red edges. A long-finned variety that almost disappeared during the early 1990s is now found with greater frequency once more.

Tench

Tinca tinca

Other common name:
Doctor Fish

Subfamily: Leuciscinae (classified as Cyprininae by some authors)

Distribution: Widespread in Europe and stretching eastward to Russia; absent from northern Scandinavia, possibly Scotland, Ireland, Iberia, and the Adriatic coastline; widely introduced into exotic locations, including the United States.

Size: Up to 28in (70cm) reported in the wild; usually much smaller.

Behavior: Bottom dweller that will rise to the surface for food. Juveniles may be kept as a shoal.

Diet: All foods accepted.

Aquarium: Large, well-filtered (for water clarity purposes) aquaria with robust vegetation. Water chemistry not critical. Temperature range: from near freezing to over 86°F (30°C), but 68–77°F (20–25°C) is perfectly adequate.

Breeding: Difficult in aquaria. Huge numbers of eggs (up to 900,000) laid among plants in late spring/early summer. Hatching takes 6–8 days.

The Tench is a traditional pondfish (predominantly in Europe) that is gradually making a transition to (large) aquaria. Until the mid-1990s two color forms were available: the green (or wild type) and a golden (sometimes mottled) variety. Since then, at least two other colors have become available: a deep orange (sometimes referred to as red) and an orange/red and white type.

Left: Green, or Wild, with dark juvenile.
Below left: Three-colored.
Below right: White.
Opposite: Gold.

CHARACOIDS

Order Characiformes

Although members of the family Characidae can be very different from each other (the Piranha and the Neon Tetra are examples of this), they share a sufficiently large number of similarities for most authorities to believe that they belong to the same family. However, pending a detailed review, they are grouped by some authors, including Nelson, (see Further Reading), into a number of different subfamilies.

Broadening the issue further, there are many other fish species that share some characteristics with the members of the Characidae; however, they also exhibit significant differences. Therefore they are not, strictly speaking, characids, but are definitely characidlike. These other fish species are grouped into a number of distinct families. They are the Anostomidae, Citharinidae, Ctenolucidae, Curimatidae,

Above: *Hyphessobrycon eques.*
Below: *Hemigrammus rodwayi.*

Erythrinidae, Gasteropelecidae, Hepsetidae, Hemiodontidae, and Lebiasinidae. Together with the Characidae, they form the order Characiformes, the so-called characiforms or characoids (as opposed to characids).

The Characiformes usually have well-developed teeth—even tiny species such as the Cardinal Tetra (*Paracheirodon axelrodi*) have excellent dentition—and an adipose fin (a second small, fleshy, rayless dorsal fin). In a few Characiformes, e.g. the Silver-tipped or Copper Tetra (*Hasemania nana*), the adipose fin is not present, but in such fish other characteristics place them firmly in one or other of the characoid families. These other characteristics include a (usually) decurved lateral line, i.e. it curves downward to a greater or lesser extent (with some exceptions), and pharyngeal ("throat") teeth. Characoids lack barbels and the upper jaw is not usually protractile, i.e. extensible. There are also several skeletal features relating to the tail bones, fin rays, and so on, which identify fish as characoids.

Within this broad framework, ten families can be identified. Within them, there is a total of about 240 genera and 1,350 species, of which around 210 genera occur in Africa; the remainder are largely distributed in Central or South America, with a relatively small number in Mexico and southwestern United States.

Marbled Headstander

Abramites hypselonotus

Other common name: High-backed Headstander

Synonym: *Abramites microcephalus*

Family: Anostomidae

Subfamily: Anostominae

Distribution: Amazon, and Orinoco and Paraguay River basins.

Size: Up to 5½in (14cm).

Behavior: Progressively more intolerant of their own species as they mature, at least in aquaria (found in shoals in the wild). Appetite for tender succulent plants. Excellent jumpers.

Diet: A range of commercial foods, as well as livefoods, accepted; vegetable component important.

Aquarium: Well covered (essential to prevent jumping out) and with bogwood or large rocks. Do not use succulent plants. Only unpalatable and/or artificial plants should be provided. Medium-hard, neutral to slightly alkaline water recommended. Temperature range: 73–81°F (23–27°C).

Breeding: No documented reports of aquarium breeding currently available.

Members of this species are sometimes split into two subspecies: *A. hypselonotus hypselonotus* from the Amazon, and *A. h. ternetzi* from the Paraguay River basin. The former is said to have its dorsal fin set farther forward and to possess a narrower caudal peduncle (the base from which the caudal fin originates). Juveniles do not have the characteristic high backs of mature specimens.

Striped Anostomus

Anostomus anostomus

Other common name:
Striped Headstander

Family: Anostomidae

Subfamily: Anostominae

Distribution: Amazon (upriver from Manáus), Orinoco, Colombia, and Guyana.

Size: Up to 7in (18cm), but generally smaller.

Behavior: Large shoals tend to get along, but small groups will scrap. Single specimens generally tolerate other species. Individuals like to shelter in vertical crevices.

Diet: A range of commercial foods, as well as livefoods, accepted; vegetable component important.

Aquarium: Roomy, well planted, well covered, with adequate bogwood and other shelters, including vertical hiding places, and with good aeration and filtration (power filtration recommended to create water current). Soft, slightly acid water preferred. Temperature range: 72–82°F (22–28°C).

Breeding: Very rare in aquaria; no details currently available.

In overall body shape, *Anostomus* species are somewhat more slender than *Abramites*. They also lack the broad vertical banding, having (in most cases) longitudinal stripes, and they possess a distinctively upturned mouth. Striped Anostomus is the most commonly seen species of its genus.

Ternetz's Anostomus

Anostomus ternetzi

Other common name:
Ternetz's Headstander

Family: Anostomidae

Subfamily: Anostominae

Distribution: Orinoco basin (Venezuela); Xingu and Araguaia Rivers (Brazil).

Size: Sometimes reported up to 7in (18cm), i.e. same size as *A. anostomus*, but usually at least ³⁄₄in (2cm) smaller.

Behavior: More peaceful toward its own species than *A. anostomus*.

Diet: A range of commercial foods, as well as livefoods, accepted; vegetable component important.

Aquarium: Roomy, well planted, well covered, with adequate bogwood and other shelters, including vertical hiding places, and with good aeration and filtration (power filtration recommended to create water current). Soft, slightly acid water preferred. Temperature range: 72–82°F (22–28°C).

Breeding: No reports of aquarium breeding currently available.

This species is superficially similar to *A. anostomus* (Striped Anostomus), but it is somewhat smaller, slimmer, and less colorful, particularly in the red dorsal and caudal fin coloration. Its major advantages for mixed aquaria are its smaller size and peaceful nature.

Many-banded Leporinus

Leporinus affinis

Synonym: *Leporinus fasciatus affinis*

Family: Anostomidae

Subfamily: Anostominae

Distribution: South America. *L. affinis* found down to the Paraguay River; *L. fasciatus* Río de la Plata.

Size: *L. affinis* around 9¾in (25cm); *L. fasciatus* up to 12in (30cm).

Behavior: Generally peaceful toward other species; may scrap with members of their own species but not over-aggressive.

Diet: Predominantly vegetable based, but will also take livefoods and some commercial formulations.

Aquarium: Spacious, well covered, and with bogwood, noncalcareous rocks, and either tough, unpalatable, or artificial plants. Power filtration to create a current also advisable. Medium-hard, slightly acid to slightly alkaline water, preferably tannin-stained, suits these fish well. Temperature range: 72–82°F (22–28°C).

Breeding: No documented reports currently available.

There are two virtually identical *Leporinus* with black body bands: this species and *L. fasciatus* (Black-banded Leporinus). Many-banded Leporinus has nine bands, while *L. fasciatus* has ten. Many-banded Leporinus also has somewhat more rounded tips to the caudal fin, and *L. fasciatus* has an orange/reddish tinge along its throat. In many books, these two fish are regarded as subspecies of *L. fasciatus*.

Spotted Cachorro

Acestrorhynchus falcatus

Family: Characidae

Subfamily: Characinae

Distribution: Guiana, Amazon and Orinoco basins.

Size: Up to 12in (30cm).

Behavior: Highly aggressive and predatory.

Diet: Feeds almost exclusively on other fishes, thus raising ethical questions about its maintenance in aquaria.

Aquarium: Large, well filtered, well covered, and with open spaces. Soft, acid water preferred. Temperature range: 73–81°F (23–27°C).

Breeding: Unknown in aquaria.

Pikelike characins, including the Spotted Cachorro, are grouped together according to certain body characteristics—usually the depth of the body in relation to its length. The *A. falcatus* group or complex is distinguished by its body depth being 4.0 to 4.75 times shorter than its body length. Members of other groups are hardly ever encountered in the hobby, while the Spotted Cachorro itself is only occasionally imported.

Bloodfin

Aphyocharax anisitsi

Other common name:
Argentinian Bloodfin

Synonym: *Aphyocharax rubripinnis*

Family: Characidae

Subfamily: Uncertain (classified by some authors as Aphyocharacinae)

Distribution: Mainly Paraná River (Argentina).

Size: Up to 3in (7.5cm) reported, but usually smaller.

Behavior: Peaceful shoaler.

Diet: Wide range of commercial diets and livefoods accepted.

Aquarium: Well planted, with some open spaces recommended. A dark substratum helps show these fish to good effect. Water chemistry not critical, but pH values above 8 should be avoided. Temperature range: 64–82°F (18–28°C).

Breeding: Soft, acid water recommended. Eggs are scattered, either in the open or among vegetation (usually in the morning), and may be eaten by the parents. Hatching takes about 1½ days.

This is the fish generally regarded within the hobby as the "true" Bloodfin, although *A. rathbuni* (Rathbun's Bloodfin) can exhibit even deeper red coloration. Coming from an area a little distance from the genuinely tropical zones of South America, this species can tolerate coldwater aquarium temperatures as long as they are not allowed to drop excessively. However, best coloration is exhibited when kept within a tropical regime. The species is long-lived, with some specimens reportedly attaining an age of ten years.

Rathbun's Bloodfin

Aphyocharax rathbuni

Family: Characidae

Subfamily: Uncertain (classified by some authors as Aphyocharacinae)

Distribution: Paraguay River basin.

Size: Up to 2in (5cm).

Behavior: Peaceful shoaler.

Diet: Wide range of commercial diets and livefoods accepted.

Aquarium: Well planted, with some open spaces recommended. A dark substratum helps show these fish to good effect. Water chemistry not critical, but pH values above 7.5 should be avoided. Temperature range: 68–82°F (20–28°C).

Breeding: Soft, acid water recommended. Eggs are scattered, either in the open or among vegetation (usually in the morning), and may be eaten by the parents. Hatching takes about 1½ days.

When in peak condition, Rathbun's Bloodfin is the most colorful *Aphyocharax* species generally available for aquaria. In *A. alburnus* (the False Flame-tailed Tetra) there is no red on the lower side of the body, while in *A. anisitsi* (the Bloodfin) the red pigmentation extends a little way into the body from the anal-fin base. In Rathbun's Bloodfin, it can extend from the front edge of the anal fin up to almost half the body width and then back toward the caudal fin, creating a most impressive conelike patch.

Red-eyed Tetra

Arnoldichthys spilopterus

Other common name:
African Red-eyed Characin

Family: Characidae

Subfamily: Alestiinae

Distribution: From the Niger delta to Lagos in west Africa.

Size: Up to 4³/₄in (12cm) reported, but usually smaller.

Behavior: Peaceful but active; should be kept as a shoal.

Diet: Range of commercial formulations accepted, but livefoods preferred.

Aquarium: Spacious, with large open swimming spaces, plants around sides and back, and dark substratum. Tannin-stained water advisable. Water chemistry is not critical, but raw water should be avoided. Temperature range: 73–82°F (23–28°C).

Breeding: Soft, acid water required. Eggs are scattered and hatch in about 1¹/₂ days.

This species is the only representative of its genus. It was first imported into Europe in 1907; since then it has always been available but has never achieved the "greatness" of some other tetras, despite its undoubted beauty. Distinguishing features include an adipose fin and conspicuously large scales. Males of the species are more brightly colored than females.

Blind Cavefish

Astyanax mexicanus

Other common names:
Blind Cave Characin,
Mexican Tetra

Synonyms: *Astyanax fasciatus, A. f. mexicanus, A. m. jordani, Anoptichthys jordani*

Family: Characidae

Subfamily: Tetragonopterinae

Distribution: Blind Cavefish form found in limestone caves in the region of San Luis Potosí, Mexico; Mexican Tetra form occurs in Texas, Mexico, and Central America through to Panama.

Size: Around 3½in (9cm).

Behavior: Active, peaceful shoaler.

Diet: All foods accepted.

Aquarium: Best effects are created in plantless, darkened aquarium with calcareous gravel and stalagmites or stalactites. Illumination can be provided by a "night" fluorescent tube. Medium-hard, good quality, alkaline water preferred. Temperature range: 59–86°F (15–30°C); 77°F (25°C) is adequate for maintenance and breeding.

Breeding: Eggs are scattered and may be eaten by the parents. Hatching takes from 1–3 days.

The Blind Cavefish and the Mexican Tetra were once believed to belong not just to different species, but to different genera, as the former name of *Anoptichthys* shows. However, they were eventually shown to be members of the same species that looked very different from each other. The Mexican Tetra is the form that inhabits aboveground watercourses, while the Blind Cavefish lives underground. There is still some debate as to whether the current name for the species is *Astyanax fasciatus* or *A. mexicanus*. Not so long ago, *A. fasciatus* appeared to be the preferred name, but in recent years the balance has moved toward the latter.

Long-finned Characin

Bryconalestes longipinnis (previously Brycinus longipinnis)

Synonym: *Alestes longipinnis*

Family: Characidae

Subfamily: Alestiinae

Distribution: Tropical west Africa.

Size: Up to 5in (13cm).

Behavior: Peaceful shoaler.

Diet: Wide range of foods accepted.

Aquarium: Roomy, well covered, well filtered, with ample swimming space, planted along sides and back; dark substratum recommended. Soft to medium-hard, slightly acid to slightly alkaline water preferred. Temperature range: 72–79°F (22–26°C).

Breeding: Soft, slightly acid water should be provided. Eggs are scattered among vegetation and take up to 6 days to hatch.

So called because of the extended dorsal-fin rays of mature males, this species should be kept as a group for best effect, despite its relatively large size. It is the most frequently encountered species of its genus, all of which are predominantly silvery-bodied fish with black bands originating in the fork of the caudal fin and extending to varying lengths into the body. Yellow-gold, reddish, or white coloration usually accompanies the bands.

Pink-tailed Chalceus

Chalceus macrolepidotus

Other common name:
Pink-tailed Characin

Family: Characidae

Subfamily: Uncertain

Distribution: Amazon basin and the Guianas.

Size: Up to 9³/₄in (25cm).

Behavior: Predatory species; should be kept only with similar-sized tankmates.

Diet: Can be weaned off livefoods and on to substantial deep-frozen or freeze-dried diets and tablet food. Juveniles will accept other formulations.

Aquarium: Large, well covered, well filtered, with ample swimming space and plants around sides and back. Water chemistry not critical. Temperature range: 73–82°F (23–28°C).

Breeding: No documented accounts currently available.

The genus *Chalceus* has a number of characteristics that place it close to the genus *Brycon*. In addition, it seems to resemble some *Brycinus* (*Alestes*) species. Nelson (whose classification is followed here) does not allocate *Brycon* to any subfamily of the Characidae, while *Brycinus* belongs to the subfamily Alestiinae. As a result, the taxonomic position of these large-scaled silvery-bodied tetras must be considered uncertain at this stage. The Pink-tailed Chalceus has pink/red fins, while the closely related *C. erythrurus* (Yellow-finned Chalceus) from the Amazon basin (believed by some to be a color form rather than a separate species) has yellow fins, except for the caudal fin, which contains some red.

Blue Tetra

Mimagoniates microlepis (previously Coelurichthys microlepis)

Synonym: *Mimagoniates microlepis*

Family: Characidae

Subfamily: Glandulocaudinae

Distribution: Southern Brazil.

Size: Around 2¹/₄in (5.5cm).

Behavior: Active but peaceful shoaler.

Diet: Wide range of commercial formulations accepted, but livefoods preferred.

Aquarium: Plants should be arranged along sides and back, leaving a large swimming area along the front. Well-filtered, well-oxygenated water required, preferably with a current. Soft, slightly acid water recommended. Temperature range: 66–78°F. (19–25°C).

Breeding: Eggs are released and attached to vegetation by female following internal fertilization.

The Blue Tetra, along with its relative *C. tenuis* (Tenuis Tetra—formerly known as *Mimagoniates barberi,* from southern Brazil, Argentina, and Paraguay)—and allied genera and species, are often referred to as croaking tetras because of the ability of some species to emit sounds. The males of all the species have a gland in the caudal fin (hence the name of the subfamily) that secretes substances believed to be effective in attracting females. *Coelurichthys* are gorgeous fish when kept under appropriate conditions, which can be a little challenging for new aquarists.

Black-finned Pacu

Colossoma macropomum

Family: Characidae

Subfamily: Serrasalminae

Distribution: Widespread in the Amazon region.

Size: Around 16in (40cm).

Behavior: Peaceful, despite its size; has a keen appetite for plants.

Diet: Large commercial formulations, plus added vegetable component, e.g. lettuce leaves.

Aquarium: Only large, deep aquaria are suitable. Use only unpalatable or artificial plants, plus large pieces of bogwood and other forms of decor. Water chemistry not critical, but water should be well filtered. Temperature range: 72–82°F (22–28°C).

Breeding: No accounts of successful aquarium breeding available.

Although this fish superficially resembles a piranha and belongs to the same subfamily, the Pacu is a plant-eating species rather than a predator. It is a large fish that is bred commercially, both for aquaria and as a food fish, and it is quite unsuitable for most home aquaria. However, in its proper setting, the species is long-lived and well worth keeping.

Exodon

Exodon paradoxus

Other common name:
Buck-toothed Tetra

Family: Characidae

Subfamily: Uncertain

Distribution: Widely but locally in the Amazon basin.

Size: Up to 6in (15cm).

Behavior: Aggressive predator, always on the move. May be kept in a large shoal, but not as small groups of two or three individuals. May also be kept with similar-sized or larger, robust fish.

Diet: Meat-based commercial formulations, deep-frozen, freeze-dried, and livefoods all accepted.

Aquarium: Large, well-covered aquarium with ample swimming space essential. Efficient filtration, thickets of vegetation (including floating plants), and subdued lighting are also required. Temperature range: 72–82°F (22–28°C).

Breeding: Eggs are scattered among vegetation. Hatching takes about 1½ days.

This is a species for more advanced hobbyists because its aggressive tendencies and relatively large size (for a tetra) make it quite unsuitable for the usual community aquarium setups. Under appropriate conditions, a shoal of Exodon make an unforgettable sight, not just because of their coloration and bold patterning, but because of their high levels of activity.

Black Widow

Gymnocorymbus ternetzi

Other common name: Black Tetra

Family: Characidae

Subfamily: Tetragonopterinae

Distribution: Paraguay River, Bolivian section of the Guaporé, and the Brazilian Mato Grosso.

Size: Wild type around 2¼in (5.5cm); larger for some cultivated varieties.

Behavior: Peaceful shoaler.

Diet: Most commercial formulations and livefoods accepted.

Aquarium: Well planted, with some open swimming spaces, and tannin-stained water recommended. Soft, acid water preferred; some deviation from this accepted, though raw water must be avoided. Temperature range: 68–82°F (20–28°C).

Breeding: Eggs are scattered among vegetation and may be eaten by the spawners. Hatching takes about 1 day.

This species has been popular ever since its introduction into Europe in 1935. For many years, the basic—and very beautiful—wild type was the only form available. However, over time several fin and color varieties have been developed, including a long-finned, large-bodied white type and a reddish/pinkish one. Two other species with the same basic requirements are also available, but not as frequently as the Black Widow: *G. socolofi* (Socolof's Tetra) from the Meta River in Colombia and *G. thayeri* (Straight-finned Black Tetra) from the Amazon and Orinoco basins.

Silver-tipped Tetra

Hasemania nana

Other common name:
Copper Tetra

Synonyms: *Hasemania marginata, Hasemania melanura, Hemigrammus nanus*

Family: Characidae

Subfamily: Tetragonopterinae

Distribution: Eastern Brazil (São Francisco basin) and western Brazil (Purus tributaries).

Size: Up to 2in (5cm) reported, but often smaller.

Behavior: Peaceful; should be kept in as large a shoal as possible.

Diet: Most small foods accepted.

Aquarium: Plant thickets, subdued light, and open swimming spaces required. Soft, slightly acid, well-oxygenated, tannin-stained water recommended. Temperature range: 72–82°F (22–28°C).

Breeding: Eggs are scattered among fine-leaved vegetation and may be eaten by the spawners. Hatching takes about 1 day.

Unusually for a characin, the Silver-tipped Tetra lacks an adipose fin. Under appropriate conditions, this tiny species lives up beautifully to both of its common names. It is a fish that, at one time or another, should form part of every aquarist's community setup.

Brilliant Rummy-nosed Tetra

Hemigrammus bleheri

Family: Characidae

Subfamily: Tetragonopterinae

Distribution: *H. bleheri* found in middle Río Negro (Brazil) and Río Vaupés (Colombia). *H. rhodostomus* in Belém region of Brazil; also reported from Venezuela.

Size: Around 1³/₄in (4.5cm).

Behavior: Peaceful shoalers; *H. bleheri* is known to "parasitize" brooding pairs of *Uaru amphiacanthoides* by feeding on the "body milk" that the uarus secrete and on which their fry feed during their early days.

Diet: Most foods accepted.

Aquarium: Well planted, with swimming spaces. Soft, slightly acid, good-quality, tannin-stained water recommended. Temperature range: 72–79°F (22–26°C). *H. rhodostomus* is a little more tolerant of temperature fluctuations.

Breeding: Very soft, acid water recommended. Eggs are scattered among vegetation or over the substratum. Hatching takes about 1¹/₂ days.

This species (largely exported from the Río Negro in Brazil and the Vaupés in Colombia, and first imported into Europe in 1965) was originally known simply as the Rummy Nose or Rummy-nosed Tetra. However, a very similar species, *H. rhodostomus*, which had been imported for many years prior to this from the Belém region in Brazil, was already known as the Rummy Nose. This led to considerable confusion, with the Río Negro Rummy Nose being often named *H. rhodostomus* instead of *H. bleheri*. Skeletal differences exist between the two, but they are impossible to determine in living specimens. Fortunately, there are several other, more easily identified distinguishing characteristics: in *H. bleheri*, the red coloration in the head region covers most of the head and extends some way into the body, while in *H. rhodostomus* it is much more restricted; the tip of the snout is more rounded in *H. bleheri*; the black band that, in *H. rhodostomus*, extends along the base of the anal fin is lacking in *H. bleheri*, as are any marks on the rays of the anal fin.

Buenos Aires Tetra

Hyphessobrycon anisitsi (previously Hemigrammus caudovittatus)

Family: Characidae

Subfamily: Tetragonopterinae

Distribution: Argentina (mainly around Río de la Plata), southeastern Brazil, and Paraguay.

Size: Up to 4³⁄₄in (12cm) reported, but usually around 2³⁄₄–3in (7–8cm).

Behavior: Generally a peaceful shoaler, but larger specimens can become progressively more aggressive with age. Has a distinct appetite for succulent plants.

Diet: Wide variety of foods accepted.

Aquarium: Plant thickets (not delicate succulent types) and open swimming spaces required. Water chemistry not critical, but quality must be good and oxygenation level high. Temperature range: 64–82°F (18–28°C).

Breeding: Eggs are scattered among vegetation and may be eaten by the parents. Hatching takes about 1 day.

This active species has been known in the hobby since 1922. It is often recommended as an ideal community fish, although its behavior does not always justify this. Specimens in peak condition exhibit very attractive red coloration in the fins, except the pectoral fins. A variant, in which the caudal fin is predominantly yellow, is occasionally available.

Glowlight Tetra

Hemigrammus erythrozonus

Family: Characidae

Subfamily: Tetragonopterinae

Distribution: Essequibo basin (Guyana).

Size: Around 1½in (4cm).

Behavior: Peaceful shoaler.

Diet: Wide range of small foods accepted.

Aquarium: Well planted, with open swimming spaces, and tannin-stained water. Soft, slightly acid water preferred, but some deviation accepted if adjustments are made gradually. Temperature range: 72–82°F (22–28°C).

Breeding: Spawning may be achieved using either pairs or a shoal. Eggs are scattered among vegetation in soft, acid water. Hatching takes about 1 day.

The Glowlight is one of the old favorites of the hobby, and deservedly so. A shoal of these tiny fish kept under appropriate conditions makes a truly impressive sight. There is some doubt regarding the assignation of this species to the genus *Hemigrammus,* and studies may eventually result in its being assigned to the genus *Cheirodon.*

Head-and-tail Light Tetra

Hemigrammus ocellifer

Other common name:
Beacon Fish

Family: Characidae

Subfamily:
Tetragonopterinae

Distribution: *H. o. falsus*
found in the Amazon basin;
H. o. ocellifer in the lower
reaches of the Amazon
and French Guiana.

Size: Around 1³/₄in (4.5cm).

Behavior: Peaceful shoaler.

Diet: Wide range of foods
accepted.

Aquarium: Well planted,
with open swimming
spaces, and tannin-stained
water. Soft, slightly acid
water preferred, but some
deviation accepted if
adjustments are made
gradually. Temperature
range: 72–79°F (22–26°C)
for *H. o. falsus*; 75–82°F
(24–28°C) for *H. o. ocellifer*.

Breeding: Spawning may
be achieved using either
pairs or a shoal. Eggs are
scattered among vegetation
in soft, acid water. Hatching
takes about 1 day.

Two subspecies are generally recognized: *H. ocellifer falsus* (first imported
into Europe in 1910, and the type most frequently encountered in aquaria);
and *H. o. ocellifer* (introduced around 1960). Both are very similar, but
H. o. ocellifer has a distinct gold-bordered black spot just behind the gill
covers; in *H. o. falsus*, this feature is indistinct. In *H. o. ocellifer*, there are
also two red patches on the top and bottom lobes of the caudal fin.

Pretty Tetra

Hemigrammus pulcher

Other common names:
Black-wedge Tetra, Garnet Tetra

Family: Characidae

Subfamily:
Tetragonopterinae

Distribution: *H. p. haraldi* found in the central Amazon around Manáus; *H. p. pulcher* has wider distribution, including the Peruvian Amazon.

Size: Around 1³⁄₄in (4.5cm).

Behavior: Peaceful shoaler.

Diet: Wide range of small foods accepted.

Aquarium: Well planted, with open swimming spaces, and tannin-stained water. Soft, slightly acid water preferred, but some deviation accepted if adjustments are made gradually. Temperature range: 73–81°F (23–27°C).

Breeding: Breeding is not difficult once a good pair has been established. Eggs are scattered among vegetation and may be eaten by the parents. Hatching takes about 1 day.

The Pretty Tetra is, indeed, very pretty, but the second (less often used) common name is far more appropriate given the black wedgelike patch that occupies the posterior section of the body. Two subspecies are generally recognized: *H. pulcher haraldi*, which is not frequently kept, and *H. p. pulcher*, the popular type.

Ulrey's Tetra

Hemigrammus ulreyi

Family: Characidae

Subfamily:
Tetragonopterinae

Distribution: Paraguay
River basin.

Size: Up to 2in (5cm).

Behavior: Peaceful,
sometimes shy shoaler.

Diet: Wide range of foods
accepted.

Aquarium: Well-planted
aquarium, with open areas
and a current (as produced
by a power filter) suits this
species well. Soft, slightly
acid to neutral water
preferred. Temperature
range: 73–81°F (23–27°C).

Breeding: No documented
accounts currently available.

This species—while lacking some of the more intense coloration of
some other tetras—is, nevertheless, every bit as beautiful when in good
condition and kept in a shoal. In such circumstances, the bold gold and
black lines that run from the tip of the snout through the eye and on to
the base of the tail stand out to great effect. Ulrey's Tetra is sometimes
confused with *Hyphessobrycon heterorhabdus* (Flag Tetra) from the
southern tributaries of the central Amazon region, which has a reddish
line, rather than a golden one, above the black body stripe.

Rosy Tetra

Hyphessobrycon bentosi

Other common name:
Bentos Tetra

Synonyms: *Hyphessobrycon bentosi bentosi, H. b. callistus, H. b. rosaceus, H. callistus, H. ornatus, H. rosaceus*

Family: Characidae

Subfamily: Tetragonopterinae

Distribution: Mainly Guyana and Lower Amazon.

Size: Around 1½in (4cm).

Behavior: All "Rosy" Tetras are generally peaceful shoalers.

Diet: Wide range of foods accepted.

Aquarium: Well planted, with ample swimming space. Tannin-stained water recommended. Dark substratum will also help. Soft, slightly acid to neutral water, preferably with gentle current. Temperature range: 75–82°F (24–28°C).

Breeding: Eggs are scattered among vegetation and may be eaten by the spawners. Hatching takes about 1 day.

The correct identity, or name, of this popular tetra has not been established with any degree of certainty. There are several similarly named species (or subspecies, depending on the literature consulted), over which there is considerable debate and confusion. Variation in the intensity of the red coloration, black shoulder spots, and white fin edging, are all complicating factors, as are the changes brought about through commercial breeding. The result is that "Rosy" Tetras are encountered under a variety of scientific names. In addition, the fish usually referred to as *Hyphessobrycon "robertsi"* (Robert's Tetra) may be a hybrid.

Bleeding Heart Tetra

Hyphessobrycon erythrostigma

Synonyms: *Hyphessobrycon rubrostigma, H. callistus rubrostigma*

Family: Characidae

Subfamily: Tetragonopterinae

Distribution: Upper Amazon basin.

Size: Up to 4³/₄in (12cm) reported, but usually smaller.

Behavior: Males may scrap among themselves, but little or no damage ever occurs. This behavior may be a necessary part of keeping them in peak reproductive condition. Otherwise tolerant of other species.

Diet: Wide range of foods accepted.

Aquarium: Spacious, well planted, with ample swimming space. Tannin-stained water recommended. Dark substratum will also help. Soft, slightly acid to neutral water, preferably with gentle current. Temperature range: 75–82°F (24–28°C).

Breeding: Challenging in aquaria. Eggs are scattered and may be eaten by the parents.

Both the "erythro" and "rubro" parts of the current valid scientific name and the alternative that is still in use mean "red," while "stigma" means "spot." Both are beautifully descriptive of this impressive tetra. The only potential drawback of this species is the relatively large size that fully mature specimens can attain, making such fish better suited for medium and large community aquaria than for the smaller, more popular, versions.

Flame Tetra

Hyphessobrycon flammeus

Synonym: *Hyphessobrycon bifasciatus*

Family: Characidae

Subfamily: Tetragonopterinae

Distribution: Southeastern Brazil (both *H. bifasciatus* and *H. flammeus*).

Size: 1½in (4cm).

Behavior: Generally a peaceful shoaler.

Diet: Wide range of foods accepted.

Aquarium: Well planted, with ample swimming space. Tannin-stained water recommended. Dark substratum will also help. Subdued lighting shows this species off well. Soft, slightly acid to neutral water, preferably with gentle current. Temperature range: 75–82°F (24–28°C).

Breeding: Eggs are scattered among vegetation and may be eaten by the spawners. Hatching takes about 1 day.

Over the years the Flame Tetra—whose name derives from its red coloration—has lost ground to its other, more vividly colored, relatives, especially their cultivated forms. It is very similar overall to *H. bifasciatus* (Copper Bifasciatus), with which it is confused to the extent that *H. bifasciatus* is often used as a synonym of *H. flammeus*. However, the true *H. bifasciatus* lacks the red coloration, has several skeletal differences, and is slightly larger. *H. griemi* (Griem's Tetra) from central Brazil is also similar to the Flame Tetra but has three instead of two shoulder patches.

Black Neon

Hyphessobrycon herbertaxelrodi

Family: Characidae

Subfamily: Tetragonopterinae

Distribution: Taquari River in the Mato Grosso (Brazil).

Size: Up to 2in (5cm), but usually smaller.

Behavior: Generally a peaceful shoaler.

Diet: Wide range of foods accepted.

Aquarium: Well planted, with ample swimming space. Tannin-stained water recommended. Dark substratum will also help. Soft, slightly acid to neutral water, preferably with gentle current. Temperature range: 75–82°F (24–28°C).

Breeding: Very soft, acid water recommended. Eggs are scattered among plants. Hatching takes about 1½ days.

Although referred to simply as a "Neon," the Black Neon is quite distinct from the "true" Neon Tetra *(Paracheirodon innesi)*. It is, nevertheless, neonlike in that it possesses an iridescent golden-green line that runs all the way from the head to the base of the caudal fin. This contrasts sharply with the bold black line that runs below it. Such coloration makes a large shoal of Black Neons a truly impressive sight.

Flag Tetra

Hyphessobrycon heterorhabdus

Family: Characidae

Subfamily: Tetragonopterinae

Distribution: Southern tributaries of the central region of the Amazon.

Size: Around 1³/₄in (4.5cm).

Behavior: Prefers to be kept in largish groups.

Diet: Wide range of foods accepted.

Aquarium: Well planted, with ample swimming space. Tannin-stained water recommended. Dark substratum will also help. Soft, slightly acid to neutral water, preferably with gentle current. Temperature range: 75–82°F (24–28°C).

Breeding: Eggs are scattered among vegetation and may be eaten by the spawners. Hatching takes about 1 day.

Although this species has been around since 1910 and belongs to a separate genus, it is still sometimes confused with *Hemigrammus ulreyi* (Ulrey's Tetra), first imported even earlier. The Flag Tetra, however, possesses a reddish line above the black body line, while in *Hemigrammus ulreyi* the red is replaced with gold. The Flag Tetra is also distinguishable—although less easily—by the lack of scales on its caudal fin (*H. ulreyi* has a scaled caudal fin).

Lemon Tetra

Hyphessobrycon pulchripinnis

Family: Characidae

Subfamily:
Tetragonopterinae

Distribution: Central Brazil.

Size: Up to 2in (5cm).

Behavior: Active, peaceful shoaler.

Diet: Wide range of foods accepted.

Aquarium: Spacious; plant thickets and ample swimming space required. Floating plants, or tall plants whose leaves or stems can extend along the water surface, subdued lighting, and dark substratum are also recommended. Tannin-stained water will enhance the brilliant-lemon streaks in the fins, as well as the red of the eye. Soft, acid water usually recommended, but will tolerate harder, more alkaline conditions as long as quality is high and any changes are carried out gradually. Temperature range: 73–82°F (23–28°C).

Breeding: Only occasionally achieved in aquaria. This is an egg-scattering, egg-eating species.

This is a truly outstanding tetra, but only when kept in appropriate conditions. When they are not provided, the colors fade, making it a rather nondescript fish. Since the appropriate conditions cannot be easily provided in shop aquaria, the fish may appear pale even if healthy. Such fish will, however, soon begin to show their true colors—quite literally— once they are settled into an appropriate home-aquarium setup.

Slender Tetra

Iguanodectes spilurus

Synonym:
Iguanodectes tenuis

Family: Characidae

Subfamily:
Tetragonopterinae

Distribution: Guyana, central Amazon, and Madeira River (Brazil).

Size: Around 2½in (6cm).

Behavior: Active but peaceful shoaler.

Diet: Wide range of foods accepted.

Aquarium: Ample swimming areas surrounded by plants should be provided. Water chemistry not critical, but quality must be good and oxygenation level must be high; a water current is also advisable. Temperature range: 73–81°F (23–27°C).

Breeding: Soft, slightly acid water recommended. Eggs are scattered and may be eaten by the spawners. Hatching can take up to 14 days.

This lively, slim-bodied tetra is often overlooked in those stores where bright lights may be used to illuminate predominantly bare tanks. Such conditions are not to its liking, and as a result it loses much of its subtle brilliance. Under appropriate conditions, though, it is a useful addition to a community aquarium.

Blue Emperor

Inpaichthys kerri

Family: Characidae

Subfamily: Tetragonopterinae

Distribution: Aripuanã River, Amazonia.

Size: Up to 2in (5cm) reported, but usually smaller.

Behavior: Peaceful shoaler.

Diet: Wide range of foods accepted.

Aquarium: Thickly planted, providing adequate shelter, and with open swimming areas. Subdued lighting and dark substratum recommended. Neutral, soft water preferred. Temperature range: 75–81°F (24–27°C).

Breeding: Eggs are laid singly among fine-leaved vegetation and may be eaten by the spawners. Hatching takes 1–2 days.

This small tetra, in which the male exhibits a reflective blue sheen on the body, is a relatively new introduction when compared to most of the other tetras encountered in the hobby. It first appeared in Germany in 1977 and since then has been consistently available, although not in large numbers. It is a good choice for community aquaria that do not house robust, overactive species.

Jelly Bean Tetra

Ladigesia roloffi

Other common name:
Sierra Leone Dwarf Characin

Family: Characidae

Subfamily: Alestiinae

Distribution: Ivory Coast, Ghana, Liberia, and Sierra Leone.

Size: Up to 1¹/₂in (4cm).

Behavior: Retiring, peaceful shoaler (but with jumping ability); should not be kept with active or robust species.

Diet: Wide range of small commercial and livefoods accepted.

Aquarium: Well covered, with subdued lighting, dark substratum, plant thickets, and floating vegetation. Soft, acid, tannin-stained water required. Temperature range: 72–79°F (22–26°C).

Breeding: Very soft, acid water recommended. Eggs are released over the substratum (which, ideally, should incorporate some peat).

This is a small, beautiful, but rarely seen tetra. For long-term success, aquarium conditions must be given close attention. In particular, the red coloration of the caudal fin will fade quickly in water that is of an inappropriate quality.

Red Phantom Tetra

Hyphessobrycon sweglesi (previously Megalamphodus sweglesi)

Other common name:
Swegles' Tetra

Synonym: *Hyphessobrycon sweglesi*

Family: Characidae

Subfamily: Tetragonopterinae

Distribution: Upper Amazon basin and possibly upper Orinoco basin.

Size: Around 1 ½in (4cm).

Behavior: Peaceful shoaler.

Diet: Wide range of foods accepted.

Aquarium: Plant thickets, open spaces, and subdued lighting required. Soft, slightly acid water is recommended, with adequate temperature and water chemistry equilibration (i.e. no temperature or water chemistry "shocks"), and with regular partial water changes. Temperature range: 68–73°F (20–23°C).

Breeding: Can be challenging in aquaria. Soft, acid water and subdued lighting recommended. Eggs are scattered over plants or the substratum. Temperature should be kept below 73°F (23°C).

This species, introduced into the hobby in the early 1960s, has bright red coloration when in peak condition. It is, however, somewhat more demanding with regard to water conditions than its close relative, *M. melanopterus* (Black Phantom Tetra). Two other *Megalamphodus* species are also occasionally available: *M. axelrodi* (Calypso Tetra) from Trinidad and *M. roseus* (Golden Phantom Tetra) from the Guianas.

Silver Dollar

Metynnis argenteus

Other common name:
Silver Pacu

Synonyms: *Metynnis anisurus*; possibly *M. altidorsalis*, *M. snethlageae*

Family: Characidae

Subfamily: Serrasalminae

Distribution: Amazon basin and the Guianas.

Size: Around 5¹/₂in (14cm).

Behavior: Peaceful shoaler.

Diet: Some commercial formulations accepted. Provide fresh vegetable matter daily.

Aquarium: Large, with open swimming areas and unpalatable, robust, or artificial plants as well as large shelters. Requires subdued lighting and dark substratum. Water chemistry is not critical, but avoid extremes. Temperature range: 75–82°F (24–28°C).

Breeding: Soft, acid, preferably tannin-stained water. Aquarium should be darkened then gradually exposed to light. Provide feathery-rooted floating plants or unpalatable fine-leaved plants. Spawning takes place among vegetation; the eggs drop to the bottom of the tank and hatch after about 3 days.

Metynnis classification is probably the most inconsistent among the characoids. The existence of naturally occurring forms that could be morphs, subspecies, or even species, adds to the confusion. Individual *Metynnis* species therefore appear under various names in both aquarium and scientific literature. A distinguishing feature of the genus, which separates it from all the other members of the subfamily, is the long-based adipose fin.

Plain Metynnis

Metynnis hypsauchen

Other common name:
Silver Dollar Pacu

Synonyms: *Metynnis calichromus, M. ehrhardti, M. fasciatus, M. orinocensis, M.schreitmuelleri*

Family: Characidae

Subfamily: Serrasalminae

Distribution: Western Amazon basin, Paraguay basin, Orinoco, and Guyana.

Size: Around 6in (15cm).

Behavior: Peaceful shoaler.

Diet: Some commercial formulations accepted. Provide fresh vegetable matter daily.

Aquarium: Large, with open swimming areas, artificial or unpalatable plants, and large shelters. Subdued lighting and dark substratum. Avoid extremes of water chemistry. Temperature range: 75–82°F (24–28°C).

Breeding: Soft, acid, preferably tannin-stained water. Darken aquarium then gradually expose to light. Provide feathery-rooted floating plants. Spawning takes place among vegetation; the eggs drop to the bottom of the tank and hatch after about 3 days.

The same nomenclatural confusion outlined for *M. argenteus* (the Silver Dollar) applies to this species, only more so. Both species have been known in the hobby since 1912–13, and both continue to be regularly available. They look particularly impressive when kept in a sizable shoal in a spacious aquarium.

Diamond Tetra

Moenkhausia pittieri

Family: Characidae

Subfamily: Tetragonopterinae

Distribution: Region of Lake Valencia (Venezuela).

Size: Up to 2¹/₂in (6cm).

Behavior: Tolerant shoaler.

Diet: Wide range of foods accepted.

Aquarium: Spacious, planted, with large open swimming areas and dark substratum. Good-quality, mature water preferred, but hard water should be avoided. Temperature range: 75–82°F (24–28°C).

Breeding: Eggs are scattered among fine-leaved vegetation and may be eaten by the parents. It is helpful to darken the aquarium during the initial prespawning stage so that the level of illumination can be gradually increased when the fish are ready to spawn. Hatching takes 2–3 days.

The male possesses a very long dorsal fin, which, when extended at the same time as the anal fin, makes this fish look quite spectacular. The glistening body scales (the "diamonds" from which the name derives) add to this effect. However, juvenile specimens—which are the type most often available in stores—lack these features and can therefore be easily overlooked.

Red-eyed Tetra

Moenkhausia sanctaefilomenae

Other common name:
Yellow-banded Tetra

Family: Characidae

Subfamily:
Tetragonopterinae

Distribution: Eastern Bolivia, western Brazil, Paraguay, and eastern Peru.

Size: Up to 2³/₄in (7cm), but often smaller.

Behavior: Tolerant shoaler.

Diet: Wide range of foods accepted.

Aquarium: Spacious, planted, with large open swimming areas and dark substratum. Good-quality mature water preferred, but a wide range of water chemistry conditions is tolerated. Temperature range: 72–79°F (23–26°C), but slightly higher and lower temperatures also tolerated.

Breeding: Eggs are scattered among the feathery roots of floating plants, such as Water Hyacinth (*Eichhornia crassipes*), or over fine-leaved vegetation. Soft, acid, tannin-stained water recommended. The spawners may eat their eggs. Hatching takes 1–2 days.

Of this fish's two common names, the Red-eyed Tetra more accurately describes the species because the intensity of the yellow band in front of the caudal fin can vary considerably. The species is superficially similar to *Moenkhausia oligolepis* (Glass Tetra), but is generally more vividly colored and does not attain the same size.

Redhook Pacu

Myloplus rubripinnis (previously Myleus rubripinnis)

Other common name:
Redhook Metynnis

Synonyms: *Mylopus rubripinnis*, possibly *Myleus asterias*

Family: Characidae

Subfamily: Serrasalminae

Distribution:
M. r. rubripinnis in Suriname and probably Guyana; *M. r. luna* in Maroni River.

Size: Some wild-caught specimens reported up to 10in (25cm); aquarium specimens usually slightly less than half this size.

Behavior: Peaceful shoaler with appetite for plants.

Diet: Some commercial formulations accepted. Fresh vegetable matter, e.g. lettuce leaves, should be provided daily.

Aquarium: Large, with open swimming areas and unpalatable, robust, and/or artificial plants, together with large shelters. Lighting should be subdued, and a dark substratum is recommended. Water chemistry not critical, but avoid extremes. Temperature range: 75–82°F (24–28°C).

Breeding: Appears not to have bred in aquaria.

Owing to its overall similarity to *Metynnis* species, this species is sometimes misleadingly referred to as the Redhook Metynnis. As both common names imply, a major characteristic of this fish is the large hooklike anal fin, which can be particularly distinctive in juvenile specimens. Two subspecies are generally recognized: *M. rubripinnis rubripinnis* and *M. r. luna*. Several other *Myleus* species are available (under a variety of scientific names owing to the confused state of the taxonomy of these fishes); all have basically similar requirements.

Silver Mylossoma

Mylossoma duriventre

Other common name:
Hard-bellied Silver Dollar

Synonyms: *Myletes duriventris*, *Mylossoma argenteum*, *M. albiscopus*, *M. ocellatum*

Family: Characidae

Subfamily: Serrasalminae

Distribution: Amazon basin.

Size: Up to 9in (23cm) reported, but usually smaller.

Behavior: Tolerant shoaler, with a voracious appetite for plants.

Diet: Some commercial formulations accepted. Fresh vegetable matter, e.g. lettuce leaves, should be provided daily.

Aquarium: Large, with open swimming areas and unpalatable, robust, and/or artificial plants, together with large shelters. Lighting should be subdued, and a dark substratum is recommended. Water chemistry not critical, but avoid extremes. Temperature range: 75–82°F (24–28°C).

Breeding: Assumed to be similar to *M. argenteus* (Silver Dollar), but this has not been confirmed.

The many names under which this fish appears in aquarium and other literature is an indication of the difficulties encountered in correctly identifying individual species. Like its close relatives, it bears a close resemblance to the piranhas, but the mouth is neither as powerful nor is it armed with sharp teeth. Of the other four or so species in the genus, one of the silver dollars, *M. aureum* (from the Amazon basin) is the most frequently encountered.

Emperor Tetra

Nematobrycon palmeri

Synonym: *Nematobrycon amphiloxus*

Family: Characidae

Subfamily: Tetragonopterinae

Distribution: Western Colombia.

Size: Up to 2¹/₂in (6cm), but usually a little smaller.

Behavior: Quiet, peaceful fish; should he kept in small groups.

Diet: Wide range of foods accepted.

Aquarium: Well planted, with ample swimming space, and dark substratum. Softish, acid to slightly alkaline water quite suitable. If possible, water should be tannin-stained. Regular partial water changes should be carried out, but any alterations to water chemistry must be made gradually. Temperature range: 73–81°F (23–27°C).

Breeding: Can be challenging. Soft, acid water and darkened aquarium recommended. Eggs are laid singly among vegetation and may be eaten by the spawning pair. Hatching takes 1–2 days.

Emperor tetras are among the longest-lived tetras: fish kept in appropriate conditions may live for up to five years. Unlike its close relative *N. lecortei* (Rainbow Emperor Tetra), this species does not possess blue marbling, and its eyes are greenish blue rather than red. *Nematobrycon amphiloxus* (sometimes written as *N. "amphiloxus"*) is believed to be a smoky colored naturally occurring morph of the Emperor Tetra.

Cardinal Tetra

Paracheirodon axelrodi

Synonyms: *Cheirodon axelrodi, Hyphessobrycon cardinalis*

Family: Characidae

Subfamily: Tetragonopterinae

Distribution: From the Orinoco (Venezuela) through the northern tributaries of the Río Negro (Brazil) to western Colombia.

Size: Up to 2in (5cm).

Behavior: Peaceful shoaler.

Diet: Wide range of foods accepted.

Aquarium: Well planted, with open spaces and subdued lighting. These fish are often found in tannin-stained water. Soft, acid water recommended, but harder, more alkaline conditions tolerated if adjustments carried out gradually. Temperature range: 73–81°F (23–27°C).

Breeding: Challenging in aquaria. Subdued lighting and very soft, acid, tannin-stained water will enhance chances of success. Eggs are scattered among vegetation and may be eaten by the parents. Hatching takes about 1 day.

The Cardinal Tetra is one of the most famous and popular species in the hobby. It is a truly magnificent fish, which forms the cornerstone of the Brazilian Amazon ornamental fishery. It is also bred commercially in several countries, most notably the Czech Republic. Various forms of the species are known within its natural range, and may represent several, rather than a single, species. A cultivated golden variety is sometimes available.

Neon Tetra

Paracheirodon innesi

Synonym: *Hyphessobrycon innesi*

Family: Characidae

Subfamily: Tetragonopterinae

Distribution: Putumayo River, eastern Peru.

Size: Around 1½in (4cm).

Behavior: Peaceful shoaler.

Diet: Wide range of foods accepted.

Aquarium: Well planted, with some open spaces and subdued lighting (e.g. provided by floating plants), recommended. These fish are often, but not invariably, found in tannin-stained water. Soft, acid water recommended, but harder, more alkaline conditions tolerated if adjustments carried out gradually. Temperature range: 68–79°F (20–26°C).

Breeding: Challenging in aquaria. Subdued lighting and very soft, acid, tannin-stained water will enhance chances of success. Eggs are scattered among vegetation and may be eaten by the parents. Hatching takes about 1 day.

At first sight, this species may be confused with *P. axelrodi* (Cardinal Tetra). However, in the Neon Tetra, the red body coloration occupies only the posterior half of the body, while in *P. axelrodi* it extends from head to tail. Traditionally, there have been two major sources of neons: wild-caught specimens from South America and captive-bred stocks from Hong Kong. However, other sources of captive-bred fish are becoming established, particularly in Sri Lanka. Several cultivated varieties of Neon are available in addition to the wild type, including Diamondhead, Gold, Albino, Brilliant, and "Mon Cheri" (yellow).

False Neon Tetra

Paracheirodon simulans

Other common name:
Green Neon Tetra

Synonym: *Hyphessobrycon simulans*

Family: Characidae

Subfamily:
Tetragonopterinae

Distribution: Jufaris or Tupari Rivers in the area of the Río Negro (Brazil).

Size: Up to 1½in (4cm), but usually a little smaller.

Behavior: Peaceful shoaler.

Diet: Wide range of foods accepted.

Aquarium: Well planted, with some open spaces and subdued lighting (e.g. provided by floating plants), recommended. These fish are often, but not invariably, found in tannin-stained water. Soft, acid water recommended. Avoid alkaline, hardwater conditions. Temperature range: 68–79°F (20–26°C).

Breeding: Challenging in aquaria. Subdued lighting and very soft, acid, tannin-stained water will enhance chances of success. Eggs are scattered among vegetation and may be eaten by the parents. Hatching takes about 1 day.

This is the least frequently encountered of the three *Paracheirodon* species featured. In overall coloration it falls somewhere in between *P. innesi* (Neon Tetra) and *P. axelrodi* (Cardinal Tetra). Despite its relative rarity, at least two varieties are known in addition to the wild type: a White Green (or False) Neon and a Gold Green (or False) Neon.

Congo Tetra

Phenacogrammus interruptus

Synonym: *Micralestes interruptus*

Family: Characidae

Subfamily: Alestiinae

Distribution: D. R. Congo.

Size: Fully mature males up to 3½in (9cm); females somewhat smaller.

Behavior: Peaceful and tolerant; may become timid in the presence of robust, hyperactive, or aggressive tankmates. May also nibble delicate or succulent plants.

Diet: Wide range of foods accepted; vegetable component recommended.

Aquarium: Spacious, well-planted, with ample swimming areas. Soft, slightly acid water is recommended—preferably tannin-stained. Temperature range: 75–81°F (24–27°C).

Breeding: Uncommon in aquaria. Bright illumination may act as a stimulus for well-matched pairs or shoals. Eggs are scattered over the substratum and take up to 6 days to hatch.

During the early part of the last decade of the 20th century the scientific name *Micralestes* to describe this species became more popular than *Phenacogrammus*. As the new millennium approached, however, *Phenacogrammus* seemed to come back into fashion. The main contributing factor to this confusion is the considerable overlap in certain characteristics between the two genera. The main distinguishing feature between the two is that in *Phenacogrammus* the lateral line is incomplete, while in *Micralestes* it is complete (although this distinction is not infallible since, in some *Micralestes*, the lateral line can also be incomplete). Whatever its true identity, the species is an elegant fish that looks splendid when kept in appropriate conditions and in a small shoal.

Glass Bloodfin

Prionobrama filigera

Other common names:
Translucent Bloodfin, Glass
Bloodfish

Synonyms: *Aphyocharax
filigerus, Prionobrama
madeirae*

Family: Characidae

Subfamily: Uncertain
(classified as Paragoniatinae
by some authors)

Distribution: Amazon
River basin.

Size: Around 2½in (6cm).

Behavior: Peaceful shoaler.

Diet: Wide range of foods
accepted.

Aquarium: Well planted
with ample swimming space
recommended. Surface
cover in the form of floating
plants also advisable.
Softish, slightly acid water
appears to be preferred, but
higher pH and hardness also
tolerated. Temperature
range: 72–86°F (22–30°C).

Breeding: Soft, acid,
tannin-stained water
recommended. Sunlight
will also help. Eggs are
scattered among fine-leaved
vegetation and hatch after
about 3 days.

Closely related to *Aphyocharax anisitsi* (Bloodfin), this species is much
less frequently seen in the hobby. This is a shame because it is an elegant,
strikingly patterned fish, with the added attraction that the male's anal fin
possesses a brilliant white, curved extension along its front edge.

X-ray Tetra

Pristella maxillaris

Other common names:
X-ray Fish, Water Goldfinch

Synonym: *Pristella riddlei*

Family: Characidae

Subfamily:
Tetragonopterinae

Distribution: Lower
Amazon, Guyana, and
Venezuela.

Size: Around 1³/₄in (4.5cm).

Behavior: Peaceful shoaler.

Diet: Wide range of foods
accepted.

Aquarium: Well planted,
with ample swimming
space; a dark substratum
and subdued lighting will
show off a shoal to great
effect. Water chemistry
not critical (although soft,
slightly acid conditions
preferred), but quality must
be good. Temperature
range: 70–82°F (21–28°C)—
low temperatures should
not be maintained on a
long-term basis.

Breeding: Sometimes
difficult if pairs are not
well matched; otherwise
spawning is easy. Eggs are
scattered and take about
1 day to hatch.

This is an undemanding species that tolerates a range of aquarium
conditions. However, for its colors to be seen to best effect, the overall
water quality must be good. The somewhat intriguing common name of
Water Goldfinch probably derives from the gold, white, black, and red
coloration, which is shared with its feathered namesake.

Red-bellied Piranha

Pygocentrus nattereri

Synonyms: *Serrasalmus nattereri, Pygocentrus altus*

Family: Characidae

Subfamily: Serrasalminae

Distribution: Amazon and Orinoco basins.

Size: Up to 12in (30cm).

Behavior: Aggressive, often toward tankmates of their own species.

Diet: Meat/fish-based diet and large livefoods. Live fish also eaten, but the ethics of this practice need to be considered before providing such a diet.

Aquarium: Large, deep, well filtered, with large pieces of bogwood laid out for shelter. Only robust and/or artificial plants suitable. Avoid bright lighting. Soft, slightly acid water preferred. Temperature range: 73–81°F (23–27°C).

Breeding: Infrequent in aquaria. Eggs have been laid among the feathery roots of large floating plants, but usually they are laid inside a depression dug in the substratum. Both parents, or one (usually the male), will defend the eggs until they hatch about 2–3 days later.

As in the case of other members of the subfamily Serrasalminae, such as the Silver Dollars (e.g. *Metynnis* and *Myleus* spp.), piranha taxonomy is currently somewhat unsettled. The former subgeneric name *Pygocentrus*, for example, is now becoming more widely accepted as a full generic name for some types of piranha. Despite its formidable reputation, the Red-bellied Piranha is not quite the indiscriminate killer it is made out to be. It is, nevertheless, a potentially dangerous species, and even small specimens must be treated with due caution, particularly when cleaning their aquaria. This species may be illegal or restricted in some U. S. states; it is best to seek advice locally before purchase.

Swordtail Characin

Corynopoma riisei (previously Stevardia riisei)

Synonym: *Corynopoma riisei*

Family: Characidae

Subfamily: Glandulocaudinae

Distribution: Meta River in Colombia, and possibly in Trinidad.

Size: Up to 2³/₄in (7cm).

Behavior: Peaceful shoaler; should not be housed with fin-nipping species such as *Barbus tetrazona* (Tiger Barb).

Diet: Wide range of foods accepted.

Aquarium: Well planted with ample swimming areas recommended. Water chemistry can range from slightly acid to slightly alkaline and from soft to medium-hard. Temperature range: 72–82°F (22–28°C).

Breeding: Unusually for a characin, the eggs are fertilized internally (hence the need for the female to adopt a precise position for mating). The eggs are subsequently released and hatch in 1–1¹/₂ days.

This basically silver-colored fish has rather unusual distinguishing physical and reproductive characteristics. Mature males possess a long extension of the lower rays of the caudal fin—the "sword" that gives the species its common name. In addition, they have a long, filamentlike extension on each gill cover, with a fleshy structure at the tip; it is believed that this "paddle" is used as a lure to attract a female into the appropriate breeding position.

Boehlke's Penguin Fish

Thayeria boehlkei

Other common names:
Hockey Stick Tetra, Black-line Thayeria

Family: Characidae

Subfamily:
Tetragonopterinae

Distribution: Peruvian Amazon and Araguaia (Brazil).

Size: Up to 3in (8cm) reported, but usually smaller.

Behavior: Peaceful shoaler.

Diet: Wide range of foods accepted.

Aquarium: Thickly planted with some swimming space recommended. Soft, slightly acid, well-oxygenated water preferred, but some deviation is tolerated, as long as changes are carried out gradually. Frequent water changes (observing this rule) also advisable. Temperature range: 72–82°F (22–28°C).

Breeding: Eggs are scattered freely among fine-leaved vegetation. Hatching takes about 1 day.

This species looks best when kept in a shoal, which emphasizes the bold black gold-bordered body band, as well as the unusual way in which the band extends into the lower part of the caudal fin. The species also adopts a characteristic angled posture when at rest, with the head pointed slightly upward and often with all the fish in a shoal facing in the same direction.

Penguin Fish

Thayeria obliqua

Other common name:
Short-striped Thayeria

Family: Characidae

Subfamily:
Tetragonopterinae

Distribution: Amazon basin.

Size: Up to 3in (8cm) reported, but usually smaller.

Behavior: Peaceful shoaler.

Diet: Wide range of foods accepted.

Aquarium: Thickly planted with some swimming space recommended. Soft, slightly acid, well-oxygenated water preferred, but some deviation is tolerated, as long as changes are carried out gradually. Frequent water changes (observing this rule) also advisable. Temperature range: 72–82°F (22–28°C).

Breeding: No documented reports available, but it is likely that eggs are scattered freely among fine-leaved vegetation and that they hatch after about 1 day.

At first sight this species can be confused with *T. boehlkei* (Boehlke's Penguin Fish). However, in the Penguin Fish the black band extends forward from the tip of the lower lobe of the caudal fin at an upwardly directed angle to a point on the back just posterior to the dorsal fin. In *T. boehlkei* the band extends all the way along the center of the body right up to the gill cover.

Narrow Hatchetfish

Triportheus angulatus

Family: Characidae

Subfamily: Uncertain (classified as Bryconinae by some authors)

Distribution: Amazon basin.

Size: Up to 8in (20cm) reported, but usually smaller.

Behavior: Generally peaceful, but may attack small tankmates.

Diet: Livefoods preferred, but will accept a range of commercial diets.

Aquarium: Large, well covered, well illuminated, with ample swimming areas recommended. Well-oxygenated water important, but composition may vary from slightly acid to slightly alkaline and from soft to medium-hard. Temperature range: 72–82°F (22–28°C).

Breeding: No documented reports currently available.

Members of the genus *Triportheus* (of which this species is the most frequently encountered in the hobby) have a keel-like chest that resembles that found in the "true" hatchetfishes (family Gasteropelecidae). It forms the anchor for powerful chest muscles that allow the fish to jump out of the water and—with the aid of winglike pectoral fins—glide for short distances, thereby escaping predators.

Lined Citharinid

Citharinus citharus

Family: Citharinidae

Subfamily: Citharininae

Distribution: From Senegal to the Nile basin.

Size: Up to 20in (50cm) reported, but usually much smaller.

Behavior: Not aggressive; may be kept in shoals, space permitting. Likes to dig in the substrate in search of food.

Diet: Wide range of foods accepted.

Aquarium: Large, deep, with ample swimming space and fine-grained substratum recommended. Neutral to alkaline, soft to medium-hard water preferred. Temperature range: 72–82°F (22–28°C).

Breeding: Believed to be an egg scatterer, but no documented accounts currently available.

This large, predominantly silvery fish has dusky dorsal, caudal, and anal fins, clear pectoral fins, and reddish pelvic fins. Only juveniles are suitable for average-sized aquaria. This species is therefore best avoided unless adequate accommodation can be provided for adults.

Silver Distichodus

Distichodus affinis

Family: Citharinidae

Subfamily: Distichodontinae

Distribution: Congo basin, D. R. Congo.

Size: Up to 5in (13cm).

Behavior: Peaceful, with a distinct liking for succulent plants.

Diet: Some commercial foods accepted, particularly vegetable flakes; lettuce, spinach, watercress, and other plants should form an important part of the diet.

Aquarium: Roomy, with rock and bogwood decor recommended. Use only unpalatable or artificial plants, and provide swimming space. Slightly acid to neutral, soft to medium-hard water. Temperature range: 73–81°F (23–27°C).

Breeding: No documented accounts currently available.

The Silver Distichodus was first imported into Europe in 1911 and has been available ever since, despite its plant-eating habits. Overall, it is similar to *D. noboli* (Nobol's Distichodus) from Upper Congo (D. R. Congo), with which it is sometimes confused. All *Distichodus* are specialist feeders and are best suited to experienced aquarists.

Long-nosed Distichodus

Distichodus lusosso

Family: Citharinidae

Subfamily: Distichodontinae

Distribution: Congo basin (D. R. Congo), Angola, Cameroon.

Size: Up to 16in (40cm) reported, but usually smaller.

Behavior: Peaceful, with a strong appetite for plants.

Diet: Some commercial foods accepted, particularly vegetable flakes; lettuce, spinach, watercress, and other plants should form an important part of the diet.

Aquarium: Roomy, with rock and bogwood decor recommended. Use only unpalatable or artificial plants. Sufficient swimming space should be provided. Slightly acid to neutral, soft to medium-hard water required. Temperature range: 72–79°F (22–26°C).

Breeding: No documented accounts currently available.

Owing to the large size attained by adults, only juveniles of this species are suitable for most aquaria. A similar-looking species, *D. sexfasciatus* (Six-lined Distichodus)—also from the Congo basin in D. R. Congo—can be confused with this species, although, as its name implies, the Long-nosed Distichodus has a somewhat longer and more pointed snout than its close relative.

One-striped African Characin

Nannaethiops unitaeniatus

Family: Citharinidae

Subfamily: Distichodontinae

Distribution: Widely distributed in tropical regions of Africa.

Size: Around 2³/₄in (7cm).

Behavior: Peaceful shoaler best kept in a species aquarium, i.e. one set up specifically for it.

Diet: Wide range of foods accepted once specimens have been adequately acclimatized.

Aquarium: Tank should be brightly lit, with ample swimming space and fine-grained substratum. Tannin-stained water advisable. Neutral, softish water preferred, but a little deviation accepted. Temperature range: 73–79°F (23–26°C).

Breeding: Morning sun appears to stimulate spawning. Eggs are scattered, and hatch in a little over 1 day.

Although it looks very different to the other members of the family featured in the previous entries, the One-striped African Characin possesses fin ray, skeletal, and tooth characteristics that identify it as a citharinid. Despite the subtle coloration of the species, it nevertheless makes an impressive display when kept in appropriate conditions. A gold-striped variety is also occasionally available.

Ansorge's Neolebias

Neolebias ansorgii

Synonym:
Neolebias ansorgei

Family: Citharinidae

Subfamily: Distichodontinae

Distribution: Widely distributed from Cameroon to D. R. Congo.

Size: Around 1 1/2 in (3.5cm).

Behavior: Peaceful, timid; best kept in a species aquarium, i.e. one set up specifically for it.

Diet: Livefoods preferred, but other foods accepted.

Aquarium: Subdued lighting, dark substratum, and ample planting are recommended, as is relatively shallow water (around 8in/20cm). Raw water must be avoided (add a good conditioner when carrying out partial changes). Slightly acid, softish water preferred. Temperature range: 73–82°F (23–28°C).

Breeding: Peat or moss base recommended. Eggs are scattered and hatch in about 1 day.

This colorful species (the most colorful of its genus) has been available since the 1920s without ever attaining the high levels of popularity it deserves. It is, nevertheless, the most widely available *Neolebias* species. Unusually for characoids, *Neolebias* species lack an adipose fin.

African Pike Characin

Phago loricatus (previously Phago maculatus)

Family: Citharinidae

Subfamily: Distichodontinae

Distribution: Niger basin in West Africa.

Size: Around 5½in (14cm).

Behavior: Unsociable and highly predatory; despite this, *Phago* can be very timid in aquaria.

Diet: May eat larger invertebrate livefoods, but shows a clear preference for live fish. This species should therefore be kept only after serious consideration of its dietary requirements.

Aquarium: Roomy, with ample swimming space and suitable shelters of bogwood or caves. Water chemistry not critical. Temperature range: 73–82°F (23–28°C).

Breeding: No accounts of successful aquarium breeding currently available.

The three members of this genus (or four members according to some literature) look quite different from the other citharinids featured in the preceding pages. The body is long and slim, and the mouth is armed with a fearsome set of cutting teeth. The snout itself is elongated into a "beak" whose top half actually lifts when the mouth is opened. Since *Phago* species are known for eating small fishes and biting the fins of larger specimens, they are often referred to as the "fin eaters."

Silver Prochilodus

Semaprochilodus taeniurus

Synonym: *Prochilodus taeniurus*

Family: Curimatidae

Subfamily: Prochilodontinae

Distribution: Brazil and western Colombia.

Size: Up to 12in (30cm).

Behavior: Peaceful, despite its size.

Diet: Wide range of foods accepted; vegetable component essential.

Aquarium: Roomy, with good illumination, fine-grained substratum, and tough or unpalatable plants (or artificial equivalents) recommended. Water chemistry not critical, but good filtration advisable. Temperature range: 72–79°F (22–26°C).

Breeding: No documented accounts of aquarium breeding currently available.

When in peak condition, the Silver Prochilodus (one of only a few prochilodontids seen with any regularity) is an extremely attractive fish in which the black-and-white markings of the dorsal and caudal fins contrast beautifully with the silvery body and the bright red pelvic fins. Its main drawbacks as an aquarium fish are its plant-eating and burrowing habits, and its relatively large size.

Golden Trahira

Hoplerythrinus unitaeniatus

Other common name:
Blackband Predator Characin

Synonyms: *Erythrinus unitaeniatus, E. gronovii, E. kessleri, E. salvus, E. vittatus*

Family: Erythrinidae

Distribution: Guyana, Paraguay, Trinidad, and Venezuela.

Size: Up to 16in (40cm).

Behavior: Solitary predator; can be kept with larger fish.

Diet: Livefoods, including fish—a factor that needs to be considered prior to obtaining a specimen. May be weaned onto dead/frozen foods and some chunky commercial diets.

Aquarium: Large, well covered, well filtered, with hiding places and robust plants recommended. Water chemistry not critical. Temperature range: 72–81°F (22–27°C).

Breeding: No documented accounts of aquarium breeding currently available.

The large number of names by which this species has been referred to in scientific and other literature indicates the difficulty encountered when dealing with a widely distributed and variable species. The Golden Trahira is unusual for a characoid in that it lacks an adipose fin. Other features include a thick layer of slippery body mucus and an ability to use its swimbladder as an auxiliary respiratory organ. The Golden Trahira is most definitely a fish for the specialist.

Wolf Fish

Hoplias malabaricus

Other common name:
South American Tiger Fish

Family: Erythrinidae

Distribution: Widespread in Central America and northern South America.

Size: Up to 20in (50cm).

Behavior: Solitary predator; can be kept with larger fish.

Diet: Livefoods, including fish—a factor that needs to be considered prior to obtaining a specimen. May be weaned onto dead/frozen foods and some chunky commercial diets.

Aquarium: Large, well covered, well filtered tank. Plenty of hiding places and robust plants are recommended. Water chemistry not critical. Temperature range: 72–81°F (22–27°C).

Breeding: Has been achieved in aquaria, but details not currently available.

The Wolf Fish is one of the best known of all predatory characoids (other than the piranhas), although it is not seen with any great frequency. Like *Hoplerythrinus unitaeniatus* (the Golden Trahira), this species is widely distributed. One other species, *Hoplias microlepis*, is very occasionally available: it is somewhat smaller and comes from southern Ecuador, Panama, and Costa Rica.

Marbled Hatchetfish

Carnegiella strigata

Synonym: *Carnegiella vesca*

Family: Gasteropelecidae

Distribution: Guianas and Amazon basin.

Size: Around 1½in (4cm).

Behavior: Peaceful shoaler; should not be kept with boisterous tankmates.

Diet: Wide range of floating foods accepted; sinking foods usually ignored once they float down below top inch (3cm) of the water column.

Aquarium: Well covered and well filtered with some clear spaces on the surface recommended. Provide plant thickets and some floating plants as shelter. Softish, slightly acid water preferred, as is a water current (produced via the outlet of a power filter or power head). Temperature range: 75–82°F (24–28°C).

Breeding: Soft, acid, heavily tannin-stained water recommended, along with subdued lighting. Eggs are deposited among the feathery roots of floating plants, though not all will remain attached. Hatching takes just over 1 day.

Two subspecies of Marbled Hatchetfish are generally recognized: *C. strigata strigata*, and *C. s. fasciata* (Dark Marbled Hatchetfish), which is found in the more southern regions of the range (although there is some overlap where "intermediate" specimens are known to occur). In *C. s. strigata* the dark band that originates from the middle of the edge of the breast keel and extends upward and backward through the body is divided into two "sub-bands" almost from its point of origin. In *C. s. fasciata* this dark band does not divide until it reaches the level of the pectoral fins. However, since this feature is variable, unequivocal identification can be difficult. A lutino morph of *C. s. strigata*, which lacks most of the body markings but (unlike albinos) possesses normal-colored eyes, is also occasionally available.

Common Hatchetfish

Gasteropelecus sternicla

Other common names:
Black-lined/Black-stroke Hatchetfish

Family: Gasteropelecidae

Distribution: Peruvian Amazon, Guianas, Suriname, Trinidad, and Mato Grosso (Brazil).

Size: Around 2½in (6.5cm).

Behavior: Peaceful shoaler; should not be kept with boisterous tankmates.

Diet: Wide range of floating foods accepted; sinking foods usually ignored once they float down below top inch (3cm) of the water column.

Aquarium: Well covered, well filtered tank, with some clear spaces on the surface recommended. Provide plant thickets and some floating plants as shelter. Softish, slightly acid water preferred, as is a water current (produced via the outlet of a power filter or power head). Temperature range: 73–82°F (23–28°C).

Breeding: No documented accounts currently available.

The Common Hatchetfish has a body that, as its name suggests, is typically "hatchet-shaped." It also has a distinctive black horizontal line running from behind the head to the base of the caudal fin. It is similar to *Thoracocharax securis* (the Silver Hatchetfish), with which it is sometimes confused.

Silver Hatchetfish

Thoracocharax securis

Other common name:
Pectorosus Hatchetfish

Synonyms: *Gasteropelecus securis, Thoracocharax stellatus, T. pectorosus*

Family: Gasteropelecidae

Distribution: If *T. stellatus* is regarded as synonymous with *T. securis*, widespread in central South America; if not, middle/upper parts of the Amazon basin.

Size: Around $3\frac{1}{2}$in (9cm).

Behavior: Peaceful shoaler; should not be kept with boisterous tankmates.

Diet: Wide range of floating foods accepted; sinking foods usually ignored once they float down.

Aquarium: Well covered, well filtered tank, with some clear spaces on the surface recommended. Provide plant thickets and some floating plants as shelter. Softish, slightly acid water preferred, as is a water current (produced via the outlet of a power filter or power head). Temperature range: 73–86°F (23–30°C).

Breeding: No documented accounts currently available.

Depending on the literature consulted, there is either one species in this genus (*T. securis*) or two, if *T. stellatus* is accepted as a valid species. Both appear almost identical, although *T. stellatus* has a black spot on the base of the dorsal fin and two or three rows of almost microscopic scales along the base of the anal fin. *Thoracocharax securis* lacks the spot and has five to six rows of tiny scales. *Thoracocharax* can be distinguished from *Gasteropelecus* by the more pronounced chest profile, whose anterior edge is almost vertical in *Thoracocharax* and more gently sloping in *Gasteropelecus*.

Slender Hemiodus

Hemiodus gracilis (previously Hemiodopsis gracilis)

Synonym: *Hemiodus gracilis*

Family: Hemiodontidae (referred to as Hemiodidae by some authors)

Subfamily: Hemiodontinae

Distribution: Amazon and Guyana.

Size: Around 6in (15cm).

Behavior: Shoaler, with distinct appetite for succulent plants.

Diet: Most foods accepted; vegetable component recommended.

Aquarium: Spacious tank with ample swimming space. Provide robust, unpalatable, or artificial plants. Well-oxygenated water important; water chemistry not critical, but soft, acid conditions preferred. Temperature range: 73–81°F (23–27°C).

Breeding: No documented accounts currently available.

The synonym (*Hemiodus*), the current generic name (*Hemiodopsis*), and the common name all reflect the uncertainty that exists regarding the classification of these characoids. The main feature quoted as distinguishing *Hemiodus* are the scales on the back of adult and semiadult specimens, which are noticeably smaller than those above the pelvic fins.

One-spot Hemiodus

Hemiodus unimaculatus

Other common name:
Yellow-tailed Hemiodus

Synonyms: *Anisitsia notata*, *Hemiodus microcephalus*

Family: Hemiodontidae (referred to as Hemiodidae by some authors)

Subfamily: Hemiodontinae

Distribution: Río Negro (Brazil), the Guianas, and the Orinoco system.

Size: Up to 7½in (19cm).

Behavior: Shoaler, with distinct appetite for succulent plants.

Diet: Most foods accepted; vegetable component recommended.

Aquarium: Spacious tank with ample swimming space. Provide robust, unpalatable, or artificial plants. Well-oxygenated water important; water chemistry not critical, but soft, acid conditions preferred. Temperature range: 73–81°F (23–27°C).

Breeding: No documented accounts currently available.

The One-spot Hemiodus possesses a distinct black body spot and a black- or cream-streaked caudal fin. In these characteristics it resembles a relative, *Hemiodopsis microlepis* (Red-tailed, or Feather, Hemiodus). In the southern parts of the range, around the Río Paraguay, there is another similar-looking species, *Hemiodus orthonops* (which has a greater number of lateral line scales). *Hemiodus rudolphoi* (Rudolph's Hemiodus), the only other species in the genus, is occasionally seen.

African Pike Characin

Hepsetus odoe

Synonym: *Sarcodaces odoe*

Family: Hepsetidae

Distribution: Across tropical regions of Africa, except the Nile basin.

Size: Up to 26–28in (65–70cm) in the wild, but usually around half this size.

Behavior: Solitary predator; can only be kept with tankmates that are too large to swallow.

Diet: Young specimens can be accustomed to chunky meat- and fish-based foods; adults are more difficult, preferring live fish—a factor that needs to be considered before obtaining a specimen.

Aquarium: Large, well covered, well filtered, with shelters constructed from bogwood and rounded rocks—sharp objects should be avoided. Water chemistry not critical, but avoid extremes. Temperature range: 79–82°F (26–28°C).

Breeding: No documented accounts in aquaria. In nature this species is known to build a bubble nest on the surface of the water, into which eggs are deposited; eggs guarded by one or both spawners.

This species is the only member of its genus and family. It is built like a pike (*Esox* spp.), as indicated by its common name, and hunts using similar techniques of stealth followed by a lightning-fast strike. Some individuals may be prone to "panic attacks" in the aquarium, crashing into the sides of the tank and anything in it. For this reason, it is advisable to avoid sharp objects on which the fish may injure themselves. This is most definitely a species for the specialist.

Red-spotted Copeina

Copeina guttata

Other common name:
Red-spotted Characin

Family: Lebiasinidae

Subfamily: Pyrrhulininae

Distribution: Amazon basin.

Size: Up to 6in (15cm) reported, but usually only about half this size.

Behavior: Peaceful, except during breeding, when males may become aggressive.

Diet: Wide range of foods accepted.

Aquarium: Large aquarium recommended, with fine-grained substratum. Plants are not eaten but they may be uprooted during nestbuilding. Tannin-stained water preferred. Water chemistry not critical, but softish, acid to neutral conditions preferred. Temperature range: 73–82°F (23–28°C).

Breeding: Male hollows out a shallow depression in the substratum, and the pair spawn in it. The eggs are guarded by male until they hatch 1½–2 days later. Recommended breeding temperature: 82–86°F (28–30°C).

Primarily distinguished from the closely related members of the genus *Copella* by its jawbone characteristics, the Red-spotted Copeina is popular for its striking coloration. Specimens in peak condition have a shiny light blue body overlaid with numerous red spots. The pelvic, anal, and lower lobe of the caudal fin all have red borders as well.

Splashing Tetra/Characin

Copella arnoldi

Other common names: Jumping Tetra/Characin, Spraying Tetra/Characin

Synonym: *Copeina arnoldi*

Family: Lebiasinidae

Subfamily: Pyrrhulininae

Distribution: Lower Amazon basin.

Size: Males up to 3¼in (8cm); females smaller.

Behavior: Peaceful; may be kept in pairs or in a shoal.

Diet: Wide range of foods accepted.

Aquarium: Well-covered aquarium essential. Surface vegetation and open swimming spaces required. Soft, slightly acid water, preferably tannin-stained recommended. Temperature range: 77–84°F (25–29°C).

Breeding: Well-covered aquarium, with lowered water level to allow some broadleaved plants to project about an inch (3cm) above the surface. The spawning pair will jump out of the water and deposit their eggs on the leaves or on the aquarium cover itself. The eggs are kept moist by spraying or splashing by male until they hatch 2–3 days later.

Splashing Tetra owes its common names to its breeding habits, which are quite unusual. This fish lays its eggs above the water line. The male and female jump out of the water together and cling to the underside of an overhanging leaf. The female deposits and the male fertilizes several eggs on the leaf. They repeat the performance many times until all the eggs have been laid in this way. The male then keeps the eggs moist by spraying or splashing them until they hatch. All other members of the genus breed in more "traditional" ways (see *C. metae*).

Meta Tetra

Copella eigenmanni (previously Copella metae)

Other common name:
Brown-banded Copella

Synonym: *Copeina metae*

Family: Lebiasinidae

Subfamily: Pyrrhulininae

Distribution: Meta River (Colombia) and Peruvian Amazon.

Size: Up to 2½in (6cm).

Behavior: Peaceful, active but timid; should be kept in shoals with other species of similar temperament.

Diet: Wide range of foods accepted.

Aquarium: Well covered with surface vegetation and subdued lighting. Submerged plants should include some broadleaved species, e.g. *Echinodorus* spp. Water chemistry can range from acid to slightly alkaline and from soft to medium-hard (adjustments must be carried out gradually). Temperature range: 73–81°F (23–27°C).

Breeding: Soft water, preferably tannin-stained. Eggs are laid on submerged broadleaved plant and guarded by male. Hatching takes just over 1 day.

Despite one of the common names (Brown-banded Copella), not all Meta Tetras exhibit the bold body band at all times. Well-banded specimens are particularly attractive when kept in a shoal under appropriate conditions. Small shoals are advisable to reduce the incidence of fighting among males.

Colombian Dwarf Predatory Tetra

Lebiasina astrigata

Other common name:
Elegant Pencilfish

Synonym: *Piabucina astrigata*

Family: Lebiasinidae

Subfamily: Lebiasininae

Distribution: Colombia and northern South America.

Size: Up to 3¼in (8cm).

Behavior: Predatory; must not be kept with small tankmates.

Diet: Primarily livefoods and deep-frozen diets, although dried formulations may also be accepted after the fish have been acclimatized to aquarium conditions.

Aquarium: Thickly planted. Water chemistry not critical. Temperature range: 72–79°F (22–26°C).

Breeding: No documented accounts currently available.

Lebiasina species are distinguished from their close relatives, *Copella*, by their four (rather than three) branchiostegal rays (slender bony rods on some of the bones that support the gill cover). They also have a relatively long upper jawbone, they are considerably more resilient in terms of environmental tolerance, and they have a very different temperament. A few other species may be occasionally available, most notably *L. multipunctata* (Multi-spotted Lebiasina), which is from northwest Colombia.

Beckford's Pencilfish

Nannostomus beckfordi

Other common name:
Golden Pencilfish

Synonyms: *N. anomalus*,
N. aripirangensis, *N. simplex*

Family: Lebiasinidae

Subfamily: Pyrrhulininae

Distribution: Central
Amazon, lower Río Negro,
and Guyana.

Size: Up to 2¹/₂in (6.5cm)
reported, but usually smaller.

Behavior: Peaceful shoaler;
can be kept with lively
tankmates as long as they
are not predatory.

Diet: Most small foods
accepted, particularly
livefoods.

Aquarium: Well (but not
excessively) planted, with
reasonable amount of cover.
Tolerant of a range of water
and lighting conditions, but
soft, acid water—preferably
tannin-stained—and
subdued illumination
preferred. Temperature
range: 75–82°F (24–28°C).

Breeding: Subdued lighting,
soft, acid water and fine-
leaved vegetation required.
Water temperature: around
86°F (30°C). Eggs are
scattered among vegetation
and may be eaten by the
spawners. Hatching takes
1–3 days.

Three generic names are often encountered in relation to the pencilfishes that form the group to which Golden Pencilfish belongs: *Poecilobrycon, Nannobrycon,* and *Nannostomus*. Features, including the presence or absence of an adipose fin (Golden Pencilfish lacks this fin), presence or absence of a canal in one of the bones surrounding the eye (not directly observable in live specimens), relative length of the snout and angle of orientation when at rest or swimming (horizontal or angled upward, i.e. head-up) have all been cited as distinguishing characteristics. However, variability of some of these, e.g. presence/absence of an adipose fin, has led to considerable debate, with *Poecilobrycon* tending to be dropped and *Nannobrycon* being retained only by some ichthyologists for two species that exhibit the "head-up" characteristic, along with an enlarged lower caudal-fin lobe. Most authorities, however, tend to regard all the species concerned as members of a single genus, *Nannostomus*. Their peaceful nature and shoaling behavior make them attractive as aquarium fish, but pencilfishes are also desirable because of their two very different color patterns: one reserved for the daylight hours and one for the night.

Two-lined Pencilfish

Nannostomus bifasciatus

Family: Lebiasinidae

Subfamily: Pyrrhulininae

Distribution: Suriname and Guyana.

Size: Up to 2in (5cm).

Behavior: Peaceful shoaler, somewhat more timid than *N. beckfordi*; should not be kept with lively tankmates.

Diet: Most small foods accepted, particularly livefoods.

Aquarium: Thickly planted and with subdued lighting. Soft, slightly acid, nitrate-free water preferred (any changes in conditions must be carried out gradually), as is tannin-stained water. Temperature range: 73–81°F (23–27°C).

Breeding: Subdued lighting, soft, acid water, and fine-leaved vegetation required. Water temperature should be maintained at around 86°F (30°C). Eggs are scattered among the vegetation and may be eaten by the spawners. Hatching takes 1–3 days.

Although this species lacks the red body coloration of prime *N. beckfordi* (Golden Pencilfish) specimens, it is nevertheless beautifully patterned with a broad, body-long, black band along the midline and a considerably narrower one above. This species lacks an adipose fin.

Harrison's Pencilfish

Nannostomus harrisoni

Synonym: *Poecilobrycon harrisoni*

Family: Lebiasinidae

Subfamily: Pyrrhulininae

Distribution: Guyana.

Size: Around 2½in (6cm).

Behavior: Peaceful shoaler, somewhat more timid than *N. beckfordi*; should not be kept with lively tankmates.

Diet: Most small foods accepted, particularly livefoods.

Aquarium: Thickly planted and with subdued lighting. Soft, slightly acid, nitrate-free water preferred (any changes in conditions must be carried out gradually), as is tannin-stained water. Temperature range: 73–81°F (23–27°C).

Breeding: Subdued lighting, soft, acid water, and fine-leaved vegetation required. Water temperature should be maintained at around 86°F (30°C). Eggs are scattered among the vegetation and may be eaten by the spawners. Hatching takes 1–3 days.

This pencilfish possesses red markings on the pelvic, anal, and caudal fins. These, added to the snout-to-tail body band, make for an impressive show when the species is kept in a large shoal. This species possesses an adipose fin.

Dwarf Pencilfish

Nannostomus marginatus

Family: Lebiasinidae

Subfamily: Pyrrhulininae

Distribution: Guyana, Suriname, and (possibly) lower reaches of the Amazon.

Size: Around 1½in (3.5cm).

Behavior: Peaceful shoaler, somewhat more timid than *N. beckfordi*; should not be kept with lively tankmates.

Diet: Most small foods accepted, particularly livefoods.

Aquarium: Thickly planted and with subdued lighting. Soft, slightly acid, nitrate-free water preferred (any changes in conditions must be carried out gradually), as is tannin-stained water. Temperature range: 73–81°F (23–27°C).

Breeding: Subdued lighting, soft, acid water and fine-leaved vegetation required. Water temperature: around 86°F (30°C). Eggs are scattered among the vegetation and may be eaten by the spawners. Hatching takes 1–3 days.

This is a delightful species that, despite its small size, creates a sparkling display. It has vivid red coloration on its fins (except the caudal fin), three prominent, dark brown bands on its body, and a splash of several red scales along the midpoint of the central band. This species lacks an adipose fin.

One-lined Pencilfish

Nannostomus unifasciatus

Synonym: *Nannobrycon unifasciatus*

Family: Lebiasinidae

Subfamily: Pyrrhulininae

Distribution: Middle and upper Amazon basin, Río Negro, Upper Río Orinoco, and Guyana.

Size: Around 2½in (6cm).

Behavior: Peaceful shoaler, timid; should not be kept with lively tankmates.

Diet: Most small foods accepted, particularly livefoods.

Aquarium: Thickly planted and with subdued lighting. Soft, slightly acid, nitrate-free water preferred (any changes in conditions must be carried out gradually), as is tannin-stained water Temperature range: 73–81°F (23–27°C).

Breeding: Subdued lighting, soft, acid water and fine-leaved vegetation required. Water temperature: around 86°F (30°C). Eggs are scattered among the vegetation and may be eaten by the spawners. Hatching takes 1–3 days.

This pencilfish is one of the few that exhibit the "head-up" orientation referred to under *N. beckfordi* (Golden Pencilfish), as well as the enlarged lower caudal-fin lobe—hence its synonym, *Nannobrycon*. The One-lined Pencilfish possesses an adipose fin.

Short-lined Pyrrhulina

Pyrrhulina brevis

Other common name:
Scaleblotch Pyrrhulina

Family: Lebiasinidae

Subfamily: Pyrrhulininae

Distribution: Amazon basin, extending into Colombia (this applies to the Short-lined Pyrrhulina in its broadest sense).

Size: Up to 3¹⁄₄in (8cm) reported, but usually around 2in (5cm).

Behavior: May react nervously to external disturbances; prefers to be kept in groups although it does not possess strong shoaling instincts.

Diet: Predominantly livefoods, but may accept deep-frozen, freeze-dried, and other commercial formulations.

Aquarium: Spacious, well planted; subdued lighting and dark substratum recommended. Slightly acid, medium-hard water preferred, particularly if tannin-stained. Temperature range: 75–79°F (24–26°C).

Breeding: No documented accounts currently available.

Superficially, members of this species are difficult to distinguish from *Copeina* and *Copella* species. There are, however, several cranial and dental characteristics that allow distinctions to be made on close examination of preserved specimens. In live specimens perhaps the most easily detectable of these features is that, in *Pyrrhulina*, the nostrils are very close to each other. Within the genus *Pyrrhulina* (which, like its close relatives, lacks an adipose fin) confusion still exists regarding the exact number of species or, in some cases, even the full characteristics of single species. The Short-lined Pyrrhulina is one of these, with some of the naturally existing variants possibly constituting subspecies, varieties, or full species in their own right.

Red-spotted Rachow's Pyrrhulina

Pyrrhulina australis (previously Pyrrhulina rachoviana)

Other common names:
Eyestroke Pyrrhulina,
Fanning Characin

Family: Lebiasinidae

Subfamily: Pyrrhulininae

Distribution: Paraná and Río de la Plata basins.

Size: Up to 2½in (6cm).

Behavior: May react nervously to external disturbances; prefers to be kept in groups although it does not possess strong shoaling instincts. Males become aggressive toward each other if kept in a single-sex group.

Diet: Predominantly livefoods, but may accept deep-frozen, freeze-dried, and other commercial formulations.

Aquarium: Spacious, well planted with subdued lighting and dark substratum. Slightly acid, medium-hard water preferred, particularly if tannin-stained. Temperature range: 75–79°F (24–26°C).

Breeding: Soft, acid water at 79–81°F (26–27°C) recommended. Adhesive eggs laid on broadleaved plant and subsequently fanned and guarded by male. Hatching takes about 1 day.

This attractively marked species has a dark band running from the tip of the snout to the base of the caudal fin and a golden band just above it. The dorsal fin carries a pronounced black blotch, and the body is covered with small red spots.

LOACHES & SUCKERS

Superfamily Cobitoidea

Within the order Cypriniformes, which includes the family Cyprinidae (carps, minnows, rasboras, etc.), there are four closely related groups of fish, three of which are referred to as loaches and one as suckers. Together these four families make up the superfamily Cobitoidea. Nelson, whose classification is followed here, divides the four families as follows (listed alphabetically):

Below: *Yasuhikotakia morleti* (=*horae*).

Balitoridae Classified as Homalopteridae by some authors, these fish are commonly referred to as river loaches (an indication of their preferred habitat). They possess three or more pairs of barbels around the mouth. Within the family two subfamilies are recognized.

Catostomidae These are the suckers, distinguished by their thick, fleshy lips, usually with plicae (folds, membranes, or wrinkles) or papillae (tiny conical protuberances).

Cobitidae This family includes most of the aquarium species generally referred to as loaches. Among the distinguishing features is an erectile spine below the eye. The Cobitidae is subdivided into two subfamilies.

Gyrinocheilidae This family contains just one genus, *Gyrinocheilus*. Of the four species only one, the Sucking Loach or Chinese Algae Eater, is known to aquarists.

Saddled Hillstream Loach

Homaloptera orthogoniata

Family: Balitoridae (classified as Homalopteridae by some authors)

Subfamily: Balitorinae

Distribution: Indonesia and Thailand.

Size: Up to 4³/₄in (12cm) reported.

Behavior: A bottom dweller, peaceful toward other species, but may be a little scrappy toward conspecifics.

Diet: Wide range of foods accepted; algal or vegetable component recommended.

Aquarium: Well filtered, well oxygenated, with water current (as produced by a powerhead outlet). Smoothly rounded rocks and other decor, including broadleaved plants, should also be included. Softish, neutral water preferred, but some deviation accepted. Temperature range: 68–75°F (20–24°C).

Breeding: No documented accounts available.

Only two species of *Homaloptera* are seen with any regularity in aquatic stores: the Saddled Hillstream Loach and *H. zollingeri* (Zollinger's Hillstream Loach). Of the two, the former is more attractively patterned and easier to maintain.

Chinese Sailfin Sucker

Myxocyprinus asiaticus

Other common names: Chinese High Fin, Banded Shark, Hilsa Herring, Rough Fish

Family: Catostomidae

Subfamily: Cycleptinae

Distribution: Yangtze River (China).

Size: Up to 39in (1m).

Behavior: A peaceful bottom dweller.

Diet: Wide range of foods accepted, but diet must include vegetable component.

Aquarium: Large, deep aquarium essential once specimens are even one-quarter of their eventual size. Efficient filtration, high oxygenation, and water current (as produced by a powerhead outlet) also recommended. Water chemistry not critical. Temperature range: below 59°F (15°C) to around 72°F (22°C).

Breeding: No documented accounts currently available.

This fish of many names began appearing in stores with considerable frequency during the last decade of the 20th century. However, the stunning juveniles grow to great length and depth of body, making this attractive species totally unsuitable for most home aquaria.

Horse-faced Loach

Acantopsis choirorhynchos (previously Acanthopsis choirorhynchus)

Other common name:
Long-nosed Loach

Family: Cobitidae

Subfamily: Cobitinae

Distribution: Southeast Asia.

Size: Up to 9in (22½cm) reported, but usually much smaller.

Behavior: A peaceful, burrowing, crepuscular/nocturnal bottom dweller.

Diet: All foods accepted, particularly sinking types, including livefoods.

Aquarium: Soft, fine-grained substratum. Protect plants from being uprooted (by making area around the roots inaccessible). Use a "moonlight" fluorescent tube for night viewing. Water chemistry not critical. Temperature range: 77–82°F (25–28°C).

Breeding: No documented accounts currently available.

This delicately marked species is a poor swimmer, which spends most of its time on the bottom or actually buried in the substratum with only its eyes poking out of the surface. It is, however, capable of producing short spurts of lightning speed.

Banded Loach

Syncrossus helodes (previously Botia helodes)

Family: Cobitidae

Subfamily: Botinae

Distribution: Southeast Asia, but not overlapping *B. hymenophysa*.

Size: Up to 8³/₄in (22cm), but usually smaller.

Behavior: Very active and potentially aggressive, particularly toward conspecifics; most active in the evening and at night; likes to burrow.

Diet: Wide range of foods accepted.

Aquarium: A fine-grained substratum and shelters should be provided, but protect plants (by making root area inaccessible). Soft, slightly acid water and subdued lighting preferred. Temperature range: 75–86°F (24–30°C).

Breeding: No documented accounts currently available.

This species is sometimes available as *B. hymenophysa*, but the true *B. hymenophysa* has a different range (Borneo, southern Malaysia, and Sumatra). Like some other *Botia* species, the Banded Loach can produce clicking sounds when excited.

Yo-yo Loach

Botia lohachata

Other common names:
Pakistani Loach, Y-loach

Family: Cobitidae

Subfamily: Botinae

Distribution: Northern and northeastern India, Bangladesh.

Size: Up to 4³/₄in (12cm) reported, but usually much smaller.

Behavior: Very active and potentially aggressive, particularly toward conspecifics; most active in the evening and at night; likes to burrow.

Diet: Wide range of foods accepted.

Aquarium: A fine-grained substratum and shelters should be provided, but protect plants (by making root area inaccessible). Soft, slightly acid water and subdued lighting preferred. Temperature range: 75–86°F (24–30°C).

Breeding: No documented accounts currently available.

Boldly marked in black and white or black and cream—although the intensity of coloration can vary—this species can prove nervous and easily frightened during the initial stages of acclimatization to a new aquarium. The coloration of the Yo-yo Loach can vary enormously but, in common with other members of the subfamily, it has four pairs of barbels.

Clown Loach

Chromobotia macracanthus (previously Botia macracantha)

Other common name:
Tiger Loach

Synonym:
Botia macracanthus

Family: Cobitidae

Subfamily: Botinae

Distribution: Borneo and Sumatra (Indonesia).

Size: Up to 12in (30cm) reported, but usually smaller.

Behavior: An active shoaler that should be kept in groups; less aggressive than some other *Botia* species and more active during the day. May lie on its side, seemingly dead or dying, for some time; such specimens are, however, perfectly healthy and appear to be resting or asleep.

Diet: Wide range of foods accepted.

Aquarium: A fine-grained substratum and shelters should be provided, but protect plants (by making root area inaccessible). Soft, slightly acid water and subdued lighting preferred. Temperature range: 75–86°F (24–30°C).

Breeding: Has been bred commercially, but only rarely in home aquaria.

This is the best known and probably the most attractive of the *Botia* loaches. Owing to its relatively large size, it is considered a food fish in its native waters. Like its relative, *B. helodes* (Banded Loach), it is known for making clicking noises when excited.

Orange-finned Loach

Yasuhikotakia modesta (previously Botia modesta)

Other common name:
 Blue Loach

Family: Cobitidae

Subfamily: Botinae

Distribution: Malaysia, Thailand, and Vietnam.

Size: Up to 9½in (24cm) reported, but usually much smaller.

Behavior: Can be timid; may be kept in a group.

Diet: Wide range of foods accepted.

Aquarium: A fine-grained substratum and shelters should be provided, but protect plants (by making root area inaccessible). Soft, slightly acid water and subdued lighting preferred. Temperature range: 75–86°F (24–30°C).

Breeding: No documented accounts currently available.

This is an unusually, but most attractively, colored species. It is sometimes confused with *B. lecontei* (Leconte's Loach). However, in Orange-finned Loach all the fins are orange to yellow, while in *B. lecontei* the dorsal fin is grayish blue.

Dwarf Loach

Ambastaia sidthimunki (previously Botia sidthimunki)

Other common name:
Chain Loach

Family: Cobitidae

Subfamily: Botinae

Distribution: Northern India and northern Thailand.

Size: Up to 2¼in (5.5cm).

Behavior: An active species that likes to rest on broad-leaved plants in full view. Unlike some other *Botia* species, it does not avoid bright lights.

Diet: Wide range of foods accepted.

Aquarium: A fine-grained substratum and shelters should be provided, but protect plants (by making root area inaccessible). Soft, slightly acid water and subdued lighting preferred. Temperature range: 75–86°F (24–30°C).

Breeding: No documented accounts currently available.

This small gem—as its common name suggests, it is the smallest member of the genus *Botia*—is now available more widely than it was during the latter decades of the 20th century. For optimum effect, it is best to maintain a shoal of a minimum of six specimens.

Zebra Loach

Botia striata

Family: Cobitidae

Subfamily: Botinae

Distribution: Western Ghats and Maharashtra (India).

Size: Up to 2¹/₂in (6cm).

Behavior: An active species but usually peaceful; lives in small groups.

Diet: Wide range of foods accepted; will include snails in its diet.

Aquarium: A fine-grained substratum, such as sand (for burrowing) required; shelters in the form of tubes and cracks should be provided close to the bottom. Soft, slightly acid water preferred. Temperature range: 73–79°F (23–26°C).

Breeding: No documented accounts currently available.

The peaceful nature of this species, together with its habit of destroying unwanted snails and other water pests, makes it an excellent choice for a community aquarium. Compared with other *Botia* species, it remains fairly small. Because of its patterning, it is sometimes confused with *B. helodes* (Banded Loach).

Spined Weather Loach

Cobitis taenia

Other common name:
Spotted Weather Loach

Family: Cobitidae

Subfamily: Cobitinae

Distribution: Widely distributed in Europe and western Asia, but not in northern regions.

Size: 4³/₄in (12cm).

Behavior: Generally peaceful; most active during the evening and at night.

Diet: Strong preference for bottom-dwelling livefoods; may be difficult to acclimatize to dry foods.

Aquarium: Well oxygenated, well filtered, with a water current (as produced by a powerhead outlet), and substratum consisting of gravel, pebbles, and rocks. Water chemistry not critical. Temperature range: around 50°F (10°C) to 64°F (18°C).

Breeding: Eggs are scattered among plants and/or over substratum.

There are several forms of this loach (regarded as subspecies by some authors). It is quite sensitive to high temperatures and is therefore strictly a species for the coldwater aquarium. In its natural habitat the species is known to be an important source of food for trout.

Lesser Loach

Lepidocephalichthys thermalis (previously Lepidocephalus thermalis)

Other common name:
Indian Stonebiter

Synonym:
Lepidocephalichthys thermalis

Family: Cobitidae

Subfamily: Cobitinae

Distribution: India and Sri Lanka.

Size: Around 3in (8cm).

Behavior: A sociable species that frequently burrows; most active during the evening and at night.

Diet: Bottom-dwelling livefoods preferred, but other diets accepted.

Aquarium: Well filtered, well oxygenated, with fine-grained substratum and some flat rocks and plants. Water chemistry not critical. Temperature range: 72–77°F (22–25°C), but higher temperatures accepted.

Breeding: No documented accounts currently available.

This small spotted species is often found in quiet, slow-flowing waters with a sandy bottom into which it sometimes burrows. It feeds mainly on detritus and algae. The Lesser Loach was originally found in an area of thermal springs, hence its scientific species name *"thermalis."*

Dojo
Misgurnus anguillicaudatus

Other common names: Chinese/Japanese Weather Loach

Family: Cobitidae

Subfamily: Cobitinae

Distribution: Dojo is widely distributed in northeast Asia; *M. fossilis* is widely distributed in central and eastern Europe.

Size: Up to 8in (20cm) or even larger reported, but usually smaller.

Behavior: Peaceful bottom dweller; most active during the evening and at night, and in the period preceding stormy weather.

Diet: Wide range of foods accepted.

Aquarium: Well oxygenated, well filtered, with a water current (as produced by a powerhead outlet) and substratum consisting of gravel, pebbles, and rocks. Water chemistry not critical. Temperature range: around 50°F (10°C)—or even lower for *M. fossilis*—to around 68°F (20°C) or a little higher.

Breeding: Infrequent in aquaria; the pair wrap their bodies around each other and scatter their eggs among vegetation.

Weather loaches, such as the Dojo, are renowned for their sensitivity to barometric pressure. When it drops—as happens preceding a storm—the drop in gas pressure in the swimbladder makes these fish very active. Thus they are said to be able to "predict" stormy weather. If the pressure drop is excessive, weather loaches (both the Dojo and its European relative, *M. fossilis*, the Pond Loach) will "burp" or "break wind." Golden forms of the Dojo and of *M. fossilis* are also available.

Kuhli Loach

Pangio kuhlii

Other common names:
Coolie Loach, Prickly Eye

Synonyms: *Cobitis kuhlii,
Acanthophthalmus fasciatus,
A. kuhlii*

Family: Cobitidae

Subfamily: Cobitinae

Distribution: Indonesia
(Java and Sumatra),
Malaysia, Singapore,
and Thailand.

Size: Up to 4in (10cm).

Behavior: Peaceful; most
active at dusk; feeds at
night and hides during
the day.

Diet: Wide range of foods
accepted.

Aquarium: Well oxygenated,
well filtered tank with a
substratum consisting
of very fine gravel or sand
(for burrowing). Water
chemistry not critical, but
soft, slightly acid water
preferred. Temperature
range: 70–75°F (21–24°C),
although short-lived
temperatures of up to 82°F
(28°C) may be tolerated.

Breeding: Infrequent (but
possible) in aquaria; the
eggs are laid beneath
the surface and stick to
the stems and roots of
floating plants.

The Kuhli Loach can be divided into two distinct subspecies on the
basis of its coloration and markings: *Pangio kuhlii kuhlii* and *P. kuhlii
sumatranus* (Sumatra Kuhli). The latter subspecies usually has fewer than
15 black circular bands along the length of its body, while *P. kuhlii kuhlii*
has narrower, redder bands, and the black areas do not totally encircle the
body. Kuhli Loaches have defensive spines close to the eyes. If threatened,
they can raise the spines, which will easily become stuck in a net or in the
mouth of a would-be predator.

Myer's Loach

Pangio myersi

Other common names:
Slimy Loach, Kuhli Loach

Synonym:
Acanthophthalmus myersi

Family: Cobitidae

Subfamily: Cobitinae

Distribution: Thailand.

Size: Up to 3in (8cm).

Behavior: All "kuhli" loaches like to burrow; often active during the day, but most active during the evening and at night.

Diet: Wide range of foods accepted, but sinking livefoods and other formulations preferred.

Aquarium: Well covered (kuhlis can squeeze through the tiniest openings), with fine-grained substratum, subdued lighting, floating vegetation, and shelters. A "moonlight" fluorescent tube will facilitate night viewing. Soft, slightly acid water preferred, but some deviation accepted. Temperature range: 75–86°F (24–30°C).

Breeding: Infrequent in aquaria. Green eggs may be scattered among surface vegetation, plant stems, or roots.

This is a variably patterned species, giving rise to speculation that the fish currently considered *P. myersi* may consist of more than just a single species, or may contain several subspecies. Similar doubts surround some of the other species in the genus, making a detailed review highly desirable. In addition to Myer's Loach, the following are the main species currently encountered in the hobby. All have similar behavioral characteristics and aquarium requirements: *P. semicinctus* (Half-banded Kuhli Loach) from the Malay Peninsula; *P. kuhlii* ("True" Kuhli Loach) from Java, Sumatra, Malaysia, Singapore, and Thailand; *P. javanicus* (Javanese Loach) from Java, and *P. shelfordi* (Shelford's Loach) from Malaysia and Borneo.

Chinese Algae Eater

Gyrinocheilus aymonieri

Other common name:
Sucking Loach

Family: Gyrinocheilidae

Distribution: Thailand.

Size: Up to 10½in (27cm), but usually much smaller.

Behavior: Juveniles peaceful toward each other; progressively territorial as they grow. May also graze on thick skin mucus of other fish.

Diet: Most foods accepted; vegetable component should be included.

Aquarium: Well planted, well oxygenated and well filtered, with adequate shelter. Water chemistry not critical. Temperature range: 70–82°F (21–28°C).

Breeding: No reports of aquarium breeding available, although the species—particularly the golden form—has been bred commercially.

Both the common names for this species are misnomers, since this fish is not a "true" loach—as in the barbel-bearing Balitoridae and Cobitidae—and it does not occur in China. It does, however, eat algae and is able to attach itself to the substratum with its suckerlike mouth. It also has special adaptations, such as an aperture in the top corner of the gill cover that allows it to take in water for respiratory purposes while still clinging onto a surface with its mouth. A golden form of this species is now widely available.

GOURAMIS & RELATIVES

Suborders Anabantoidei, Channoidei, Percoidei

Gouramis, along with some of their close relatives, such as the Siamese Fighting Fish (*Betta splendens*) and the Combtail (*Belontia signata*), have been strong favorites within the hobby for the best part of 100 years. For example, the Dwarf Gourami (*Colisa lalia*) was first imported into Europe in 1903, while the Paradise Fish (*Macropodus opercularis*) has been known even longer, being the first "tropical" fish to be imported into Europe way back in 1869.

These fish, along with the Pikehead (*Luciocephalus pulcher*—family Luciocephalidae), make up the suborder Anabantoidei, commonly referred to as the labyrinthfishes. Closely related to them is the suborder Channoidei, with its single family, the Channidae (the snakeheads).

Other fish, such as the Badis (*Badis badis*) and its relatives, the leaf fishes (*Monocirrhus*, *Polycentrus,* and other species) constitute the family Nandidae (suborder Percoidei). The nandids are deemed by some authorities to have some affinity with the Anabantoidei.

Anabantoids possess an auxiliary respiratory organ known as the labyrinth. This allows them to take in air at the water

surface and thus survive in conditions in which the oxygen concentration fluctuates from time to time (and may even fall to dangerously low levels). The labyrinth is located in a special chamber just above and behind the gills, and consists of folds of tissue served by a rich blood supply. Air is gulped in at the water surface and passed into the labyrinth chamber, where the oxygen is extracted, enabling labyrinth-bearing fish to survive in oxygen-deficient waters that would be unbearable for many other fish. Most species of anabantoids have become so dependent on the labyrinth that they will actually drown if prevented from surfacing for air.

The labyrinth is also used by many anabantoids to construct bubble nests, either at the water surface or under a broad submerged leaf or other appropriate surface. In these species, spawning occurs under the nest. The eggs are deposited among the bubbles by one or both parents, one of whom (the male) subsequently mounts guard until the eggs hatch and the resulting fry become free swimming. Other species dispense with nests altogether. Alternatively, they may incubate their eggs orally until they hatch. Both types of anabantoids (nestbuilding and mouthbrooding) will be featured in this section.

Among them will be all the well-known species referred to as "gouramis." Although many of the best-known anabantoids are known as gouramis, the term itself cannot be precisely defined. It is simply one that over the years has been applied to some species in a genus but not others, to some genera but not others, and to some families of anabantoids but not others. If there is a "true" gourami at all, it is the Giant Gourami (*Osphronemus goramy*). Fish carrying the gourami name tag occur in various genera, families, and subfamilies.

Opposite: *Belontia hasselti*. **Below:** *Parachanna africana.*

Climbing Perch

Anabas testudineus

Other common name:
Walking Perch

Synonyms: *A. elongatus*,
A. macrocephalus,
A. scandens, and others

Family: Anabantidae

Distribution: Widely
distributed in tropical Asia.

Size: Up to 10in (25cm)
reported, but usually
smaller.

Behavior: Retiring, but can
be aggressive in the confines
of an aquarium.

Diet: Livefoods preferred, but
other formulations may be
accepted.

Aquarium: Well covered,
with adequate shelter and
surface vegetation. Water
chemistry not critical.
Temperature range: around
59°F (15°C) to 86°F (30°C).

Breeding: Insignificant nest
is built (or none at all). The
floating eggs receive very
little or no parental care.
Hatching takes about 1 day
at the higher end of the
temperature range.

This tough, durable species was first imported into Europe in 1891,
making it one of the oldest tropical fish in the hobby. It has been reported
as being able to "walk" on land and even to climb trees. The former
behavior is known to be within the species' capabilities, e.g., during wet
weather and perhaps in moving from one pond to another, but its climbing
powers are somewhat exaggerated. A yellow (xanthistic) form has been
reported, but is rarely seen, as is a second species, the High-bodied
Climbing Perch (*A. oligolepis*), from India and Bangladesh.

Leopard Ctenopoma

Ctenopoma acutirostre

Other common names:
Spotted Ctenopoma, Bushfish, Climbing Perch

Family: Anabantidae

Distribution: Lower and central Congo basin.

Size: Up to 8in (20cm) reported, but usually smaller.

Behavior: Generally shy and retiring, but predatory; most active during the evening and at night.

Diet: Livefoods and a range of commercial diets accepted.

Aquarium: Well planted, with shelters and open swimming spaces. Subdued lighting during the day and a "moonlight" fluorescent tube for night viewing are both recommended. Water chemistry is not critical. Temperature range: 73–82°F (23–28°C).

Breeding: Eggs are laid in male-built bubble nest, though nest quality is variable and may consist of very few bubbles, if any. Little parental care occurs.

The Leopard Ctenopoma, along with some other members of its genus, is now encountered with greater regularity than in the past, thanks to the efforts of specialist anabantoid societies in several countries. The species belongs to the "larger" *Ctenopoma*—a group of species that exceed 6 inches (15cm) in length. A nonspotted and a violet morph are occasionally available. *Sandelia* sp., a close relation of both *Anabas* and *Ctenopoma*, is hardly ever seen in the hobby.

Orange Bushfish

Microctenopoma ansorgii (previously Ctenopoma ansorgii)

Synonym: *Microctenopoma ansorgii*

Family: Anabantidae

Distribution: Congo River basin.

Size: Up to 3in (8cm), but often smaller.

Behavior: One of the more peaceful *Ctenopoma* species.

Diet: A range of livefoods and commercial formulations accepted.

Aquarium: Well planted, with shelters and open swimming spaces. Subdued lighting during the day and a "moonlight" fluorescent tube for night viewing recommended. Water chemistry is not critical. Temperature range: 73–82°F (23–28°C).

Breeding: Male builds bubble nest and cares for the eggs and newly hatched fry. Hatching takes about 1 day.

Although one of the smaller members of the genus at barely 3 inches (8cm) in length, the Orange Bushfish is probably the most beautiful of all the *Ctenopoma* species, ranging in color from orange to bluish-green. Some variation in body coloring and patterning occurs in wild-caught specimens.

Tailspot Bushfish

Ctenopoma kingsleyae

Synonym: Possibly *Ctenopoma argentoventer*

Family: Anabantidae

Distribution: West Africa, from Gambia to Cameroon.

Size: Up to 8in (20cm), but often smaller.

Behavior: Placid, especially with similar-sized tankmates.

Diet: Wide range of foods accepted.

Aquarium: Well planted, with shelters and open swimming spaces. Subdued lighting during the day and a "moonlight" fluorescent tube for night viewing recommended. Water chemistry is not critical. Temperature range: 73–82°F (23–28°C).

Breeding: Up to 20,000 eggs are laid; they float on the surface and should be removed; if the eggs are transferred to water with a temperature of 84°C (29°C), larvae will hatch out in 1 day and become free-swimming 2 days later.

This is a plainly colored species with a distinct black spot on the caudal peduncle and often a yellowish tinge on the anal and pectoral fins. The tail spot is usually ringed in gold in juvenile specimens. Several morphs are known to exist in the wild.

Mottled Ctenopoma

Ctenopoma weeksii

Other common name: Mottled Bushfish

Synonyms: *C. oxyrhynchum,* *C. oxyrhynchus*

Family: Anabantidae

Distribution: D. R. Congo.

Size: Up to 4³/₄in (12cm), but often a little smaller.

Behavior: Generally peaceful toward similar-sized tankmates, but males become aggressive and territorial during breeding season.

Diet: Wide range of foods accepted.

Aquarium: Well planted, with shelters and open swimming spaces. Subdued lighting during the day and a "moonlight" fluorescent tube for night viewing recommended. Water chemistry not critical. Temperature range: 73–82°F (23–28°C).

Breeding: Eggs are laid in male-built bubble nest, though nest quality is variable and may consist of very few bubbles, if any. No parental care occurs. Hatching takes 3–4 days.

This is a laterally compressed species with a mottled appearance. It may show a central body spot and banding in the caudal fin. Young Mottled Ctenopomas have a different pattern than the adults, exhibiting two dark brown stripes behind the eyes, and their pelvic fins are black at first.

Java Combtail

Belontia hasselti

Other common name:
Honeycomb Combtail

Family: Belontiidae

Subfamily: Belontiinae

Distribution: Borneo, Malaysia, Singapore, and Sumatra; also said to occur in Java.

Size: Up to 8in (20cm), but often smaller.

Behavior: Relatively peaceful except during breeding when males become territorial and aggressive.

Diet: Primarily livefoods and deep-frozen/freeze-dried formulations; other commercial preparations also accepted; vegetable component recommended.

Aquarium: Large, well planted, well illuminated, with good (but not over-turbulent) water filtration. Water chemistry is not critical, but alkaline, hardish conditions are preferred. Temperature range: 77–86°F (25–30°C).

Breeding: Shallow water preferred; a bubble nest is usually, but not always, built. Hatching takes 1–2 days.

The second, less frequently used, common name of this species beautifully describes the delicate reticulated scale and fin patterns of this handsome fish. The basic body coloration of both sexes is brownish, but females lose the meshlike pattern when they are in spawning condition.

Combtail

Belontia signata

Family: Belontiidae

Subfamily: Belontiinae

Distribution: Sri Lanka.

Size: Up to 6in (15cm) reported, but often smaller.

Behavior: Can be quite aggressive, particularly at breeding time.

Diet: Primarily livefoods and deep-frozen/freeze-dried formulations; other commercial preparations also accepted; vegetable component recommended.

Aquarium: As for *B. hasselti*, (Java Combtail), but less alkaline conditions and slightly lower temperatures preferred.

Breeding: Shallow water preferred; a bubble nest is usually, but not invariably, built. Hatching takes about 1½ days.

Adult specimens exhibit extended rays in the caudal fin, which gives rise to the common name of this impressive species. Two subspecies are generally recognized: *B. s. signata* (the "traditional" Combtail) and *B. s. jonklaasi* (Pectoral Spot Combtail), also from Sri Lanka. There is also a dark-bodied morph named "Kottawa Forest."

Slender Betta

Betta bellica

Family: Belontiidae

Subfamily: Macropodinae

Distribution: Mainly Perak region of peninsular Malaysia.

Size: Around 4¹/₄in (11cm).

Behavior: Relatively peaceful, despite its bellica ("warlike") species name.

Diet: Livefoods, deep-frozen, and freeze-dried diets preferred, but other foods may also be accepted.

Aquarium: Densely planted tank (including floating vegetation), with a number of shelters. Illumination should be not too bright. Soft, acid water preferred. Temperature range: 75–82°F (24–28°C).

Breeding: A challenging bubble-nesting species.

Both adult males and females of this species have a yellowish-brown anterior half, with bluish-green scales appearing progressively down the body. The fins also have this bluish-green sheen. Males have longer, more pointed fins than do females.

Wine Red Fighter

Betta coccina

Other common name:
Claret Betta

Family: Belontiidae

Subfamily: Macropodinae

Distribution: Reported from southern peninsular Malaysia and central Sumatra.

Size: Up to 2¼in (5.5cm) reported, but often smaller.

Behavior: Timid, retiring; must not be kept with boisterous tankmates.

Diet: Livefoods, deep-frozen and freeze-dried diets preferred, but other foods may also be accepted.

Aquarium: Densely planted (including some floating vegetation), with a number of shelters. Illumination should be subdued. Soft, acid water preferred. Temperature range: 75–82°F (24–28°C).

Breeding: A challenging bubble-nesting species.

This exceptionally marked species has a reddish-brown body with longitudinal bands and a central spot, which is not always visible. The dorsal and caudal fins are delicately edged in bluish white. The male of the species exhibits the more intense wine-red color implied in its common name, while the female tends to be a more dull brown color.

Crescent Betta

Betta imbellis

Other common name:
Peaceful Betta

Family: Belontiidae

Subfamily: Macropodinae

Distribution: Western Borneo, northeast Sumatra, and Malaysia.

Size: Around 2in (5cm).

Behavior: Relatively peaceful, except at breeding time or when a new specimen is introduced into the aquarium.

Diet: Livefoods, deep-frozen, and freeze-dried diets preferred, but other foods may also be accepted.

Aquarium: Densely planted (including some floating vegetation), with a number of shelters. Illumination should be not too bright. Soft, acid water preferred. Temperature range: 75–82°F (24–28°C).

Breeding: Easier than in *B. bellica* (Slender Betta) and *B. coccina* (Wine Red Fighter). Male builds bubble nest under floating or submerged leaves; spawning is nonviolent, and male guards the eggs and newly hatched fry. Hatching can take up to 3 days.

The crescent, from which one of the common names for this species is derived, is particularly well exhibited on the caudal fin of males in peak condition. The deep red of this crescent is also evident on the anal and pelvic fins.

Penang Mouthbrooding Betta

Betta pugnax

Family: Belontiidae

Subfamily: Macropodinae

Distribution: Malaysia.

Size: Up to 4¾in (12cm), but usually smaller.

Behavior: Relatively peaceful except during breeding.

Diet: Livefoods, deep-frozen and freeze-dried diets preferred, but other foods may also be accepted.

Aquarium: Densely planted (including some floating vegetation), with a number of shelters. Illumination should be not too bright. Soft, acid water preferred, preferably slow flowing and tannin stained. Temperature range: 75–82°F (24–28°C).

Breeding: A mouthbrooding species in which male retains the eggs and larvae in his mouth for about 10 days.

This was one of the early *Betta* species to be imported, arriving in 1905. It has never become widespread in the hobby, having been overshadowed by its more spectacular relative, *B. splendens* (Siamese Fighting Fish). It is nevertheless a delicately colored species worthy of greater recognition. Several naturally occurring color morphs are known.

Emerald Betta

Betta smaragdina

Other common names:
Smaragd Betta/Fighter

Family: Belontiidae

Subfamily: Macropodinae

Distribution: Cambodia, Laos, northeastern and eastern Thailand.

Size: Up to 2³/₄in (7cm).

Behavior: Males are aggressive toward each other. They will accept several females in the same aquarium, but they should not be kept with boisterous tankmates.

Diet: Livefoods, deep-frozen and freeze-dried diets preferred, but other foods may also be accepted.

Aquarium: Densely planted (including some floating vegetation), with a number of shelters. Illumination should be not too bright. Soft, acid water preferred. Temperature range: 75–82°F (24–28°C).

Breeding: A bubble nester that can be relatively easily bred. Nests may be built at water surface, or under submerged leaf or other surface. Male guards the eggs and newly hatched fry.

Although introduced only around 1970, the Emerald Betta has become one of the more popular *Betta* species in the hobby. It is a truly magnificent species when in peak condition, rivaling both *B. imbellis* (Crescent Betta) and *B. splendens* (Siamese Fighting Fish) in beauty.

Siamese Fighting Fish

Betta splendens

Other common names:
Siamese Fighter, Betta

Family: Belontiidae

Subfamily: Macropodinae

Distribution: Southeast Asia, but self-sustaining populations have become established in nonnative locations e.g., Laos, Myanmar, and Colombia.

Size: Up to 2½in (6cm).

Behavior: Males will fight (sometimes to the death), becoming territorial during breeding and aggressive toward females after spawning; otherwise, a tolerant species that should not be kept with boisterous tankmates.

Diet: Wide range of live-foods and commercial formulations accepted.

Aquarium: Densely planted (including some floating vegetation), with a number of shelters. Illumination not too bright. Soft, acid water. Temperature range: 75–82°F (24–28°C).

Breeding: Male builds a bubble nest at the water surface and guards the eggs and newly hatched fry for several days. Hatching takes about 1 day.

This famous old favorite was imported into Europe during the last decade of the 19th century and has been popular ever since. It was originally renowned not just for its coloration but for its fighting qualities. As far as the aquarium hobby is concerned, however, the species' ongoing popularity is owed to the exceptionally colorful long-finned varieties that have been developed over the years. This is a "must-keep" fish for every aquarist at some stage.

Above: Siamese Fighter.
Right: Roundtail, Green
  Turquoise.
Opposite: Fantail Violet.

Above (clockwise from top left): Fantail Turquoise; Fantail Multicolor; Doubletail Turquoise. **Opposite above:** Doubletail Multicolor. **Opposite below:** Fantail Blue.

Above: Fantail Red.
Right: Pan Bak Bara.

Noble Gourami

Ctenops nobilis

Other common names:
Indian Gourami, Ctenops

Family: Belontiidae

Subfamily: Macropodinae

Distribution: Eastern India and Bangladesh.

Size: Up to 4³/₄in (12cm), but usually smaller.

Behavior: Shy, retiring; must not be kept with boisterous tankmates.

Diet: Livefoods preferred, but deep-frozen, freeze-dried, and some other commercial diets may be accepted.

Aquarium: Heavily planted, tranquil, with subdued lighting and numerous bogwood shelters. Softish, neutral water advisable, with a little deviation tolerated. Temperature range: 77–86°F (25–30°C).

Breeding: Very challenging and infrequent in aquaria. Small numbers of eggs are incubated orally by female who releases free-swimming fry 10–15 days after spawning.

Although the Noble Gourami was imported into Europe during the early decades of the 20th century, it never attained wide popularity owing to its "challenging" requirements and delicate nature. This is, undoubtedly, a species that should be kept only by experienced aquarists. Kept in appropriate conditions, it is a truly beautiful fish.

Black Paradise Fish

Macropodus spechti (previously Macropodus concolor)

Synonym: *Macropodus opercularis concolor*

Family: Belontiidae

Subfamily: Macropodinae

Distribution: Cambodia and Vietnam.

Size: Males around 4³/₄in (12cm); females somewhat smaller.

Behavior: Considerably less aggressive than *M. opercularis* (Paradise Fish), but territorial during breeding.

Diet: Wide range of foods accepted.

Aquarium: Spacious, well planted, with some open areas and shelters. Water chemistry not critical. Temperature range: 68–79°F (20–26°C).

Breeding: Male builds bubble nests and vigorously defends nest, eggs, and subsequent fry until they are free swimming. Hatching takes about 1 day.

There has long been controversy regarding the status of this fish. Some believe it to be a subspecies of the better-known *M. opercularis* (Paradise Fish), while others see it merely as a naturally occurring morph. Most modern opinion, however, tends toward regarding it as a valid species in its own right, despite the ease with which it hybridizes with *M. opercularis* to produce the Dark Paradise Fish.

Chinese Paradise Fish

Macropodus ocellatus

Other common name:
Round-tailed Paradise Fish

Synonym: *Macropodus chinensis*

Family: Belontiidae

Subfamily: Macropodinae

Distribution: Southern China and (possibly) Korea.

Size: Males around 3in (8cm); females smaller.

Behavior: Considerably less aggressive than *M. opercularis* (Paradise Fish), but territorial during breeding.

Diet: Wide range of foods accepted.

Aquarium: Spacious, well planted, with some open areas and shelters. Water chemistry not critical. Temperature range: around 61°F (16°C) to 79°F (26°C).

Breeding: Male builds bubble nests and vigorously defends nest, eggs, and subsequent fry until they become free swimming. Hatching takes about 1 day.

This exceptionally beautiful species is seen much less frequently than its two closest relatives, *M. concolor* (Black Paradise Fish) and *M. opercularis* (Paradise Fish). Despite one of its common names, the caudal fin of fully adult males tends to have a blunted-tip profile rather than a smoothly rounded one. This species is known to hybridize with *M. opercularis*: the hybrids are sometimes referred to as Matte's Paradise Fish.

Paradise Fish

Macropodus opercularis

Family: Belontiidae

Subfamily: Macropodinae

Distribution: Southern China, Vietnam, Korea, Taiwan, and other islands in the region.

Size: Males up to 4³/₄in (12cm); females smaller.

Behavior: More aggressive and territorial than its relatives; keep only 1 male per aquarium.

Diet: Wide range of foods accepted.

Aquarium: Spacious, well-planted, with some open areas and shelters. Water chemistry not critical. Temperature range: 61–82°F (16–28°C), but can tolerate slightly lower temperatures.

Breeding: Male builds bubble nests and vigorously defends nest, eggs, and subsequent fry until they are free swimming. Hatching takes about 1 day.

This was the first "tropical" fish to be imported into Europe (arriving in 1869). It soon became popular because of its hardiness, coloration, and interesting breeding habits. Today, it is still widely available and popular in a range of colors, from the wild type through a "blue" to an albino form. This species hybridizes easily with its two closest relatives, *M. concolor* (Black Paradise Fish) and *M. ocellatus* (Chinese Paradise Fish).

Above: Redback.
Below left: Blue (male).
Below right: Albino.
Opposite: Blue (female).

Licorice Dwarf Gourami

Parosphromenus deissneri (previously Parosphromenus deisneri)

This is by far the most frequently available of all the licorice gourami species. It has a long history in the hobby, having first been imported in 1914, but its rather demanding requirements mean that it is often not seen at its best in aquatic stores—a factor that has undoubtedly contributed to its somewhat limited occurrence in home aquaria.

Other common names: Liquorice/Splendid Dwarf Gourami

Family: Belontiidae

Subfamily: Macropodinae

Distribution: Banka and Sumatra (Indonesia) and peninsular Malaysia.

Size: Around 1½in (4cm), although 3in (7.5cm) reported.

Behavior: Gentle, slow moving; must not be kept with boisterous tankmates.

Diet: Small livefoods preferred, but some commercial diets may also be accepted.

Aquarium: Quiet, well covered, well planted, with surface plants, a number of shelters, subdued lighting, and dark substratum. Water soft and acid, although some deviation may be accepted. Temperature range: 75–82°F (24–28°C).

Breeding: Male builds bubble nest (usually in a cave), often after egg release. Hatching can take 3 days. Male guards the eggs and newly hatched fry.

Spike-tailed Paradise Fish

Pseudosphromenus cupanus

Other common name:
Red-eye Spiketail

Synonym: *Macropodus cupanus*

Family: Belontiidae

Subfamily: Macropodinae

Distribution: Probably from southern India originally; now found in Sri Lanka and (possibly) Bengal, Myanmar (Burma), Sumatra, and Tonkin (north Vietnam.)

Size: Around 2½in (6cm).

Behavior: Peaceful; should not be kept with boisterous tankmates.

Diet: Wide range of foods accepted.

Aquarium: Heavily planted, with caves or other shelters and dark substratum. Water chemistry is not critical. Temperature range: around 68°F (20°C) to 82°F (28°C).

Breeding: Male builds bubble nest under broad leaf or in a cave. Egg care usually undertaken by male, but female may participate. Eggs hatch after about 2 days.

Although the synonym for this fish is now disappearing from aquarium literature, it is still encountered from time to time. The name is a relic of the days when this species and *P. dayi* (Day's Spike-tailed Paradise Fish) were believed to be more closely related to *Macropodus opercularis* than they actually are. Both *Pseudosphromenus* were also once believed to be subspecies, rather than distinct valid species.

Day's Spike-tailed Paradise Fish

Pseudosphromenus dayi

Other common names: Brown Spike-tailed Paradise Fish, Day's Spiketail

Synonym: *Macropodus dayi*

Family: Belontiidae

Subfamily: Macropodinae

Distribution: Range said to include southern and western India, Sri Lanka, Vietnam, Sumatra, Myanmar (Burma), and the Malabar Coast.

Size: Up to 3in (7.5cm) reported, but usually smaller.

Behavior: Peaceful; should not be kept with boisterous tankmates.

Diet: Wide range of foods accepted.

Aquarium: Heavily planted, with caves or other shelters and dark substratum. Water chemistry is not critical. Temperature range: around 68°F (20°C) to 82°F (28°C), but may be even wider.

Breeding: Normally a bubble nester (like *P. cupanus*); but in colder parts of its range has been reported as spawning like cichlids.

Adult males of this species possess fine extensions on the central rays of the caudal fin, along with bright greenish-blue fin edges. There are also two dark bands on the body, which run all the way from the head to the caudal peduncle. Hybridization between the two *Pseudosphromenus* species is known to occur, with the resulting hybrids being fertile.

Dwarf Croaking Gourami

Trichopsis pumilus

Other common name:
Pygmy Croaking Gourami

Synonym: *Trichopsis pumila*

Family: Belontiidae

Subfamily: Macropodinae

Distribution: Indonesia, Malaysia, and Thailand.

Size: Up to 1½in (4cm).

Behavior: Peaceful; must not be kept with boisterous tankmates.

Diet: Wide range of foods accepted.

Aquarium: Heavily planted, with caves or other shelters and dark substratum. Water should be close to the soft, acid end of the chemistry spectrum. Temperature range: 77–82°F (25–28°C).

Breeding: Bubble nest of variable quality is built, and the eggs and newly hatched fry are guarded by male. Hatching takes about 2 days.

The three species belonging to the genus *Trichopsis* are capable of producing croaking sounds, hence the common names of this species and *T. vittatus* (Croaking Gourami). All three are slender species with pointed snouts resembling some of the *Parosphromenus* species, to which they are related. The Dwarf Croaking Gourami is, reportedly, capable of hybridizing with *T. schalleri*, with the resulting offspring being fertile.

Sparkling Gourami

Trichopsis schalleri

Other common name:
Schaller's Gourami

Family: Belontiidae

Subfamily: Macropodinae

Distribution: Southern Thailand.

Size: Up to 2$\frac{1}{2}$in (6cm).

Behavior: Peaceful; must not be kept with boisterous tankmates.

Diet: Wide range of foods accepted.

Aquarium: Heavily planted, with caves or other shelters and dark substratum. Water should be close to the soft, acid end of the chemistry spectrum. Temperature range: 77–82°F (25–28°C).

Breeding: Bubble nest of variable quality is built, and the eggs and newly hatched fry are guarded by male. Hatching takes about 2 days.

This is perhaps the most beautiful of the three *Trichopsis* species, with specimens in peak condition living up to the "sparkling" label. Sparkling Gourami is reported to produce fertile hybrids in crosses with its two close relatives, *T. pumilis* (Dwarf Croaking Gourami) and *T. vittatus* (Croaking Gourami).

Croaking Gourami

Trichopsis vittata (previously Trichopsis vittatus)

Synonym: *Trichopsis vittata*

Family: Belontiidae

Subfamily: Macropodinae

Distribution: Widely distributed in Southeast Asia.

Size: Up to 2³/₄in (7cm), but often smaller.

Behavior: Peaceful; must not be kept with boisterous tankmates.

Diet: Wide range of foods accepted.

Aquarium: Heavily planted, with caves or other shelters and dark substratum. Water should be close to the soft, acid end of the chemistry spectrum. Temperature range: 72–82°F (22–28°C).

Breeding: Bubble nest is built, and the eggs and the newly hatched fry are guarded by male. Male *T. vittatus* may build more substantial bubble nest than his *T. pumilus* and *T. schalleri* counterparts. Hatching takes about 1 day.

Several forms of this species are known in the wild, including a two-spot type and a blue one (sometimes referred to as *T. harrisi*). Owing to its widespread distribution and variability, some doubts remain regarding the correct identification of the various types. The Croaking Gourami is known to interbreed with *T. schalleri* (Sparkling Gourami), with the resulting offspring being fertile.

Honey Gourami

Trichogaster chuna (previously Colisa chuna)

Other common name:
Honey Dwarf Gourami

Synonym: *Colisa sota*

Family: Belontiidae

Subfamily: Trichogasterinae (classified as Trichogastrinae by some authors)

Distribution: Northeastern India and Bangladesh.

Size: Up to 2³/₄in (7cm), but generally smaller.

Behavior: Peaceful, retiring; should not be kept with boisterous tankmates.

Diet: Most foods accepted.

Aquarium: Heavily planted, tranquil, with surface vegetation and adequate shelter. Water chemistry not critical. Temperature range: 72–82°F (22–28°C).

Breeding: Male builds good bubble nest, and guards the eggs and newly hatched fry. Hatching takes about 1 day.

The scientific name of this, the smallest member of the genus *Colisa*, has oscillated over time, with current opinion settling on *Colisa chuna*. The Honey Gourami is different from the other *Colisa* species in that it lacks oblique body bands. Males in nuptial coloration are particularly impressive, especially when they "stand on their tails" during courtship displays. Golden, peach, and mottled varieties are frequently available.

Giant Gourami

Trichogaster fasciata (previously Colisa fasciata)

Other common names:
Banded/Striped/ Indian/ Gourami

Family: Belontiidae

Subfamily: Trichogasterinae (classified as Trichogastrinae by some authors)

Distribution: Most of India, except south and southwest; also reported from Myanmar.

Size: Up to 4³/₄in (12cm) reported, but usually a little smaller.

Behavior: Peaceful toward other species, except during breeding; males somewhat less peaceful toward each other.

Diet: Most foods accepted.

Aquarium: Heavily planted, tranquil, with surface vegetation and adequate shelter. Water chemistry not critical. Temperature range: 72–82°F (22–28°C).

Breeding: Male builds good bubble nest, and guards the eggs and newly hatched fry. Hatching takes about 1 day.

This species has been known in the hobby for more than 100 years. However, unlike the three other members of the genus, it has never been developed into fin or color varieties. The Giant Gourami will interbreed with its closest relatives, *C. labiosa* (Thick-lipped Gourami) and *C. lalia* (Dwarf Gourami); the resulting hybrids from *C. labiosa* crosses are fertile.

NOTE: The common name Giant Gourami also applies to *Osphronemus gorami*.

Thick-lipped Gourami

Trichogaster labiosa (previously Colisa labiosa)

Other common name:
Thicklip Gourami

Family: Belontiidae

Subfamily: Trichogasterinae (classified as Trichogastrinae by some authors)

Distribution: Irrawaddy River, Myanmar (Burma).

Size: Up to 4in (10cm) reported, but usually smaller.

Behavior: Peaceful toward other species, except during breeding; males somewhat less peaceful toward each other.

Diet: Most foods accepted.

Aquarium: Heavily planted, tranquil, with surface vegetation and adequate shelter. Water chemistry not critical. Temperature range: 72–82°F (22–28°C).

Breeding: Male builds good bubble nest and guards the eggs and newly hatched fry. Hatching takes about 1 day.

Closely related to *C. fasciata* (Giant Gourami), the Thick-lipped Gourami can be immediately recognized by its smaller head and (in fully mature males) the elegantly extended tip of the dorsal fin. *C. labiosa x fasciata* hybrids are fertile, while *C. labiosa x lalia* are not. A peach-colored variety is widely available.

Dwarf Gourami

Trichogaster lalius (previously Colisa lalia)

Family: Belontiidae

Subfamily: Trichogasterinae (classified as Trichogastrinae by some authors)

Distribution: Northern India.

Size: Up to 2$\frac{1}{2}$in (6cm), but usually smaller.

Behavior: More tolerant of conspecific males than are *C. fasciata* and *C. labiosa*.

Diet: Most foods accepted.

Aquarium: Heavily planted, tranquil, with surface vegetation and adequate shelter. Water chemistry not critical. Temperature range: 72–82°F (22–28°C).

Breeding: Male builds exceptional bubble nest containing interwoven vegetation and guards the eggs and newly hatched fry. Hatching takes about 1 day.

The Dwaft Gourami is the most widely kept *Colisa* species. It has been developed into a number of color forms, the best known being the Sunset (Red), Rainbow, Blue, Neon, and Multicolored. *Colisa lalia* will hybridize with both *C. fasciata* (Giant Gourami) and *C. labiosa* (Thick-lipped Gourami), although the hybrids are infertile.

False Chocolate Gourami

Parasphaerichthys ocellatus

Family: Belontiidae

Subfamily: Trichogasterinae (classified as Trichogastrinae by some authors)

Distribution: Mountain streams in northern Myanmar.

Size: Up to 2½in (6cm) reported, but usually smaller.

Behavior: Shy, retiring; can be kept only with quiet tankmates.

Diet: Small livefoods, although some deep-frozen/ freeze-dried foods may be accepted; dried formulations may be accepted only reluctantly.

Aquarium: Well planted tank. Surface vegetation and subdued lighting are important. Soft, slightly acid to neutral water preferred. Temperature range: 72–77°F (22–25°C).

Breeding: No documented accounts available; may be a mouthbrooder like *Sphaerichthys* (see following entries).

Although described as long ago as 1929, the False Chocolate Gourami remains one of the rarely seen species. It is a somewhat more elongate fish than *Sphaerichthys osphromenoides* (Chocolate Gourami) with a rounded tail. Exacting in its demands, it is undoubtedly one for the specialist and best avoided by new aquarists.

Chocolate Gourami

Sphaerichthys osphromenoides

Family: Belontiidae

Subfamily: Trichogasterinae (classified as Trichogastrinae by some authors)

Distribution:
S. o. osphromenoides found in Indonesia and Malaysia; *S. o. selatanensis* in Borneo.

Size: Up to 2¹/₂in (6cm), but usually smaller.

Behavior: Retiring and peaceful; must not be kept with boisterous tankmates.

Diet: Small livefoods, although some deep-frozen/freeze-dried foods may be accepted; dried formulations may be accepted only reluctantly.

Aquarium: Well planted tank. Surface vegetation and subdued lighting are important; pH should be maintained within the acid part of the spectrum. Temperature range: 77–86°F (25–30°C).

Breeding: Challenging in aquaria; female orally incubates the eggs and fry for up to 2 weeks.

This is by far the most famous member of its genus, having first been imported into Europe in 1905. In the late 1970s, a red-finned "Chocolate" —the Crossband Chocolate Gourami—was described and afforded subspecific status: *S. o. selatanensis*. At that point, *S. osphromenoides* became *S. o. osphromenoides*.

Vaillant's Chocolate Gourami

Sphaerichthys vaillanti

Family: Belontiidae

Subfamily: Trichogasterinae (classified as Trichogastrinae by some authors)

Distribution: Borneo.

Size: Up to 3in (8cm), but usually smaller.

Behavior: Retiring and peaceful; must not be kept with boisterous tankmates.

Diet: Small livefoods, although some deep-frozen/ freeze-dried foods may be accepted; dried formulations may be accepted only reluctantly.

Aquarium: Well planted, with surface vegetation and subdued lighting important. Soft, slightly acid water preferred. Temperature range: 77–86°F (25–30°C).

Breeding: Challenging in aquaria; eggs and fry are orally incubated for up to 2 weeks, but some doubt exists regarding the sex of the mouthbrooding parent.

Although it is not the "youngest" of the *Sphaerichthys* species, Vaillant's Chocolate Gourami is perhaps the most recent one to appear with any degree of regularity. It is also a beautifully marked species when in peak condition.

Pearl Gourami

Trichopodus leerii (previously Trichogaster leeri)

Other common names:
Lace/Leeri/Mosaic Gourami

Family: Belontiidae

Subfamily: Trichogasterinae (classified as Trichogastrinae by some authors)

Distribution: Peninsular Malaysia, Borneo, Sumatra, (possibly) Java, and around Bangkok (Thailand).

Size: Up to 6in (15cm) reported, but usually considerably smaller.

Behavior: Generally peaceful, except at breeding time when males become territorial.

Diet: Most foods accepted.

Aquarium: Large, covered, well planted, with some surface vegetation and an open central area. Subdued illumination recommended. Water chemistry not critical. Temperature range: 73–82°F (23–28°C).

Breeding: Substantial bubble nest may be built at water surface by male. The eggs and newly hatched fry are also guarded by male. Hatching takes about 1 day.

Once seen, a large mature male Pearl Gourami in full breeding regalia is never forgotten. This is another of those "must-keep" fish. A golden form appeared in outdoor ponds in Florida in the early 1990s, but the colors faded and were replaced by normal wild-type coloration over a period of a few weeks once the fish were transferred to indoor aquaria.

Moonlight Gourami

Trichopodus microlepis (previously Trichogaster microlepis)

Other common names:
Moonbeam Gourami,
Thinlip Gourami

Family: Belontiidae

Subfamily: Trichogasterinae
(classified as Trichogastrinae
by some authors)

Distribution: Cambodia,
Malaysia, Singapore, and
Thailand.

Size: Up to 8in (20cm)
reported, but usually
considerably smaller.

Behavior: Generally
peaceful, except at breeding
time when males become
territorial.

Diet: Most foods accepted.

Aquarium: Large, covered,
well planted, with some
surface vegetation and an
open central area. Subdued
illumination recommended.
Water chemistry not critical.
Temperature range: 73–82°F
(23–28°C).

Breeding: Substantial bubble
nest may be built at water
surface by male, which may
tear off bits of submerged
vegetation for inclusion in
bubble nest. The eggs and
newly hatched fry are also
guarded by male. Hatching
takes about 1 day.

This is an elegant silvery fish with extremely long filamentlike pelvic fins.
Neither it nor any of the other gouramis in its genus, or within *Colisa*,
should be kept with fin-nipping species such as *Barbus tetrazona* (Tiger
Barb), which would—sooner or later—damage these delicate fins.

Snakeskin Gourami

Trichopodus pectoralis (previously Trichogaster pectoralis)

Family: Belontiidae

Subfamily: Trichogasterinae (classified as Trichogastrinae by some authors)

Distribution: Cambodia, Vietnam, and Thailand, but also introduced elsewhere in Southeast Asia and other regions, including Sri Lanka and Haiti.

Size: Up to 8in (20cm).

Behavior: Very peaceful despite its size.

Diet: Most foods accepted.

Aquarium: Large, covered, well planted, with some surface vegetation and an open central area. Subdued illumination recommended. Water chemistry not critical. Temperature range: 73–82°F (23–28°C).

Breeding: Bubble nest (which can be fairly small) may be built at water surface by male. The eggs and newly hatched fry are also guarded by male. Hatching takes about 1 day.

While not spectacularly colored, the brown shades and patterns of the Snakeskin Gourami, suffused overall with a delicate purplish sheen, make it a very attractive fish. It is much loved by the anabantoid enthusiasts that have kept and bred it.

Blue Gourami

Trichopodus trichopterus (previously Trichogaster trichopterus)

Other common names:
Spotted Gourami, Two-spot/Three-spot Cosby; Opaline/Opal/Platinum/Lavender/Golden/Amethyst/Brown Gourami; Hairfin

Family: Belontiidae

Subfamily: Trichogasterinae (sometimes Trichogastrinae)

Distribution:
T. t. trichopterus Indochina, Malaysia, Indonesia, Thailand, and neighboring regions; *T. t. sumatranus* is restricted to Sumatra.

Size: Up to 6in (15cm), but often smaller.

Behavior: Males somewhat intolerant of each other.

Diet: Most foods accepted.

Aquarium: Large, covered, well planted, with central open area. Surface vegetation and subdued illumination recommended. Water chemistry not critical. Temperature range: 73–82°F (23–28°C).

Breeding: Bubble nest (the quality of which may vary from small, single layer of bubbles to major construction) may be built at water surface by male. Eggs and newly hatched fry are also guarded by male. Hatching takes about 1 day.

This species, in its numerous color varieties, is—along with *Colisa lalia* (Dwarf Gourami)—the most widely kept of all the gouramis. Two subspecies are generally recognized: *T. t. trichopterus*, which occurs in various (nonblue) natural forms, such as the Brown and Lavender Gourami; and *T. t. sumatranus*, a blue form found exclusively in Sumatra. According to some authorities, the blue *"sumatranus"* is no more than yet another color morph and not a distinct subspecies.

Above: Blue. **Below left:** Blue Marble Cosby. **Below right:** Steel Blue. **Opposite:** Cosby.

Kissing Gourami

Helostoma temminckii

Synonym: *Helostoma rudolfi*

Family: Helostomatidae

Distribution: Widely distributed (and introduced) in Southeast Asia.

Size: Up to 12in (30cm), but usually around half this size.

Behavior: Generally peaceful despite its size (and strength trials); exhibits a strong appetite for delicate plants.

Diet: All foods accepted; vegetable component recommended.

Aquarium: Large, well covered, and with a selection of hardy and/or unpalatable plants. A gravel substratum, with several large pieces of decor, e.g., rocks or bogwood, also recommended. Water chemistry not critical. Temperature range: 72–86°F (22–30°C).

Breeding: Spawning may occur in the absence of bubble nest or in the presence of a token one. No strong egg/fry care exhibited. Hatching takes about 1 day, or slightly less at high temperatures.

This large species is famous for its "kissing" habit and fleshy lips. The kissing, however, has little to do with affection and a great deal to do with gaining or maintaining territory; it is, in fact, a mouth-to-mouth trial of strength, which results in no damage to either party. There are three color forms available: the green or wild type, a pink-bodied version, and a mottled one.

Pikehead

Luciocephalus pulcher

Family: Luciocephalidae

Distribution: Southeast Asia.

Size: Up to 8in (20cm).

Behavior: Predatory; stalks its prey.

Diet: Almost exclusively livefoods, e.g., insects, but also fish—a factor that needs due consideration prior to purchase.

Aquarium: Well covered, with adequate shelter, open spaces, and subdued lighting. Soft, slightly acid water preferred. Temperature range: 72–84°F (22–29°C).

Breeding: No documented accounts available; assumed to be a mouthbrooder.

Built like a torpedo and armed with a large mouth, the Pikehead is an efficient predator. It is a fish for the specialist who can cater to its needs. A second, as yet unidentified, species, the Spotted Pikehead, was collected in the late 1990s but has not yet become widespread.

Giant Gourami

Osphronemus goramy

Family: Osphronemidae

Distribution: Widely distributed and introduced in tropical Asia, but probably originating in Borneo, Java, and Sumatra.

Size: Up to 24in (60cm) or slightly larger.

Behavior: Sedate and tolerant.

Diet: Wide range of foods accepted; vegetable component recommended.

Aquarium: Juveniles may be kept in community setup, but special provision must be made as they grow: a large, well-filtered, well-covered aquarium, with some large decorations (including large unpalatable or artificial plants), and adequately wide and deep swimming areas. Water chemistry not critical. Temperature range: 66–86°F (19–30°C).

Breeding: Difficult to achieve in aquaria. Bubble nest is built on water surface or below, with plant material incorporated. Eggs and fry are guarded by male. Hatching takes around 2 days.

As its name implies, this is a large fish that can be kept on a long-term basis only by aquarists who can accommodate it. It is usually available as juveniles of various colors, including (mainly) the wild type and a golden-bodied one. The Red-finned Giant Gourami, which began becoming available in the 1990s, is probably *O. laticlavus*, originally from Sabah, Borneo. The *O. septemfasciatus* (Sevenstripe Giant Gourami) is only rarely seen. Both these last species were described only during the early 1990s. NOTE: The common name Giant Gourami also applies to *Colisa fasciata*.

Above left: Gold (juvenile). **Above right:** Wild (juvenile). **Below:** Wild (adult).

Red Snakehead

Channa micropeltes

Family: Channidae

Distribution: Widely distributed in tropical Asia.

Size: Up to 39in (1m).

Behavior: Stealthy predator; can be kept only with tankmates that are too large to swallow.

Diet: Chunky meat- and/or fish-based foods, plus live fish—a factor that needs due consideration prior to purchase.

Aquarium: Large, well covered, well filtered, with coarse gravel, large decor, and caves, e.g., lumps of bogwood. Subdued lighting recommended. Water chemistry not critical. Temperature range: 75–82°F (24–28°C).

Breeding: Difficult to achieve. No bubble nest is built. Eggs float on water surface and are guarded by male. The young fish are cannibalistic.

This is the most widely available *Channa* species, usually sold as strikingly marked striped juveniles with red areas around the caudal and pectoral fins. These markings are gradually lost until the fish becomes more irregularly marked with little or no red. It is, nevertheless, a very attractive fish, even in its adult form. Like all its relatives in the genus and the family, it is predatory and large—beginners would be wise to avoid it. This species may be illegal or restricted in some U.S. states and in parts of Canada; it is best to seek advice locally before purchase.

Dark African Snakehead

Parachanna obscura (previously Channa obscura)

Family: Channidae

Distribution: Widely distributed in western Africa.

Size: Around 13¾in (35cm).

Behavior: Stealthy predator; can be kept only with tankmates that are too large to swallow.

Diet: Chunky meat- and/or fish-based foods, plus live fish—a factor that needs due consideration prior to purchase.

Aquarium: Large, well covered, well filtered, with coarse gravel, large decor, and caves, e.g., lumps of bogwood. Subdued lighting recommended. Water chemistry not critical. Temperature range: 75–82°F (24–28°C).

Breeding: Difficult to achieve. No bubble nest is built. Eggs float on water surface and are guarded by male. The young fish are cannibalistic.

This is one of the smaller species in the genus and therefore easier to accommodate. However, it is just as predatory as its close relatives; like them, it is capable of delivering a nasty bite to an unsuspecting human hand. Adult specimens exhibit excellent black body markings. This species may be illegal or restricted in some U.S. states and in parts of Canada; it is best to seek advice locally before purchase.

Badis

Badis badis

Other common name:
Chameleon Fish

Family: Nandidae

Subfamily: Badinae
(classified as Badidae by
some authors).

Distribution: *B. b. badis*
found in India; *B. b.
burmanicus* in Myanmar;
B. b. siamensis in Phuket
(Thailand); *B. b. assamensis*
in Assam.

Size: Males up to 3in (8cm);
females a little smaller.

Behavior: Generally
peaceful, although males
may become territorial.

Diet: Wide range of foods
accepted.

Aquarium: Heavily planted,
with sandy substratum
and numerous shelters.
Water chemistry not critical.
Temperature range: 73–82°F
(23–28°C).

Breeding: Eggs are usually
laid in caves. Male guards
eggs and also cares for
the fry until they are free
swimming. Hatching takes
about 3 days.

The other common name, Chameleon Fish, refers to this fish's ability
to change color rapidly according to mood. Two basic color forms have
been known for a long time in the wild, and they are usually regarded
as separate subspecies: *B. b. badis* (Blue Dwarf), with bluish fins, and
B. b. burmanicus (Burmese Badis/Chameleon Fish), a reddish form. More
recently, a darker form: *B. b. siamensis* (Siamese Badis/Chameleon Fish)
has begun appearing in the hobby. A less colorful, fourth Badis (probably
B. b. assamensis) has also been recorded.

South American Leaf Fish

Monocirrhus polyacanthus

Family: Nandidae

Subfamily: Nandinae

Distribution: Peruvian Amazon.

Size: Up to 4in (10cm).

Behavior: Slow-moving, stalking predator; should be kept only with tankmates that are too large to swallow.

Diet: Livefoods, including live fish—a factor that needs due consideration prior to purchase.

Aquarium: Heavily planted, well filtered (but with little water turbulence), with numerous shelters. Soft, acid water important. Temperature range: 72–77°F (22–25°C).

Breeding: Challenging in aquaria. Eggs are laid on broad leaves or flat surfaces and are guarded by male. Hatching takes about 4 days.

Aptly named, the South American Leaf Fish floats in midwater, head angled downward, creating the perfect impression of a drifting leaf. The large mouth is a clear indication of the diet of this very challenging fish. Its effective camouflage coloration enables it to drift very close to unsuspecting fish, at which point it opens its mouth wide and sucks in its victim.

Common Nandus

Nandus nandus

Family: Nandidae

Subfamily: Nandinae

Distribution: India, Myanmar, and Thailand.

Size: Up to 8in (20cm).

Behavior: Predatory, nocturnal loner.

Diet: Livefoods, but more adaptable in its requirements than *M. polyacanthus*; may accept some commercial preparations.

Aquarium: Heavily planted, well filtered (but with little water turbulence), with numerous shelters. Neutral to alkaline, medium-hard water with 1 teaspoon aquarium salt per 1 Imp. gal (1⅕ U.S. gal./4.5 l) added. Temperature range: 72–79°F (22–26°C).

Breeding: Challenging. The water should not contain salt. Eggs are scattered over substratum; no parental care occurs. Hatching takes about 2 days.

Although a leaf fish, Common Nandus does not exhibit the head-down posture of *Monocirrhus polyacanthus* (South American Leaf Fish) and is not as leaflike. It exhibits more normal swimming activity, but it has an equally large mouth and similar feeding habits.

Schomburgk's Leaf Fish

Polycentrus schomburgkii (previously Polycentrus schomburgki)

Family: Nandidae

Subfamily: Nandinae

Distribution: Guyanas, Trinidad, and Venezuela.

Size: Around 4in (10cm).

Behavior: Predatory, nocturnal loner.

Diet: Livefoods, including live fish—a factor that needs due consideration prior to purchase.

Aquarium: Heavily planted, well filtered (but with little water turbulence), with numerous shelters. Neutral to alkaline, medium-hard water with 1 teaspoon aquarium salt per 1 Imp. gal (1⅕ U.S. gal./4.5 l) added. Temperature range: 72–79°F (22–26°C).

Breeding: Challenging in aquaria. Eggs are laid on broad leaves or flat surfaces and are guarded by male. Hatching takes about 3 days.

Adults of this species have a somewhat more rounded head profile than *Monocirrhus polyacanthus* (South American Leaf Fish) and *Nandus nandus* (Common Nandus). Some specimens have very attractive dark mottling.

RAINBOWS & BLUE-EYES

Order Atheriniformes

The first rainbowfish was described in 1843 as *Atherina nigrans*. Some 20 years later it was reassigned to a new genus, *Melanotaenia,* and it is this genus that contains most of the species that have become popular aquarium species over the years.

Over time these beautiful fish and their relatives have been well studied, and gradually their biology and relationships have been worked out. However, there remain doubts as to the exact status of the various recognized groups—all of which share certain characteristics, such as two dorsal fins, a long-based anal fin, a deeply forked mouth, and large eyes.

One of the most widely accepted classifications and the one followed here (Nelson 1994; see Further Reading), separates the rainbows and their relatives into the following families:

Atherinidae (silversides), **Bedotiidae** (Madagascan rainbows), **Dentatherinidae** (only one species), **Melanotaeniidae** (rainbowfishes), **Nothocheiridae** (Isonidae— exclusively marine), **Phallostethidae** (species with an exceptional copulatory appendage, the priapium), **Pseudomugilidae** (blue-eyes), and **Telmatherinidae** (Celebes rainbowfishes).

Left: *Melanotaenia praecox.*

Madagascar Rainbowfish

Bedotia madagascariensis

Other common name:
Bowfish

Synonym: *Bedotia geayi*

Family: Bedotiidae

Distribution: Madagascar.

Size: Up to 6in (15cm) reported, but usually smaller.

Behavior: A peaceful shoaler.

Diet: Wide range of (mainly) floating formulations accepted. Food that sinks to the bottom is ignored.

Aquarium: Spacious, well planted, with large, central, open swimming area. Water chemistry not critical, as long as quality is good, but neutral to slightly alkaline, medium-hard water preferred, with frequent partial water changes. Temperature range: 68–77°F (20–25°C).

Breeding: Eggs are scattered among fine-leaved vegetation. Hatching can take around 7 days.

This slender-bodied aquarium favorite is the only rainbowfish of African origin. It is a colorful species, the males being multicolored, and the females yellow. A large shoal kept under appropriate conditions creates an unforgettable sight.

Salmon Red Rainbowfish

Glossolepis incisus

Family: Melanotaeniidae

Distribution: Lake Sentani and surrounding areas in Irian Jaya (New Guinea).

Size: Up to 6in (15cm) reported, but usually smaller.

Behavior: A peaceful, though active, shoaler.

Diet: Livefoods preferred, but some commercial formulations also accepted.

Aquarium: Spacious, well planted, with large, central, open swimming area. Water chemistry is not critical as long as quality is good; neutral to slightly alkaline, hard water accepted, with frequent partial water changes. Temperature range: 68–77°F (20–25°C).

Breeding: Eggs are scattered among fine-leaved vegetation. Hatching can take around 7 days.

This is easily the most widely available species in the genus. It first made its appearance in the hobby in 1973 and since then has been widely bred commercially. Some mature cultivated males have particularly deep coloration. There is also a marbled variety.

Threadfin Rainbowfish

Iriatherina werneri

Family: Melanotaeniidae

Distribution: Irian Jaya (New Guinea) and northern Australia.

Size: Up to 2in (5cm) reported.

Behavior: A peaceful shoaler.

Diet: Livefoods preferred, but many commercial diets also accepted.

Aquarium: Well planted and with no fin-nipping tankmates—e.g., Tiger Barbs (*Barbus tetrazona*) or Mosquito Fish (*Gambusia* spp.)—present. Subdued lighting and relatively soft, slightly acid water preferred. Temperature range: 72–84°F (22–29°C).

Breeding: Eggs are scattered —over a period of several days—among fine-leaved vegetation. Hatching can take 10–12 days, depending on temperature.

This is the only species in its genus. It is distinguished from other members of the family by its slender body and threadlike fin extensions. Despite its delicate appearance, Threadfin Rainbowfish is relatively hardy. A light-bodied, dark-eyed form (Lutino) is also occasionally available. *Rhadinocentrus ornatus* (Ornate Rainbowfish)—a slim-bodied species from Queensland and Victoria, Australia—can be easily distinguished from Threadfin Rainbowfish by its long-based anal fin, lack of fin extensions, and blunt snout.

Northern Rainbowfish

Melanotaenia affinis

Other common name:
North New Guinea Rainbowfish

Synonyms: *Rhombatractus affinis, Rhombosoma sepikensis*

Family: Melanotaeniidae

Distribution: Northern New Guinea.

Size: 5½in (14cm).

Behavior: Active swimmer; nonaggressive, suitable for community aquarium.

Diet: Prefers live foods, but many commercial diets also accepted.

Aquarium: Spacious, well planted, with large open central area, dense background vegetation, and sandy bottom. Neutral to slightly alkaline medium-hard water recommended. Temperature range: 77–82°F (25–28°C).

Breeding: Not difficult; eggs are laid—over a period of a few days—among fine-leaved plants or plant roots. Hatching takes about 12 days.

This is a peaceful, active shoaling rainbowfish that is well suited to life in a community aquarium. Male Northern Rainbowfish are grayish silver in color and have a wide blue horizontal bar running from the eye to the tail. Their fins are blue and yellow. Females exhibit similar coloring, but they are duller overall.

Boeseman's Rainbowfish

Melanotaenia boesemani

Family: Melanotaeniidae

Distribution: Ajamaru Lakes and surrounding areas in Irian Jaya (New Guinea).

Size: Up to 4³/₄in (12cm) reported, but usually smaller.

Behavior: Generally peaceful, though active, shoaler.

Diet: Wide range of foods accepted.

Aquarium: Spacious, well planted, with large open central area. Short, fine-leaved/fronded plants, such as Java moss (*Vesicularia dubyana*), may be used along bottom of swimming area. Soft, slightly acid to neutral, well-filtered but not turbulent water recommended; Temperature range: 77–86°F (25–30°C).

Breeding: Eggs are scattered —over a period of a few days—among fine-leaved vegetation, e.g., Java moss. Hatching takes approximately 7 days.

This splendid fish was first imported into Europe in 1980. Its strikingly unusual coloration, best seen in mature males in peak condition, quickly made it popular with aquarists. The vast majority of specimens available for aquaria are now captive bred.

Lake Tebera Rainbowfish

Melanotaenia herbertaxelrodi

Family: Melanotaeniidae

Distribution: Lake Tebera (Papua New Guinea).

Size: Up to 5in (13cm), but usually smaller.

Behavior: Generally peaceful shoaler.

Diet: Wide range of foods accepted.

Aquarium: Spacious, well planted, with large open central area. Short, fine-leaved or fronded plants, such as Java moss (*Vesicularia dubyana*), may be used along bottom of swimming area. Medium-hard, slightly alkaline, well filtered but not turbulent water recommended. Temperature range: 68–79°F (20–26°C).

Breeding: Eggs are scattered —over a period of a few days—among fine-leaved vegetation, e.g., Java moss. Hatching takes approximately 7 days.

This species was first described in 1981 and has been popular ever since. The appearance of fully mature specimens is very impressive, owing not just to their coloration but also to the depth of their bodies. A dark central band runs along the midline of these fish, and during the spawning period males develop a blue or white stripe that runs from the dorsal fin down over the head.

Turquoise Rainbowfish

Melanotaenia lacustris

Other common name:
Lake Kutubu Rainbowfish

Family: Melanotaeniidae

Distribution: Lake Kutubu (Papua New Guinea).

Size: Up to 4³/₄in (12cm), but usually smaller.

Behavior: Generally peaceful shoaler.

Diet: Wide range of foods accepted.

Aquarium: Spacious, well planted, with large open central area. Short, fine-leaved or fronded plants, such as Java moss (*Vesicularia dubyana*), may be used along bottom of swimming area. Medium-hard, slightly alkaline, well filtered but not turbulent water recommended. Temperature range: 68–79°F (20–26°C).

Breeding: Eggs are scattered —over a period of a few days—among fine-leaved vegetation, e.g., Java moss. Hatching takes approximately 7 days.

Although this magnificent species was described in 1964, it was not until the 1980s—when commercially bred stocks became more widely available —that it began to be seen on a regular basis. Mature males make a truly impressive sight in their metallic-blue and silvery-white livery.

MacCulloch's Rainbowfish

Popondichthys furcatus (previously Melanotaenia maccullochi)

Other common names: Black-lined/Dwarf/Australian Rainbowfish

Family: Melanotaeniidae

Distribution: Northeast Australia and southeast Papua New Guinea.

Size: Up to 2³/₄in (7cm).

Behavior: Generally peaceful shoaler.

Diet: Wide range of foods accepted.

Aquarium: Spacious, well planted, with large open central area. Short, fine-leaved or fronded plants, such as Java moss (*Vesicularia dubyana*), may be used along bottom of swimming area. Medium-hard, slightly alkaline, well filtered but not turbulent water recommended. Temperature range: 68–86°F (20–30°C).

Breeding: Eggs are scattered —over a period of a few days—among fine-leaved vegetation, e.g., Java moss. Hatching takes approximately 7 days.

This is one of the "earlier" rainbows, first imported into Europe in 1934. It is also one of the smaller species, whose popularity has gradually been eclipsed by the more recent and more colorful additions to the range of species that are available. At least two naturally occurring color variants are known.

Parkinson's Rainbowfish

Melanotaenia parkinsoni

Family: Melanotaeniidae

Distribution: Southeastern Papua New Guinea.

Size: Fully mature males reported up to 5$\frac{1}{2}$in (14cm).

Behavior: Generally peaceful shoaler.

Diet: Wide range of foods accepted.

Aquarium: Spacious, well planted, with large open central area. Short, fine-leaved or fronded plants, such as Java moss (*Vesicularia dubyana*), may be used along bottom of swimming area. Medium-hard, slightly alkaline, well filtered but not turbulent water recommended. Temperature range: 77–84°F (25–29°C).

Breeding: Eggs are scattered —over a period of a few days—among fine-leaved vegetation, e.g., Java moss. Hatching takes approximately 7 days.

Parkinson's Rainbowfish is an unusually colored and patterned fish in which a sparkling bluish base color is liberally mottled in yellow, gold, and orange in the posterior half of the body. The same yellow, gold, and orange coloration extends into the unpaired fins. A red form is also available.

Splendid Rainbowfish

Melanotaenia splendida

Family: Melanotaeniidae

Distribution:
M. s. splendida found in Queensland, Australia; *M. s. inornata* in Northern Territory, Australia; *M. s. rubrostriata* in Aru Island and southern New Guinea; *M. s. australis* in Western Australia and Northern Territory, Australia.

Size: *M. s. splendida* 5¹/₂in (14cm); *M. s. inornata* 4³/₄in (12cm); *M. s. rubrostriata* 6in (15cm); *M. s. australis* 4¹/₄in (11cm).

Behavior: Generally peaceful shoaler.

Diet: Wide range of foods accepted.

Aquarium: Spacious, well planted, with large open central area. Short, fine-leaved or fronded plants, such as Java moss (*Vesicularia dubyana*), may be used along bottom of swimming area. Medium-hard, slightly alkaline, well filtered but not turbulent water recommended. Temperature range: 70–82°F (21–28°C).

Breeding: Eggs are scattered —over a period of a few days—among fine-leaved vegetation. Hatching takes approximately 7 days.

Four subspecies of this popular rainbow are known: *M. s. splendida* (Eastern Rainbowfish), *M. s. australis* (Western Rainbowfish), *M. s. inornata* (Checkered Rainbowfish), and *M. s. rubrostriata* (Red-striped Rainbowfish). All have the same basic requirements.

Furcata Rainbowfish

Popondichthys furcatus (previously Pseudomugil furcatus)

Other common names:
Fork-tailed Blue-eye,
Fork-tailed Rainbowfish

Synonym: *Popondichthys furcatus*

Family: Pseudomugilidae

Distribution: Eastern Papua New Guinea.

Size: Up to 2¹/₂in (6cm), but often smaller.

Behavior: Peaceful, though active, shoaler; must not be kept with larger, more boisterous tankmates.

Diet: Livefoods preferred, but deep-frozen, freeze-dried, and some dry formulations may also be accepted.

Aquarium: Heavily planted, with central open swimming area. Surface cover in the form of floating vegetation also recommended. Soft to medium-hard, neutral to slightly alkaline water preferred. Temperature range: 73–79°F (23–26°C).

Breeding: Eggs are scattered (usually over several days) among feathery roots of floating plants or among fine-leaved vegetation. Hatching can take up to 20 days, depending on temperature.

Owing to their dietary preferences and small size, members of this genus can prove somewhat more challenging to keep than *Melanotaenia* rainbows. A good shoal in peak condition, however, is nothing short of magnificent. The Furcata Rainbowfish and *P. signifer* (Australian Blue-eye) are the largest species in the genus.

Australian Blue-eye

Pseudomugil signifer

Other common name:
Pacific Blue-eye

Family: Pseudomugilidae

Distribution: Queensland and Victoria (eastern Australia).

Size: Up to 2½in (6cm) reported, but often smaller.

Behavior: Peaceful but active shoaler, although males from some populations can become a little aggressive; must not be kept with larger, more boisterous tankmates.

Diet: Livefoods preferred but some commercial formulations also accepted.

Aquarium: Heavily planted, with central open swimming area and surface cover in the form of floating vegetation. Medium to slightly hard, slightly alkaline water recommended. Some salt (slightly less than 1oz per gal/500mg per liter) may be added to the water, but this is not essential. Temperature range: 73–82°F (23–28°C).

Breeding: Eggs are scattered among feathery roots of floating plants or among fine-leaved vegetation. Hatching can take up to 20 days, depending on temperature.

The Australian Blue-eye shows considerable variation throughout its range. Some populations are more colorful or larger. In addition, some of the more northern ones may be more aggressive than those in other parts of its range. One characteristic of the species, as its common name implies, is the bright blue iris.

Celebes Rainbowfish

Marosatherina ladigesi

Other common name:
Sailfish

Synonym: *Telmatherina ladigesi*

Family: Telmatherinidae

Distribution: Sulawesi (Indonesia).

Size: Up to 3in (7.5cm), but usually smaller.

Behavior: Peaceful, though active, shoaler.

Diet: Wide range of livefoods and commercial diets accepted.

Aquarium: Set up as for *Pseudomugil furcatus* (Furcata Rainbowfish). Softish, slightly acid conditions may be accepted, but it seems to do better at higher pH and hardness values. Water quality must be good. Temperature range: 68–82°F (20–28°C).

Breeding: Breeding season lasts several months. Eggs are scattered among fine-leaved vegetation. Hatching takes 8–12 days, depending on temperature.

This species has been available since 1933, and although it has never achieved the popularity of *Melanotaenia* rainbows, it has always been popular among specialist fishkeepers. It does well only in good-quality water and in the absence of larger and more aggressive tankmates.

KILLIFISH

Families Aplocheilidae, Fundulidae, and Cyprinodontidae

Although some killifish have been known to aquarists for around 100 years, debate regarding the overall classification of the group continues. Old classifications tended to lump all the species within a single family, the Cyprinodontidae. As further information has come to light, various classifications have been put forward, all of them resulting in the splitting of the Cyprinodontidae into new families.

One of the most influential of the revisions was by Lynne Parenti in 1981 (see Further Reading), which was largely adopted by Nelson (1994)—whose classification is followed in this book. Nelson, however, does not adopt the Parenti classification with regard to the Old World rivulines (which he gives the status of subfamily Aplocheilinae within the Aplocheilidae) and the New World rivulines (which he regards as the subfamily Rivulinae within the Aplocheilidae). Parenti, on the other hand, lists them as families. For purposes of comparison, both the Parenti and Nelson interpretations are indicated in the pages that follow. Some species of the reduced family Cyprinodontidae are also included.

Whatever their scientific status, killifish are fascinating aquarium fish that should be kept by every experienced aquarist at one time or another. Some species are annual. They live for just one season, during which they lay eggs that survive buried in the dried-up substratum of the pond or ditch until the next rains arrive. Others live for several years and spawn among plants. Some species are highly territorial and aggressive, and some are spectacularly colored. Some are extremely demanding in terms of aquarium requirements, while others are hardy.

Left: *Aphyosemion bivittatum.*

Lyretail
Aphyosemion australe

Other common names:
Cape Lopez Lyretail,
Lyre-tailed Panchax

Family: Aplocheilidae (*sensu* Parenti and Nelson)

Subfamily: Aplocheilinae (*sensu* Nelson)

Distribution: Western Africa, including Gabon, Cameroon, and southern D. R. Congo.

Size: Males around 2½in (6cm); females smaller.

Behavior: Peaceful; should not be kept with boisterous tankmates.

Diet: Livefoods preferred, but will accept other diets.

Aquarium: A "quiet" tank preferred—heavily planted, with subdued lighting, dark substratum (incorporating some peat), and preferably tannin-stained, soft, acid water. Temperature range: 64–75°F (18–24°C), but avoid prolonged exposure to the lower temperature.

Breeding: Eggs are scattered among fine-leaved vegetation or a spawning mop (strands of nontoxic wool attached to a cork that is floated on the water surface). Hatching takes about 2 weeks.

This splendid fish first made its appearance in the hobby around 1913. It is one of the longer-lived killies—a life span of around three years is common. Only mature males exhibit the characteristic lyre-shaped tail that gives this species its common name. Several naturally occurring color forms are available as well as some cultivated ones.

Red-seam Killifish

Aphyosemion calliurum

The Red-seam Killifish is a stumpier species than *Aphyosemion australe* (Lyretail), and it lacks the long extensions to the tail that are characteristic of its relative. Several naturally occurring color forms are known. In this species males are far more colorful than the smaller females.

Other common name: Banner Lyretail

Family: Aplocheilidae (*sensu* Parenti and Nelson)

Subfamily: Aplocheilinae (*sensu* Nelson)

Distribution: West Africa, including Cameroon and Niger delta.

Size: Males around 1³/₄in (4.5cm); females smaller.

Behavior: Quarrelsome and territorial toward rivals.

Diet: Livefoods preferred, but will accept other diets.

Aquarium: A "quiet" tank preferred—heavily planted, with subdued lighting, dark substratum (incorporating some peat), and preferably tannin-stained water. Soft to medium-hard, slightly acid water recommended. Temperature range: 75–79°F (24–26°C).

Breeding: Eggs are scattered among fine-leaved vegetation or a spawning mop (strands of nontoxic wool attached to a cork that is floated on the water surface). Hatching takes about 2 weeks.

Blue Killifish

Fundulopanchax filamentosus (previously Aphyosemion filamentosum)

Other common name:
Plumed Killifish

Synonym: *Fundulopanchax filamentosum*

Family: Aplocheilidae (*sensu* Parenti and Nelson)

Subfamily: Aplocheilinae (*sensu* Nelson)

Distribution: Western Africa (Togo, southern Benin, and western Nigeria).

Size: Around 2¼in (5.5cm) for males; females smaller.

Behavior: Generally peaceful; territorial during breeding.

Diet: Livefoods preferred, but will accept other diets.

Aquarium: As for *A. australe,* but water chemistry less critical. Temperature range: 72–77°F (22–25°C).

Breeding: Ensure lowered water level, a thick layer of peat on the bottom, and subdued lighting. Introduce 1 male and several females. Eggs buried in peat. After spawning, remove peat and squeeze gently to eliminate excess moisture. Store at around 72°F (22°C) for about 3 months, ensuring it does not dry out. After this resting period cover the eggs with aquarium water. Hatching will occur over a number of days.

The males of some populations of this species, such as those from southern Togo, possess a great deal of blue on their bodies, hence one of the common names. Confusingly, some other populations from the same region are orange-red. Most populations from other locations contain varying amounts of blue, orange-red, and reddish brown.

Blue Gularis

Fundulopanchax sjostedti (previously Aphyosemion sjoestedti)

Other common names: Red Amphyosemion, Golden Pheasant

Synonym: *Fundulopanchax sjoestedti*

Family: Aplocheilidae (*sensu* Parenti and Nelson)

Subfamily: Aplocheilinae (*sensu* Nelson)

Distribution: West Africa (southern Nigeria, western Cameroon, and Ghana.

Size: Males up to 4³/₄in (12cm); females smaller.

Behavior: Active; aggressive, especially with conspecifics.

Diet: Mainly livefoods.

Aquarium: Spacious and heavily planted with dark substratum (incorporating some peat). Soft, acid, tannin-stained water preferred. Temperature range: 73–79°F (23–26°C).

Breeding: Ensure lowered water level, thick layer of peat, and subdued lighting. Introduce 1 male and several females. Eggs buried in peat. After spawning, remove peat and squeeze gently to eliminate excess moisture. Store at 64–68°F (23–26°C) for 4–6 weeks, then cover eggs with aquarium water. Eggs hatch over a number of days.

Blue Gularis is another species of killifish that has a number of different color forms. However, it is not split into subspecies. While possessing some blue (as indicated by one of its common names), most forms exhibit attractive red patches and stripes on the body.

Clown Killifish

Epiplatys annulatus (previously Aplocheilus [Pseudepiplatys] annulatus)

Other common names:
Comet Panchax, Rocket Panchax

Synonyms: *Epiplatys annulatus, Pseudepiplatys annulatus*

Family: Aplocheilidae (*sensu* Parenti and Nelson)

Subfamily: Aplocheilinae (*sensu* Nelson)

Distribution: West Africa, including Guinea, Liberia, and Sierra Leone.

Size: Up to 1½in (4cm), but often smaller.

Behavior: Peaceful surface swimmer; must not be housed with larger or more boisterous tankmates.

Diet: Livefoods preferred, but other formulations may be accepted.

Aquarium: Well planted, with some floating plants, a peat substratum, and subdued lighting. Softish, slightly acid water preferred. Temperature range: 73–79°F (23–26°C).

Breeding: Eggs are laid among fine-leaved vegetation and ignored by the spawners (a spawning mop, as for *Aphyosemion australe*, will also be acceptable). Hatching takes about 8–10 days.

Traditionally, the Clown Killifish and its closest relatives have been classified as *Epiplatys*. In 1990, following an earlier paper on the subject, Scheel (see Further Reading) placed *Epiplatys* within *Aplocheilus*. Owing to distinct body patterning and unique color distribution on the caudal fin, along with some skeletal and behavioral differences, Scheel also regarded *A. annulatus* as in a sufficiently "isolated position in *Aplocheilus*" to warrant its own subgenus, *Pseudepiplatys* (already considered as a valid genus by some earlier authors).

Chaper's Panchax

Epiplatys chaperi (previously Aplocheilus chaperi)

Synonym: *Epiplatys chaperi*

Family: Aplocheilidae (*sensu* Parenti and Nelson)

Subfamily: Aplocheilinae (*sensu* Nelson)

Distribution: Western Africa (Ghana and Ivory Coast).

Size: Up to $2^3/_4$in (7cm).

Behavior: Peaceful, but not as retiring as *A. annulatus.*

Diet: Livefoods preferred, but other formulations may be accepted.

Aquarium: Well planted, with some floating plants, a peat substratum, and subdued lighting. Softish, slightly acid water preferred. Temperature range: 72–82°F (22–28°C).

Breeding: Eggs are laid among fine-leaved vegetation and ignored by the spawners (a spawning mop, as in *Aphyosemion australe*, will also be acceptable). Hatching takes about 8–10 days.

Two subspecies of *A. chaperi* are known: Chaper's Panchax (*A. c. chaperi*) and Schreiber's Panchax (*A. c. schreiberi*). Both have varying numbers of backward-slanting, narrow, oblique dark bands that are more pronounced in females than in males. However, in both subspecies of *A. chaperi* the body is somewhat sturdier than in *A. annulatus* (Clown Killifish), and the caudal fin lacks the central fin ray extensions.

Blue Panchax

Aplocheilus panchax

Family: Aplocheilidae (*sensu* Parenti and Nelson)

Subfamily: Aplocheilinae (*sensu* Nelson)

Distribution: Southeast Asia.

Size: Up to 3in (8cm).

Behavior: Relatively peaceful surface swimmer, although very small fry may be regarded as food; males are somewhat aggressive toward each other.

Diet: Livefoods preferred, but other diets also accepted.

Aquarium: Well covered and spacious, with some floating plants, dense plant shelter around the edges and back, and some open swimming spaces along the front. Subdued lighting is also advisable, as are bogwood and other types of shelter. Water chemistry not critical, but quality must be good. Temperature range: 68–77°F (20–25°C).

Breeding: Eggs are laid among fine-leaved vegetation or spawning mops (see *Aphyosemion australe*) over a period of days. Hatching takes up to 2 weeks.

The Blue Panchax is one of the earliest species imported into Europe (1899). Despite this, it has never become as widespread within the hobby as its obvious beauty deserves. It has a greenish body with blue coloring along both sides that serves to highlight the outline of the scales.

Six-barred Panchax

Epiplatys infrafasciatus (previously Aplocheilus sexfasciatus)

This species has similar oblique body bands to *A. chaperi* (Chaper's Panchax). As its common name suggests, it has six of these vertical bands. It is extremely variable, both in color and body patterning, and there are five known subspecies, each exhibiting variability according to location.

Other common name: Six-barred Epiplatys

Synonym: *Epiplatys sexfasciatus*

Family: Aplocheilidae (*sensu* Parenti and Nelson)

Subfamily: Aplocheilinae (*sensu* Nelson)

Distribution: Western Africa, including Togo, Gabon, Cameroon, and (at least) Taylor Creek in Nigeria.

Size: Around 3in (8cm), but individuals up to 4¹⁄₄in (11cm) reported.

Behavior: A surface-living species that may prey on very small fish.

Diet: Livefoods preferred, but other formulations may be accepted.

Aquarium: Well planted, with some floating plants, a peat substratum, and subdued lighting. Softish, slightly acid water preferred. Temperature range: 72–82°F (22–28°C).

Breeding: Eggs are laid among fine-leaved vegetation and ignored by the spawners (a spawning mop, as in *Aphyosemion australe*, will also be acceptable). Hatching takes about 8–10 days.

Günther's Nothobranch

Nothobranchius guentheri

Family: Aplocheilidae (*sensu* Parenti and Nelson)

Subfamily: Aplocheilinae (*sensu* Nelson)

Distribution: Zanzibar, but also reported from the Tanzanian mainland.

Size: About 2in (5cm); larger sizes sometimes quoted.

Behavior: Males aggressive toward each other.

Diet: Livefoods preferred, but other diets may be accepted.

Aquarium: This species is best kept in a tank set aside specifically for it and in groups of 1 male and several females. To keep several males, the tank must be large enough to accommodate territories that do not overlap. Provide several shelters and some open swimming spaces surrounded by vegetation and a dark, soft substratum (peat is ideal). Soft, slightly acid water recommended. Temperature range: 72–79°F (22–26°C).

Breeding: Eggs are buried in substratum. Treat them as for *A. filamentosum* for 3–4 months before resoaking.

This colorful annual species, known in the hobby since the mid-1910s, is one of the best-known representatives of its genus. *Nothobranchius* species are highly variable and often cause confusion with regard to precise identification. Some aquarium strains are also known. Like many other killifish, it is available only occasionally in general aquatic outlets.

Palmqvist's Nothobranch

Nothobranchius palmqvisti

Family: Aplocheilidae (*sensu* Parenti and Nelson)

Subfamily: Aplocheilinae (*sensu* Nelson)

Distribution: Coastal regions of southern Kenya and Tanzania.

Size: Up to 2in (5cm).

Behavior: Males are particularly aggressive toward each other.

Diet: Sometimes reluctant to accept non-livefoods.

Aquarium: This species is best kept in a tank set aside specifically for it and in groups of 1 male and several females. To keep several males, the aquarium must be large enough to accommodate territories that do not overlap. Provide several shelters and some open swimming spaces surrounded by vegetation and a dark, soft substratum (peat is ideal). Soft, slightly acid water recommended. Temperature range: 72–79°F (22–26°C).

Breeding: Eggs are buried in the substratum. Treat as for *A. filamentosum* for 3–4 months before resoaking. Adults die at the end of the breeding season.

Palmqvist's Nothobranch is one of several species in which the caudal fin is blood-red throughout. As in so many other *Nothobranchius* species, the body coloration shows variation, depending on locality of origin. Generally, it has a bluish body with a network of red lines covering it. Females are smaller and duller in color than the males.

Argentine Pearl

Austrolebias bellottii (previously Cynolebias bellotti)

Family: Aplocheilidae (*sensu* Nelson); Rivulidae (Parenti)

Subfamily: Rivulinae (*sensu* Nelson)

Distribution: Río de la Plata basin (Argentina).

Size: Males up to 2¾in (7cm); females smaller.

Behavior: Active; males are sometimes aggressive.

Diet: Livefoods preferred, but other diets also accepted.

Aquarium: Single-species aquarium, with a peat substratum and vegetation clumps. Soft, slightly acid, good-quality water required. Temperature range: 59–72°F (15–22°C). Very low and very high temperatures, e.g. 39°F (4°C) and 86°F (30°C), are temporarily tolerated.

Breeding: Use 1 male to 2 or 3 females. Eggs are buried in the peat. Squeeze gently to remove excess water and store for 3–4 months without allowing it to dry out. Resoak eggs in aquarium water—they will begin hatching, sometimes within hours. Females must be removed immediately after spawning, otherwise they will be harassed by the male, which can spawn again straightaway.

The Argentine Pearl was among the first New World killifish to be introduced into the hobby almost 100 years ago, but there is ongoing debate surrounding the classification of *Cynolebias*. Some authors classify the genus as *Austrolebias*, *Nematolebias*, or *Simpsonichthys*. Mirroring the lifestyle of their Old World relatives in the genus *Nothobranchius*, the Argentine Pearl and other *Cynolebias* species are annual fishes—their reproductive behavior is virtually identical.

Black-finned Argentine Pearl

Austrolebias nigripinnis (previously Cynolebias nigripinnis)

Other common name:
Dwarf Argentine Pearl

Family: Aplocheilidae (*sensu* Nelson); Rivulidae (Parenti)

Subfamily: Rivulinae (*sensu* Nelson)

Distribution: Argentina.

Size: Males up to 2in (5cm); females smaller.

Behavior: Active; males are sometimes aggressive.

Diet: Livefoods preferred, but other diets also accepted.

Aquarium: Single-species aquarium, with a peat substratum and vegetation clumps. Soft, slightly acid, good-quality water required. Temperature range: 64–77°F (18–25°C) recommended, but slightly higher and lower temperatures are tolerated.

Breeding: Use 1 male to 2 or 3 females. Eggs are buried in the peat. Squeeze gently to remove excess water and store in the dark for 3–4 months, but do not allow it to dry out. Resoak the eggs in aquarium water; they will begin hatching, sometimes within a few hours. Remove the females immediately after spawning, since they will be harassed by the male, which can spawn again straightaway.

Many authors recognize two subspecies of *C. nigripinnis*: *C. n. nigripinnis* (Black-finned, or Dwarf, Argentine Pearl) and *C. n. alexandri* (Entre Río Argentine Pearl). Others—perhaps a majority—consider each one to be a valid species in its own right. While being overall similar to each other, *C. n. alexandri* males have brownish, almost vertical bands on the body. *C. n. nigripinnis* lacks the bands but has the characteristic black fins that are indicated in both the scientific and common names.

White's Pearl

Nematolebias whitei (previously Cynolebias whitei)

Family: Aplocheilidae (*sensu* Nelson); Rivulidae (Parenti)

Subfamily: Rivulinae (*sensu* Nelson)

Distribution: Brazil.

Size: Males up to 3in (8cm); females smaller.

Behavior: Active; males are sometimes aggressive.

Diet: Livefoods preferred; dried food accepted only reluctantly.

Aquarium: Single-species aquarium, with a peat substratum and clumps of vegetation. Soft, slightly acid, good-quality water is important. Temperature range: 68–73°F (20–23°C).

Breeding: Use 1 male to 2 or 3 females. Eggs are buried in the peat. Squeeze it gently to remove excess water and store in the dark for 3–4 months. Do not allow it to dry out. Resoak eggs in aquarium water; they will begin hatching, sometimes within hours. Females must be removed immediately after spawning, since they will be harassed by the male, which can spawn again straightaway.

As in the other *Cynolebias* species featured, the body in male *C. whitei* is spangled with numerous white, cream, or bluish "pearls." Males also exhibit a brownish base body color and elongated dorsal and anal fins. An aquarium-bred albino form is occasionally available.

Lace-finned Killifish

Pterolebias zonatus

Family: Aplocheilidae (*sensu* Nelson); Rivulidae (Parenti)

Subfamily: Rivulinae (*sensu* Nelson)

Distribution: Venezuela.

Size: Up to 6in (15cm), but usually much smaller.

Behavior: Males are aggressive toward each other; less so as they age.

Diet: Predominantly livefoods; other diets usually accepted only with reluctance.

Aquarium: Single-species aquarium, with a peat substratum and vegetation clumps. Soft, slightly acid, good-quality water is important. Temperature range: 64–73°F (18–23°C).

Breeding: Use 1 male to 2 or 3 females. Eggs are buried in the peat. Squeeze gently to remove excess water and store in the dark for 3–4 months, but do not allow it to dry out. Resoak the eggs in aquarium water; they will begin hatching, sometimes within a few hours. Remove the females immediately after spawning, since they will be harassed by the male, which can spawn again straightaway.

The Lace-finned Killifish is a truly magnificent species. It has brownish speckling and body bands on a light metallic-blue base color. Fully mature males have an almost sail-like anal fin and a substantial caudal fin. Of the other four species in the genus, *P. longipinnis* (the Long-finned Killifish) is the most frequently encountered. Its requirements are similar to those of the Lace-finned Killifish.

Green Rivulus

Rivulus cylindraceus

Family: Aplocheilidae (*sensu* Nelson); Rivulidae (Parenti)

Subfamily: Rivulinae (*sensu* Nelson)

Other common names: Brown/Cuban Rivulus

Distribution: Cuba (in mountain streams).

Size: Around 2¼in (5.5cm).

Behavior: Generally peaceful but active; exhibits good jumping ability.

Diet: Predominantly livefoods, but other diets will also be accepted.

Aquarium: Well covered, with a dark substratum, some clumps of fine-leaved vegetation, and subdued lighting. Water chemistry not critical, but neutral, medium-hard water is preferred. Temperature range: 22–24°C (72–77°F) with some deviation tolerated on either side.

Breeding: Use a trio of 1 male and 2 females. Eggs are laid mainly on fine-leaved vegetation or on a spawning mop (as in *Aphyosemion australe*). Spawning may occur on top of the mop and the exposed eggs may survive exposure for a week or more. The submerged eggs hatch after 12–14 days.

Unlike some other members of the family, *Rivulus* species do not bury their eggs. If pools dry out in the wild, the eggs of some species may withstand desiccation for a while, but they do not go into the extended resting period (diopause) exhibited by annual species. *Rivulus* species tend to live for 18 months or more, and Green Rivulus has a life span of up to four years.

Blue-striped Rivulus

Laimosemion xiphidius (previously Rivulus xiphidius)

This is probably the most spectacularly colored of all the *Rivulus* species. It is also one of the smallest and more challenging members of the genus and is definitely not a fish for beginners. It has a life span of about two and a half years. Females are smaller than the males, and they lack the blue-and-orange coloration. Instead, they have a dark gray vertical band.

Other common name: Band-tailed Rivulus

Family: Aplocheilidae (*sensu* Nelson): Rivulidae (Parenti)

Subfamily: Rivulinae (*sensu* Nelson)

Distribution: French Guyana (in forest springs); Amazon region (Brazil); also (possibly) Suriname.

Size: Up to 1³/₄in (4.5cm) but often smaller.

Behavior: Retiring and placid, with good jumping ability.

Diet: Almost exclusively livefoods.

Aquarium: Well covered, with subdued lighting and some plant thickets. Soft, slightly acid water is important. Temperature range: 72–79°F (22–25°C).

Breeding: Challenging in aquaria. Use a trio of 1 male and 2 females. Eggs are laid mainly on fine-leaved vegetation or on a spawning mop (as in *Aphyosemion australe*); spawning may occur on top of the mop, and the exposed eggs may survive exposure for a week or more. Submerged eggs hatch after around 14 days.

Golden Top Minnow

Fundulus chrysotus

Other common name:
Golden-eared Killifish

Family: Fundulidae (*sensu* Nelson and Parenti)

Distribution: Gulf Coast plain of North America, including South Carolina and Florida and westward to the Trinity River drainage in Texas.

Size: Up to 3in (7.5cm).

Behavior: Quite tolerant. Rivalry intensifies among males at breeding time.

Diet: Livefoods preferred, but other formulations, particularly deep-frozen ones, will be accepted.

Aquarium: Spacious, well covered, with surface vegetation, plant thickets, and pieces of bogwood. Water chemistry not critical; 1 teaspoonful aquarium salt per 1 Imp. gal (1$\frac{1}{5}$ U.S.gal/4.5 l) may be added for stocks that originate from brackish-water regions. Temperature range: 64–72°F (18–22°C); some deviation tolerated.

Breeding: Use 1 male and 2 or more females. Eggs are laid over a period of about a week among fine-leaved vegetation and ignored by the spawners. Hatching takes several days.

This species has a characteristic golden patch on the gill cover directly behind the eyes, hence its common names. In males the greenish body is liberally covered in small reddish-brown spots. Females are drabber but they have numerous glistening light-colored spots.

Arabian Killifish

Aphanius dispar

Other common name:
Mother of Pearl Killifish

Family: Cyprinodontidae

Subfamily: Cyprinodontinae

Distribution: Middle East, including Dubai, Jordan, Iran, and north Somalia.

Size: Around 2³/₄in (7cm).

Behavior: Adult males become scrappy.

Diet: Wide range of foods accepted; vegetable component important.

Aquarium: Well planted tank (using salt-tolerant plant species) with suitable retreats. Well-filtered, hard, alkaline water important. Preferably add 1 teaspoonful aquarium salt per 1 Imp. gal (1¹/₅ U.S.gal/4.5 l). Preferred temperature range: 61–84°F (16–29°C).

Breeding: Eggs are laid among fine-leaved vegetation or spawning mop (as in *Aphyosemion australe*). Hatching takes about 7 days.

Of the 30 or so species in this genus, two are seen much more often than any others: the Arabian Killifish and *A. mento* (Black Persian Minnow or Killifish, mainly from Israel and Turkey). Two subspecies of Arabian Killifish are generally recognized: *A. d. dispar* and *A. d. richardsoni* (from Jordan). Both have similar aquarium requirements. *Aphanius mento*, on the other hand, has lower temperature requirements (50–77°F, or 10–25°C). It can also tolerate wider pH and hardness ranges (from slightly acid and soft to alkaline and hard).

Florida Flagfish

Jordanella floridae

Other common name:
American Flagfish

Family: Cyprinodontidae

Subfamily: Cyprinodontinae

Distribution: From Florida southward to the Yucatán peninsula in Mexico.

Size: Males up to 2½in (6.5cm); females slightly smaller.

Behavior: Males territorial and often aggressive toward rivals, but more tolerant of other species.

Diet: All types of food accepted; vegetable component important.

Aquarium: Thickly planted, with some open swimming areas and fine-grained substratum. Water chemistry not critical but quality must be good. Temperature range: 66–77°F (19–25°C).

Breeding: Eggs are either scattered among fine-leaved vegetation or laid in a depression prepared by the male; male also guards eggs. Hatching takes about 6–9 days.

This old favorite continues to hold its own against some of the more colorful killifishes of both the New and Old Worlds. It is a tough, easy-to-breed species in which mature males in peak condition constantly display toward each other as well as toward prospective mates.

LIVEBEARERS

Families Poeciliidae, Anablepidae, Goodeidae, and Hemiramphidae

This section covers a group of four families, in which many of the species produce live young. The family Poeciliidae contains the most popular aquarium fish that produce live young. Many beginners start with the guppy (*Poecilia reticulata*), progressing to swordtails such as *Xiphophorus helleri*. One major reason for the popularity of the group—apart from the ease with which they can generally be kept—is the development of many colorful domestic strains of guppies, swordtails, platies, and mollies.

As part of the order Cyrinodontiformes, the group has been subjected to many taxonomic revisions. Here we take the view according to the Parenti review of 1981 (see Further Reading). The Poeciliidae contains the subfamilies Poeciliinae (the typical platies, swordtails, mollies, and guppies),

Aplocheilichthyinae (the lampeyes), and Fluviphylacinae (a single species, *Fluviphylax pygmaeus*). The four-eyed fishes (*Anableps* sp.) and one-sided livebearers (*Jenynsia* sp.) belong to the subfamily Anablepinae. With the Oxyzygonectinae, they make up the family Anablepidae. The Poeciliidae and the Anablepidae form the superfamily Poecilioidea.

The Goodeidae is divided into two subfamilies: Empetrichthyinae, which contains two egg-laying genera, and the Goodeinae. With the Cyprinodontidae (covered in the section on Killifish), they form the superfamily Cyprinodontoidea. This classification is becoming accepted by scientists, although there is still much aquarium literature that does not use it.

Finally, this section covers the family Hemirhamphidae, which are not related to the other groups, but do bear live young.

Below: *Hemiramphus far.*

Four-eyed Fish

Anableps anableps

Other common names:
Striped Four-eyed Fish,
Four Eyes

Family: Anablepidae

Subfamily: Anablepinae

Distribution: Southern
Mexico to northern South
America (in both freshwater
and brackish water).

Size: Males about 6in (15cm);
females to 10½in (27cm).

Behavior: Surface-swimming
shoaler.

Diet: Livefoods preferred,
but some commercial diets
accepted.

Aquarium: Long covered
tank only half to three-
quarters full (to see the
above/below-water eye
orientation). moderately
hard alkaline water required,
with 1 teaspoonful of
aquarium salt per 1 Imp. gal
(1⅕ U.S.gal/4.5–5 l) added.
Temperature range: 72–86°F
(22–30°C); some deviation
at either end tolerated.

Breeding: In males the anal
fin is modified into a
gonopodium via which
sperm are transferred into
the vent of the female. Eggs
are fertilized internally and
retained by female. She
gives birth to small broods
(as few as 6 offspring) of
large fry about twice a year.

This species' common name is derived from the two pigmented horizontal
flaps of tissue that extend across the eye to meet (but not fuse) in the
center of the pupil, effectively dividing the eye into an upper and a lower
portion. Modifications to the eye lens allow *Anableps* to see above and
below the water simultaneously. This ability is enhanced by a split retina:
one part receives the incoming light rays from above the water, while the
other receives those that originate underwater. The Four-eyed Fish is an
interesting but large and somewhat challenging species. Two other species
with similar characteristics, size, and requirements are also occasionally
available: *A. dowei* (Pacific Four-eyed Fish) from Mexico to Nicaragua; and
A. microlepis (Fine-scaled Four-eyed Fish) from the Orinoco delta to the
Amazon delta.

Lampeye Panchax

Poropanchax luxophthalmus (previously Aplocheilichthys luxophthalmus)

Other common names:
Big-eye, Iridescent Lampeye

Synonym: *Aplocheilichthys macrophthalmus*

Family: Poeciliidae

Subfamily:
Aplocheilichthyinae

Distribution: Western Africa, including Cameroon, Nigeria (Niger delta), and Togo.

Size: Up to 1½in (4cm).

Behavior: Active, peaceful shoaler.

Diet: Livefoods preferred, but other diets also accepted.

Aquarium: Heavily planted, with open swimming spaces and surface vegetation. Dark substratum and subdued lighting are recommended Neutral or slightly alkaline, medium-hard water is preferred. Temperature range: 72–79°F (22–26°C).

Breeding: Eggs are scattered among any fine-leaved vegetation or the finely divided roots of floating plants. Lowering the water level is recommended. Hatching takes 10–14 days.

Two subspecies of this delightful lampeye are now recognized: *A. l. luxophthalmus* (Lampeye Panchax itself), and *A. l. hannerzi* (Hannerz's Lampeye) from the lower Cross River drainage in Nigeria. To see either fish at its best, close attention must be paid to achieving optimum aquarium conditions.

Tanganyika Lampeye

Lacustricola pumilus (previously Aplocheilichthys pumilus)

Family: Poeciliidae

Subfamily: Aplocheilichthyinae

Distribution: East African crater lakes, including Lake Tanganyika and Lake Victoria.

Size: Around 2¼in (5.5cm).

Behavior: Timid, peaceful shoaler.

Diet: Livefoods preferred, but other diets also accepted.

Aquarium: Heavily planted, with open swimming spaces and surface vegetation. Dark substratum and subdued lighting are recommended Neutral or slightly alkaline, medium-hard water is preferred. Water should be thoroughly aerated. Preferred temperature range: 75–79°F (24–26°C).

Breeding: Eggs are scattered among any fine-leaved vegetation or the finely divided roots of floating plants. Lowering the water level is recommended. Use soft, slightly acid water. Hatching takes 10–14 days.

In reflected light the sides of the body—particularly in males that are in peak condition—are silvery blue and divided longitudinally by a dark stripe. The caudal fin is thinly edged in gold, while the other fins are orange-brown with some blue speckling. These colors are only really apparent under ideal aquarium conditions.

Tanganyika Pearl Killifish

Lamprichthys tanganicanus

Family: Poeciliidae

Subfamily: Aplocheilichthyinae

Distribution: Lake Tanganyika (Africa).

Size: Up to 5in (13cm).

Behavior: Active shoaler.

Diet: Livefoods preferred, but other formulations also accepted.

Aquarium: Spacious and covered, with some plant thickets and ample open swimming space. At least one group of rocks or blocks of bogwood should be placed closely together to provide crevices. Top-quality alkaline medium-hard to hard water is important. Temperature range: 72–77°F (22–25°C).

Breeding: Eggs are generally deposited in cracks or crevices in rocks or bogwood and are best left to develop in the dark for over a week.

This exceptionally beautiful species is the sole representative of the genus *Lamprichthys* and the largest member of the subfamily Aplocheilichthyinae. It is a streamlined fish with a series of lines of small, metallic-blue scales that are particularly resplendent in reflected light. It can prove challenging to keep in peak condition.

Knife Livebearer

Alfaro cultratus

Family: Poeciliidae

Subfamily: Poeciliinae

Distribution: Costa Rica, Nicaragua, and Panama.

Size: Males up to 3½in (9cm); females slightly larger.

Behavior: Can be shy and easily frightened in sparsely decorated aquaria. Males are sometimes aggressive toward each other but not excessively so when kept in a shoal that includes several other males. Aggression is highest when only 2 males are present.

Diet: Livefoods preferred, but other diets also accepted.

Aquarium: Spacious, well planted, and covered, with some open swimming spaces and shelters. Neutral or slightly alkaline medium-hard, well-filtered water with some movement (as produced by a powerhead outlet) is recommended. Temperature range: 75–82°F (24–28°C).

Breeding: Fertilization is internal. Females give birth to as many as 100 fry every 4–5 weeks (although broods are generally much smaller than this).

While not the most colorful of the poeciliines, Knife Livebearer makes a dazzling display when kept in a shoal. The "knife" consists of a series of scales on the lower edge of the body located between the vent and the beginning of the caudal fin. *Alfaro huberi* (Orange Rocket) from Guatemala, Honduras, and Nicaragua has a central body spot, is smaller (around 2¾in/7cm), and is less frequently available.

Pike Top Livebearer

Belonesox belizanus

Other common names:
Pike Top Minnow/Killifish

Family: Poeciliidae

Subfamily: Poeciliinae

Distribution:
B. b. belizanus found from Veracruz (Mexico) south to Guatemala, Honduras, and Nicaragua; *B. b. maxillosus* in the Yucatán Peninsula (Mexico).

Size: Males up to 4³/₄in (12cm); females 8in (20cm).

Behavior: Predatory; must be housed only with similar-sized tankmates; large females may even prey on small males of their own species.

Diet: Livefoods, deep-frozen, and freeze-dried diets.

Aquarium: Spacious, covered, well planted tank, with some shelters. Water should be well filtered, neutral to alkaline hard, with 1 teaspoonful of aquarium salt per 2 Imp. gal (2²/₅ U.S. gal/9–10 l) added. Temperature range: 79–86°F (26–30°C) or slightly higher.

Breeding: Up to 100 large fry (up to 1in/2.5cm) produced every 4¹/₂–7 weeks, following internal fertilization.

This streamlined, beak-mouthed, saber-toothed species has been in the hobby for nearly 100 years. One of the livebearers "with character," it is undoubtedly a species for the specialist who likes something a little different. Two subspecies are sometimes recognized: *B. b. belizanus* and *B. b. maxillosus* (Yellow Pike Top Livebearer) from the Yucatán in Mexico. Some authorities doubt the validity of the second subspecies, however.

The Bishop

Brachyraphis episcopi

Family: Poeciliidae

Subfamily: Poeciliinae

Distribution: Both oceanic slopes of Panama.

Size: Males up to 1½in (3.5cm); females 2in (5cm).

Behavior: Relatively aggressive toward smaller and even some similar-sized tankmates; exhibits fin-nipping tendencies, but may be kept as a shoal.

Diet: Predominantly livefoods, but other diets accepted (flakes often rejected).

Aquarium: Well planted and well filtered. Neutral to alkaline medium-hard water preferred. Temperature range: 75–79°F (24–26°C).

Breeding: Small broods of around 20 fry produced every 4 weeks or so.

The Bishop is perhaps the best known of the nine or so *Brachyraphis* species (the total number is uncertain because some are awaiting scientific description). It is a distinctive fish with netlike scale patterning, a red line, and dark spots running down the body. It also has a red-edged dorsal fin and the characteristic "brachy" black spot around the vent and extending into the anal fin. It is challenging to maintain in peak condition.

Blackline Mosquitofish

Gambusia vittata (previously Flexipenis vittata)

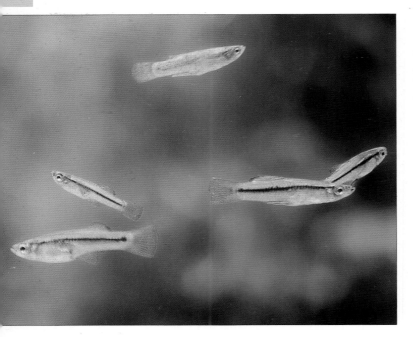

Synonyms: *Flexipenis vittatus, Gambusia vittata*

Family: Poeciliidae

Subfamily: Poeciliinae

Distribution: Atlantic side of Mexico.

Size: Males around 1³/₄in (4.5cm); females around 2¹/₂in (6cm).

Behavior: Surprisingly unaggressive for a "Gambusia-type" species; may be kept in a shoal.

Diet: Wide range of foods accepted.

Aquarium: Well-planted, well-lit, covered tank. Neutral softish water, with some deviation on either side accepted. Temperature range: 72–77°F (22–25°C).

Breeding: Broods of around 20 fry produced every 4–6 weeks.

There is considerable debate regarding the true identity of this beautiful fish. Some authorities believe it to be the single representative of the genus *Flexipenis*, while others (probably a majority) believe it to be a *Gambusia*. Whatever its classification, with the characteristic black line running along its body, it is a delightful fish for the aquarium.

Western Mosquitofish

Gambusia affinis

Synonym: *G. affinis affinis*

Family: Poeciliidae

Subfamily: Poeciliinae

Distribution: *G. affinis* found from northern Veracruz (Mexico) north to southern Indiana and east to Alabama; *G. holbrooki* from central Alabama east to Florida and north up to New Jersey.

Size: Males to 1½in (4cm); females up to 2¾in (7cm).

Behavior: Has distinct fin-nipping tendencies; voracious appetite toward anything of a swallowable size. Both species should be kept as a shoal.

Diet: Livefoods preferred.

Aquarium: Well-planted, covered tank. Provide surface vegetation with feathery roots (to offer protection for fry). Water chemistry is not critical, but quality must be good. Temperature range: from below 50°F (10°C) to above 86°F (30°C).

Breeding: Broods vary from 10–80 fry and are produced every 5–8 weeks during the warmer months. Parents are highly cannibalistic toward their offspring.

Together with its closest relative, *G. holbrooki* (Eastern Mosquitofish), the Western Mosquitofish is undoubtedly the most widely distributed of all the livebearers, having been introduced into numerous tropical and subtropical regions as a biological means of malaria control. While they have proved effective in this role—by eating large quantities of malaria mosquito larvae—both species have proved very invasive and have often displaced native species.

Eastern Mosquitofish

Gambusia holbrooki

Other common names:
Large Mosquitofish,
Holbrook's Mosquitofish

Family: Poeciliidae

Subfamily: Poeciliinae

Distribution: North America
from New Jersey south to
Florida and west to central
Alabama.

Size: Males up to 1 1/4in
(3.5cm); females from
1 1/2 –2 1/2in (4–6cm).

Behavior: Occasionally
aggressive; keep only with
hardy tankmates.

Diet: Livefoods preferred.

Aquarium: Well-planted,
covered tank. Provide
surface vegetation with
feathery roots (to offer
protection for fry). Water
chemistry not is critical,
but quality must be good.
Temperature range: 68–82°F
(20–28°C).

Breeding: Mature females
produce 10–80 fry every
5–8 weeks or so.

The Eastern Mosquitofish is sometimes regarded as a subspecies of
Gambusia affinis (Western Mosquitofish). The Eastern Mosquitofish
is slightly smaller than *G. affinis* and often has diamond-checkered
markings across its body, with lighter underparts. Males have varying
quantities of black patches on their body, and melanic (black or black-
mottled) morphs are commonly found in the wild.

Girardinus Topminnow

Girardinus metallicus

Other common names:
Metallic/Black-bellied
Metallic Topminnow

Family: Poeciliidae

Subfamily: Poeciliinae

Distribution: Most of Cuba.

Size: Males up to 2in (5cm);
females up to 3½in (9cm).

Behavior: Lively shoaler.

Diet: Wide range of foods
accepted.

Aquarium: Planted, covered,
well filtered, with some
gentle water movement.
Slightly alkaline, medium-
hard water preferred.
Temperature range:
72–84°F (22–29°C).

Breeding: At the higher
temperatures, broods of
up to 100 fry (but usually
fewer) are produced every
5 weeks or so.

Of the eight species making up the genus *Giardinus*, Giardinus Topminnow
is the most frequently seen. In some males, the gonopodium has black
coloration that extends forward into the chest area (hence the "black-
bellied" part of one of the common names). Both males and females have
a metallic sheen and vertical black body bands.

Mosquitofish

Heterandria formosa

Other common names: Dwarf Livebearer, Dwarf Topminnow, Least Killifish

Family: Poeciliidae

Subfamily: Poeciliinae

Distribution: From southeast North Carolina southward, including eastern and southern Georgia, Florida, the Gulf Coast (as far as New Orleans), and Louisiana.

Size: Males up to $^3/_4$in (2cm); females up to 1$^1/_4$in (3cm).

Behavior: Peaceful shoaler. Best kept in a tank set up exclusively for it.

Diet: Small livefoods preferred, but other diets also accepted; a regular vegetable supplement is recommended.

Aquarium: Thickly planted and covered. Alkaline hardish water preferred, but other conditions also accepted. Temperature range: from 61°F (16°C) to around 84°F (29°C).

Breeding: Small numbers of relatively large fry are released on an almost daily basis over a period of 10–14 days (this is known as superfetation).

Of the alternative common names listed above, the last should cease to be used because this delightful, minute species is not a killifish at all. It ranks among the smallest vertebrates known to science. A fish for the specialist, it should be regarded as a "must" by any aquarist who has developed the appropriate level of husbandry skills.

Black-bellied Limia

Poecilia melanogaster (previously Limia melanogaster)

Synonym: *Poecilia melanogaster*

Family: Poeciliidae

Subfamily: Poeciliinae

Distribution: Jamaica

Size: Males up to 1³/₄in (4.5cm); females up to 2¹/₂in (6cm).

Behavior: Active shoaler.

Diet: Wide range of foods accepted; regular vegetable component important.

Aquarium: Well planted, covered tank with open swimming area. Provide good illumination to encourage growth of green encrusting algae (a natural source of vegetable food) on the aquarium panes. (Leave the sides and back unscraped during aquarium maintenance.) Alkaline, hardish, good-quality water preferred. Temperature range: 72–82°F (22–28°C).

Breeding: Broods of about 20 fry are produced every 5–8 weeks. Considerable variation, however, exists, in the size and frequency of broods.

In peak condition, this is a superb little fish for a community aquarium. Males have a bluish sheen and yellow coloration in the caudal and dorsal fins, and females have a large black belly patch. Males in particular are always on the move, displaying to each other and attempting to mate with females of their own species and with those of closely related ones. If they succeed in mating with related species, fertile hybrids may be produced.

Humpbacked Limia

Poecilia nigrofasciata (previously Limia nigrofasciata)

Other common name:
Black-barred Limia

Synonym: *Poecilia nigrofasciata*

Family: Poeciliidae

Subfamily: Poeciliinae

Distribution: Lake Miragoane in Haiti.

Size: Males around 2¼in (5.5cm); females up to 2½in (6cm).

Behavior: Peaceful shoaler.

Diet: Wide range of foods accepted; regular vegetable component important.

Aquarium: As for *Limia melanogaster* (Black-bellied Limia), but water need not be as hard and alkaline. Temperature range: 75–82°F (24–28°C).

Breeding: Temperature appears to affect the sex ratio of fry, with the higher end of the scale reportedly resulting in more females. Broods of around 60 fry are produced every 4–10 weeks.

The humped back of this Limia is particularly evident in fully mature males, a group of which create an impressive sight in any aquarium. Hybridization with closely related species is not uncommon. Two very similar species: *L. grossidens* (Largetooth Limia) and *L. miragoanensis* (Miragoane Limia)—both also from Lake Miragoane—are thought by some authors to be synonymous with Humpbacked Limia.

Cuban Limia

Poecilia vittata (previously Limia vittata)

Synonym: *Poecilia vittata*

Family: Poeciliidae

Subfamily: Poeciliinae

Distribution: Cuba; some populations occur in brackish waters.

Size: Males up to 2½in (6.5cm); females up to 4¾in (12cm) but usually smaller.

Behavior: Active shoaler.

Diet: Wide range of foods accepted; regular vegetable component important.

Aquarium: As for *Limia melanogaster*. A little aquarium salt—about 1 teaspoonful per 1 Imp. gal (1⅕ U.S.gal/4.5 l) may be added to the water, but this is not essential. Temperature range: 75–82°F (24–28°C).

Breeding: Large broods of up to 100 fry are produced every 4–6 weeks.

This is another extremely attractive *Limia* species that hybridizes easily with its closest relatives. It is also highly variable, with some specimens having very little spotting, whereas others—particularly some of the aquarium-bred strains—are richly spotted with yellow and black.

Merry Widow

Phallichthys amates

Synonym: *Phallichthys amates amates*

Family: Poeciliidae

Subfamily: Poeciliinae

Distribution: Atlantic slope of southern Guatemala and northern Honduras.

Size: Males up to 1½in (4cm); females up to 2¾in (7cm).

Behavior: Quiet shoaler. Must not be kept with active tankmates.

Diet: Range of foods accepted; vegetable component necessary.

Aquarium: Thickly planted, with little or no water movement and subdued lighting preferred. Water chemistry not critical, but extremes must be avoided. Temperature range: 72–82°F (22–28°C).

Breeding: Up to 150 fry may be produced by large females every 4–6 weeks.

Superficially males of this species resemble those of *Carlhubbsia stuarti* (Banded Widow) but they lack the bold vertical body bands of the latter fish. Two other species are also available occasionally: *P. fairweatheri* (Elegant Widow) from Guatemala and *P. pittieri* (Orange-dorsal Widow) from Costa Rica, western Panama, and Nicaragua.

One-spot Livebearer

Phalloceros caudimaculatus

Other common names: Golden One-spot/Spotted/ Golden Spotted Livebearer, The Caudo

Synonyms: *Phalloceros caudimaculatus auratus* and *P. c. a. reticulatus*

Family: Poeciliidae

Subfamily: Poeciliinae

Distribution: Southern Brazil, Paraguay, and Uruguay; introduced into some locations outside its range, e.g. Malawi and western Australia.

Size: Males around 1¼in (3cm); females up to 2in (5cm).

Behavior: Peaceful shoaler.

Diet: Range of foods accepted; vegetable component required.

Aquarium: Tank should be well planted and well lit. Water chemistry not critical, but alkaline, medium-hard conditions are preferred. Temperature range: 64–82°F (18–28°C).

Breeding: Up to 80 fry may be produced every 5–6 weeks.

Owing to its great variability, with some specimens bearing one body spot, others none at all, and yet others being golden and/or mottled (reticulated), this species has a wide range of common and scientific names. Modern-day thinking is that all are representatives of a highly variable single species, *P. caudimaculatus*.

Sailfin Molly

Poecilia latipinna

Family: Poeciliidae

Subfamily: Poeciliinae

Distribution: The Carolinas, Florida, Texas, Virginia, and the Atlantic coast of Mexico.

Size: Males around 4in (10cm); females around 4³/₄in (12cm).

Behavior: Peaceful shoaler; males constantly display toward each other.

Diet: Range of foods accepted; vegetable component essential.

Aquarium: Spacious, planted tank, with some open swimming space. Alkaline, medium-hard water with 1 teaspoonful salt per 1 Imp. gal (1¹/₅ U.S. gal/4.5 l) important for long-term health. Temperature range: 77–82°F (25–28°C).

Breeding: Broods of well over 100 fry are common every 8–10 weeks.

Despite its common name, not all wild males of this species develop the full sail-like dorsal fin. The pure wild form of the species is hardly ever seen within the hobby. Instead, cultivated color varieties or, more often, fertile hybrids between sailfins and two of their closest relatives—*Poecilia sphenops* (Sphenops Molly) and *P. velifera* (Yucatán Molly)—are seen.

Above: Wild. **Below left:** Wild. **Below right:** Yellow. **Opposite:** Black.

Guppy

Poecilia reticulata

Other common name: Millions Fish

Family: Poeciliidae

Subfamily: Poeciliinae

Distribution: Widely distributed north of the Amazon and extensively introduced into tropical and subtropical regions outside of the range.

Size: Wild males up to 1¼in (3cm); wild females around 2in (5cm). Cultivated varieties generally larger.

Behavior: Peaceful shoaler. Should not be kept with boisterous or fin-nipping tankmates, e.g. *Barbus tetrazona* (Tiger Barb).

Diet: Wide range of foods accepted; a vegetable component recommended.

Aquarium: Well planted, well illuminated, with some open swimming space. Water chemistry not critical, but alkaline, medium-hard conditions are preferred. Temperature range: 64–82°F (18–28°C).

Breeding: Large females can produce over 150 fry every 4–6 weeks.

In the hobby since the early 1900s, the Guppy is one of the best known and most popular aquarium fishes of all time. It is an adaptable, hardy fish whose inherent genetic variability has been exploited over the years to produce a bewildering array of fin and color permutations. As a result, the original short-finned wild type of the species is hardly ever seen, except in the aquaria of specialist livebearer enthusiasts. Endler's Livebearer is a particularly beautiful wild form.

Above: Neon Red Sri
   Lanka.
Right: Cobra Red Sri Lanka.
Opposite: Triangletail
   nigrocaudatus (male
   and female).

Above: Triangletail
 Snakeskin.
Far Right: Triangletail
 Gray Multicolored.
Right: Triangletail
 Halfblack Blue.

Clockwise from bottom left: Neon Blue Sri Lanka; Triangletail Mosaic Tuxedo; Triangletail Halfblack Blonde; Roundtail Wild; Lyretail Wild.

Sphenops Molly

Poecilia sphenops

Other common names:
Green/Black/Liberty/
Mexican/Pointed-mouth
Molly

Family: Poeciliidae

Subfamily: Poeciliinae

Distribution: From Texas
south as far as Colombia;
also introduced elsewhere.

Size: Males around 2½in
(6cm); females around
3¼in (8cm).

Behavior: Peaceful shoaler.

Diet: Wide range of foods
accepted; a vegetable
component is essential.

Aquarium: Spacious,
planted, with some open
swimming space. Alkaline,
medium-hard water with
1 teaspoonful aquarium salt
per 1 Imp. gal (1⅕ U.S. gal/
4.5 l) important for long-
term health. Temperature
range: 77–82°F (25–28°C).

Breeding: Broods of around
80 fry produced every 5–7
weeks.

This highly variable, widely distributed species has given rise to a vast
array of cultivated varieties (many through hybridization), the best known
of which is the Black Molly. According to some authorities, it is the closely
related—and very similar—*P. mexicana* (Atlantic Molly) that is the true
ancestor of the aquarium strains. The confusion seems to have arisen
because both species were once regarded as one and the same. The
Liberty Molly, a form of Sphenops Molly, possesses a short but very
attractively colored and patterned dorsal fin. Both *P. mexicana* and
Sphenops Molly hybridize with *P. latipinna* (Sailfin Molly) and *P. velifera*
(Yucatán Molly).

Yucatán Molly

Poecilia velifera

Other common name:
Sailfin Molly

Family: Poeciliidae

Subfamily: Poeciliinae

Distribution: Yucatán
Peninsula (Mexico).

Size: Males up to 6in (15cm);
females up to 7in (18cm).

Behavior: Peaceful shoaler.
Males constantly display
toward each other.

Diet: Range of foods
accepted; a vegetable
component is essential.

Aquarium: Spacious,
planted, with some open
swimming space. Alkaline,
medium-hard water with
1 teaspoonful aquarium salt
per 1 Imp. gal (1⅕ U.S. gal/
4.5 l) important for long-
term health. Temperature
range: 77–82°F (25–28°C).

Breeding: Broods numbering
100 fry produced every 6–8
weeks are not uncommon.

Wild specimens of this species look similar to those of *P. latipinna*
(Sailfin Molly). However, Yucatán Molly is larger, and has a fuller
sail-like dorsal fin, with a greater number of fin rays (18 or 19 as
opposed to 14). Ease of hybridization between this species, *P. latipinna,*
and/or *P. sphenops* (Sphenops Molly) has resulted in a spectacular
range of aquarium varieties.

Black-barred Livebearer

Quintana atrizona

Other common name:
Barred Topminnow

Family: Poeciliidae

Subfamily: Poeciliinae

Distribution: Western Cuba.

Size: Males up to 1in
(2.5cm); females up to
1½in (4cm).

Behavior: Retiring shoaler.
Must not be kept with
boisterous tankmates.

Diet: Livefoods preferred,
but other diets accepted;
a vegetable component is
recommended.

Aquarium: Densely planted,
with surface vegetation
and little water movement.
Clean, slightly alkaline,
medium-hard water is
preferred. Temperature
range: 75–82°F (24–28°C).

Breeding: Broods numbering
on average around 25–30
fry are produced every 5–8
weeks.

When it is in peak condition, the Black-barred Livebearer is a delightful
species with vertical black body bars, black patches in the dorsal fin, light
blue in the pelvic and anal fins, and a silvery chest and belly. This small
species can be kept in very small tanks—in fact, in aquaria that are too
large, Black-barred Livebearers have a tendency toward dwarfism.

Swordtail

Xiphophorus helleri

Family: Poeciliidae

Subfamily: Poeciliinae

Distribution: Atlantic drainages in Central America and from Mexico to northwestern Honduras; also introduced into numerous locations outside its range, including Sri Lanka and South Africa.

Size: Males around 4in (10cm) excluding the sword; females around 4in (10cm); larger sizes also reported but generally not attained.

Behavior: Active shoaler. Males can be scrappy among themselves; either one male or a group should be maintained (if only two males are kept, one is likely to suffer).

Diet: Livefoods preferred, but other diets also accepted; a vegetable component is important.

Aquarium: Heavily planted, covered tank with some open space. Alkaline, medium-hard water is preferred. Temperature range: 70–77°F (21–25°C).

Breeding: Up to 200 fry are produced every 4–6 weeks.

True wild-type swordtails are hardly ever seen within the general hobby today. Considerable numbers of this highly variable species are, however, kept by livebearer enthusiasts who represent the best source of such specimens. Elsewhere, the vast majority of swordtails are available in a wide range of color and fin varieties that have been developed over many decades. Many of these cultivated fish are the result of crosses between Swordtail and one or other of two of its close relatives, *X. maculatus* (Southern Platy) and *X. variatus* (Sunset Platy).

Above: Red Green Wag Lyretail.

Above: Green.
Far left: Normal Finned Tricolor Swordtail.
Left: Normal Finned Green Neon Swordtail.
Above right: Green (Red form).
Right: Red Wag Lyretail.

Above: Normal Finned
   "Hamburg" Swordtail.
Right: Normal Finned
   "Berlin" Swordtail.

Southern Platy

Xiphophorus maculatus

Other common name:
Moonfish

Family: Poeciliidae

Subfamily: Poeciliinae

Distribution: From Veracruz in Mexico to Belize and Guatemala.

Size: Males to 1½in (4cm); females up to 2½in (6cm); cultivated varieties and hybrids may be larger.

Behavior: Placid shoaler.

Diet: Livefoods preferred, but other diets also accepted; a vegetable component is important.

Aquarium: Heavily planted, covered tank with some open space. Alkaline, medium-hard water preferred. Temperature range: 64–77°F (18–25°C).

Breeding: Around 50 fry are produced every 4–6 weeks.

Just like its famous relative, *X. helleri* (Swordtail), this species is inherently highly variable and has been developed into numerous color varieties. It has also been hybridized with both *X. helleri* and *X. variatus* (Sunset Platy). The best places to find true wild-type specimens are specialist livebearer societies.

Above left: Normal Finned
Comet Pineapple.
Left: Normal Finned
Multicolored Wagtail.
Inset: Normal Finned
Redback.

Slender Pygmy Swordtail

Xiphophorus pygmaeus

Other common name:
Dwarf Swordtail

Family: Poeciliidae

Subfamily: Poeciliinae

Distribution: Río Huichihuayan and lower part of Río Tancuilin (Mexico).

Size: Males up to 1½in (3.5cm); females very slightly larger.

Behavior: A very peaceful species, but best suited to a single-secies tank or a tank with other smaller species.

Diet: Live and dry foods accepted; a vegetable component is important.

Aquarium: Well planted tank with some surface vegetation and open spaces. Well-oxygenated, well-filtered water with slight movement is required; alkaline, medium-hard water is preferred. Temperature range: 75–79°F (24–26°C).

Breeding: Aquarium should always have more males than females. Females give birth among vegetation and the fry reach maturity after about 5 months.

Two naturally occurring forms of *Xiphophorus pygmaeus* are officially recognized: "Yellow" and "Blue." Overall, the background color of Slender Pygmy Swordtail is a grayish brown, fading to white on the belly. In the blue form, individuals have iridescent blue coloring on the sides; in the yellow form, known as Gold Pygmaeus, only the males exhibit the bright yellow coloring.

Sunset Platy

Xiphophorus variatus

Other common name:
Variatus Platy

Family: Poeciliidae

Subfamily: Poeciliinae

Distribution: Atlantic slope of Mexico.

Size: Males up to 2¼in (5.5cm); females approximately 2¾in (7cm); cultivated varieties may be larger.

Behavior: Peaceful shoaler.

Diet: Livefoods preferred, but other diets also accepted; vegetable component important.

Aquarium: Heavily planted, covered, with some open space. Alkaline medium-hard water preferred. Temperature range: 61–81°F (16–27°C).

Breeding: Usually around 50 fry (but up to 100) produced every 4–6 weeks.

This fish is more slender than *X. maculatus* (Southern Platy) and carries a number of bars on its body (which are lacking in *X. maculatus*). Many aquarium *X. variatus* specimens are hybrids between these two platy species or between *X. variatus* and *X. helleri* (Swordtail). At least one such variety even exhibits a pronounced sword, which is a characteristic of *X. helleri*, but not of either platy species.

Golden Bumblebee Goodeid

Allotoca dugesii (previously Allotoca dugesi)

Family: Goodeidae

Subfamily: Goodeinae

Distribution: Lerma River basin in Jalisco; several localities in Michoacán and Guanajuato (all Mexico).

Size: Males up to 2½in (6cm), usually smaller; females slightly larger.

Behavior: Can become aggressive. Best kept as a pair or as trio of one male and two females.

Diet: Live and dry foods accepted; a vegetable component is important.

Aquarium: Well planted tank with some surface vegetation, subdued lighting, and some rock shelter. Alkaline, medium-hard water is preferred. Temperature range: 64–75°F (18–24°C).

Breeding: Up to 76 fry reported, but broods generally smaller and produced at around 8-week intervals during breeding season (spring/summer).

Most males exhibit a beautiful golden-yellow sheen in the lower half of the body (below a dark horizontal body stripe). Females are often mottled and exhibit some blue in the lower half of the body. This is the most commonly seen species in the genus, although *A. maculata* (Opal Allotoca) from Jalisco, *A. catarinae* (Green Allotoca) from Michoacán, and *A. goslinei* (Banded Allotoca) from Jalisco, are also occasionally seen.

Ameca

Ameca splendens

Other common name:
Butterfly Goodeid

Family: Goodeidae

Subfamily: Goodeinae

Distribution: Ameca River basin in Jalisco (Mexico).

Size: Males up to 3in (8cm); females up to 4³/₄in (12cm).

Behavior: Active, generally tolerant species; older specimens may develop into fin-nippers.

Diet: All foods accepted; vegetable component is important.

Aquarium: Spacious, well planted tank with some floating vegetation and some open swimming spaces. Alkaline, medium-hard water is preferred. Temperature range: 64–84°F (18–29°C) tolerated, but 72–77°F (22–25°C) advisable in the long term.

Breeding: Up to 40 large fry can be produced during the warmer months of the year at around 8-week intervals.

The best known of the goodeids, Ameca caused a stir in the early 1970s when it was introduced into the hobby, largely because of its unusual reproductive strategy. Unlike in poeciliids, male goodeids do not have a gonopodium; instead, they have a distinct notch (a spermatopodium). Fertilization of eggs is internal, but the females cannot store sperm, so each brood requires separate insemination. After an egg has been fertilized within its egg sac, the female ejects it into the ovarian cavity, where development takes place. When the fry are born they are large and well developed. Although Ameca is under threat in the wild, the species itself is safe since all specimens currently in the hobby are captive bred.

Rainbow Goodeid

Characodon lateralis

Family: Goodeidae

Subfamily: Goodeinae

Distribution: Durango, Mexico (mainly Los Beros and Upper Mezquital River).

Size: Males up to 2½in (6cm) but usually smaller; females reported up to 3in (7.5cm) but usually smaller.

Behavior: Generally retiring. Best kept as a trio of 1 male and 2 females or a mixed shoal in a species tank set up specifically for it.

Diet: All foods accepted; a vegetable component is important.

Aquarium: Spacious, well planted tank with some floating vegetation and some open swimming spaces. Alkaline, medium-hard water is preferred. Temperature range: 64–75°F (18–24°C).

Breeding: Generally fewer than 20 fry produced at 8-week intervals.

This is one of the most colorful species in the family Goodeidae. It is also very variable, although most males in peak condition exhibit a great deal of red coloration, bluish-green reflective scales, and yellow-golden undersides. *C. audax* (Black Prince or Bold Goodeid)—also from Durango, Mexico—lacks the red coloration but has impressive black finnage.

Black-finned Goodeid

Goodea atripinnis

Family: Goodeidae

Subfamily: Goodeinae

Distribution: Durango and Jalisco in Mexico.

Size: Males up to 4³/₄in (12cm); females up to 8in (20cm).

Behavior: Occasional fin-nipper, best kept as a shoal in a species tank set up specifically for this species.

Diet: All foods accepted; a vegetable component is essential.

Aquarium: Spacious, well-planted tank with some floating vegetation and some open swimming spaces. Alkaline, medium-hard water is preferred. Temperature range: 64–75°F (18–24°C).

Breeding: Around 50 fry produced every 6–8 weeks.

At least four subspecies of this substantial species are known: *G. a. atripinnis* and *G. a. martini* (Martin's Black-finned Goodeid) from Río de Morelia and Lago de Cuitzeo (Michoacán), *G. a. luitpoldi* (Luitpold's Goodeid) from Lago de Patzcuaro (Michoacán), and *G. a. xaliscone* from Laguna Chapala (Jalisco). They differ slightly in coloration and small details but have similar characteristics and requirements.

Gold-breasted Ilyodon

Ilyodon furcidens

Family: Goodeidae

Subfamily: Goodeinae

Distribution: Mesa Central in Mexico.

Size: Males around 3½in (9cm); females around 4in (10cm).

Behavior: Active, generally peaceful shoalers.

Diet: All foods accepted; vegetable component important.

Aquarium: Spacious, well-planted tank with some floating vegetation and some open swimming spaces. Alkaline, medium-hard water is preferred. Temperature range: 64–77°F (18–25°C).

Breeding: Around 35 fry produced every 7–8 weeks during the warmer months.

There is considerable difference of opinion regarding the identity of the four *Ilyodon* "species." Some authors believe them to be valid species in their own right, while others consider them all to be subspecies of *I. furcidens*. Generally speaking, *I. furcidens* and *I. xantusi* (Xantus' Ilyodon) are believed to be very similar to each other—possibly variants of the single species, *I. furcidens*. Similarly, *I. lennoni* (Lennon's Ilyodon) and *I. whitei* could be variants of *I. whitei* (White's Ilyodon). All have similar behavior characteristics and aquarium requirements.

Green Goodeid

Xenoophorus captivus

Other common name:
Captivus

Family: Goodeidae

Subfamily: Goodeinae

Distribution: San Luis de Potosí (Mexico).

Size: Males up to 2¹/₂in (6cm); females slightly larger.

Behavior: Active, generally tolerant species. Older specimens may develop into fin-nippers.

Diet: All foods accepted; a vegetable component is important.

Aquarium: Spacious, well-planted tank with some floating vegetation and some open swimming spaces. Alkaline, medium-hard water is preferred. Temperature range: 68–77°F (20–25°C).

Breeding: Up to 40 large fry can be produced during the warmer months of the year at around 8-week intervals.

This robust species is similar in overall appearance to *Ameca splendens* (Ameca). Males in peak condition are richly adorned with greenish-blue reflective scales on a dark background. In the wild the Green Goodeid is on the brink of extinction, although three geographical variants are known: *captivus*, *erro*, and *exsul*.

Orange-tailed Goodeid

Xenotoca eiseni

Other common name:
Red-tailed Goodeid

Family: Goodeidae

Subfamily: Goodeinae

Distribution: Nayarit and
Jalisco (Mexico).

Size: Males around 2¹⁄₂in
(6cm); females around
2³⁄₄in (7cm).

Behavior: Shoaling; displays
fin-nipping tendencies.

Diet: All foods accepted;
a vegetable component
is important.

Aquarium: Spacious, well-
planted tank with some
floating vegetation and
some open swimming
spaces. Alkaline, medium-
hard water is preferred.
Temperature range: 64–84°F
(18–29°C) tolerated, but
72–77°F (22–25°C) advisable
in the long term.

Breeding: Around 30 fry are
produced every 7–8 weeks.

Mature males possess an impressive hump behind the head and a
very deep body. The two dominant colors in mature males are blue—
particularly on the posterior half of the body—and an orange or reddish
caudal peduncular area. Several forms of the species are known: one with
a great deal of blue in the body (Nayarit), a blotched one (San Marco), and
one with some body spots (Spotted). Of these, the San Marco type is the
only one found in the wild—around San Marco in Jalisco, Mexico.

Crescent Goodeid

Zoogoneticus tequila

Family: Goodeidae

Subfamily: Goodeinae

Distribution: Ameca River drainage system in Río Teuchitlán, Mexico.

Size: Males up to 2¹⁄₂in (6cm); females up to 3in (8cm).

Behavior: Calm, peaceful species; likes to hide among vegetation.

Diet: Livefoods; floating freeze-dried, deep-frozen, and other diets.

Aquarium: Well planted with plenty of vegetation at the sides and on the surface. Water chemistry not critical but hard to medium-soft water is preferred, with different degrees of hardness causing slight color variation. Temperature range: 72–79°F (22–26°C).

Breeding: Females give birth to 3–18 reasonably large fry at a time, usually every 4–6 weeks during breeding season.

Zoogoneticus tequila is commonly known as the Crescent Goodeid because of the crescent-shaped band of orange exhibited on the tail of the males. Since its discovery and classification in the 1990s, this species has become extinct in the wild, but conservation work is being undertaken to preserve these fish.

Wrestling Halfbeak

Dermogenys pusilla (previously Dermogenys pusillus)

Other common name:
Malayan Halfbeak

Synonym: *Dermogenys pusilla*

Family: Hemirhamphidae

Subfamily: Hemirhamphinae

Distribution: Malaysia and surrounding regions.

Size: Males reported up to 2½in (6cm) but usually smaller; females up to 3in (8cm) but usually smaller.

Behavior: Surface swimmer; often quarrelsome and sometimes nervous.

Diet: Livefoods; floating freeze-dried, deep-frozen, and other diets.

Aquarium: Well covered tank with plenty of open surface space (free of vegetation), subdued lighting, and submerged vegetation planted in clumps along sides and back. Neutral to alkaline medium-hard water with 1 teaspoonful of salt per 1 Imp. gal (1⅕ U.S. gal/ 4.5 l) recommended. Temperature range: 64–86°F (18–30°C).

Breeding: Up to 40 (but usually fewer) very large fry produced every 4–8 weeks.

Of the 15 or so species in the genus *Dermogenys*, *D. pusillus* is the only one encountered with any regularity. Two subspecies are generally recognized: *D. p. borealis* with bright yellow and/or red coloration on the dorsal, caudal, and anal fins, and *D. p. pusillus*, whose coloration is mainly restricted to the dorsal fin. A golden variant of *D. p. borealis* is occasionally available.

Long-snout Halfbeak

Hemirhamphodon pogonognathus

The six *Hemirhamphodon* species—including *H. pogonognathus*, the aptly named Long-snout Halfbeak—are all found in freshwater from the southern part of the Malay Peninsula south to Sumatra and east to Borneo. They can easily be distinguished from the *Dermogenys* halfbeaks by the presence of teeth in their lower jaw and by the positioning of the dorsal fin, the base of which lies in front of the anal fin.

Other common names: Long-nosed Halfbeak, Thread-jawed Halfbeak

Synonyms: *Dermogenys pogonognathus*, *Hemirhamphus pogonognathus*

Family: Hemirhamphidae

Subfamily: Hemirhamphinae

Distribution: Southern Thailand, Malaysia, Singapore, and Indonesia.

Size: Males up to 3½in (9cm); females up to 2½in (6cm).

Behavior: Lively surface swimmer; aggressive toward members of its own species.

Diet: Livefoods preferred.

Aquarium: Well covered tank with background vegetation, floating plants, and plenty of open space required; subdued lighting and a slight current are recommended. Neutral to alkaline medium-hard water. No salt required. Temperature range: 72–82°F (22–28°C).

Breeding: Female produces 30–40 fry (on average 1–4 per day) over a period of 2–3 weeks; fry are about ½in (12mm) long at birth and have very large eyes.

Celebes Halfbeak

Nomorhamphus liemi

Family: Hemirhamphidae

Subfamily: Hemirhamphinae

Distribution: Areas around Maros in southern Sulawesi.

Size: Males around 6cm (2½in); females reported up to 4in (10cm).

Behavior: Surface swimmer; considerably more peaceful than *Dermogenys pusillus* (Wrestling Halfbeak).

Diet: Livefoods; floating freeze-dried, deep-frozen, and other diets.

Aquarium: Well covered, with plenty of open surface space (i.e. free of vegetation), subdued lighting, and submerged vegetation planted in clumps along sides and back of aquarium. Neutral to alkaline medium-hard water. No salt required. Temperature range: 72–79°F (22–26°C).

Breeding: 10–15 very large fry are produced every 4–8 weeks.

Of the eight or so species in this genus, Celebes Halfbeak is the most frequently available. Its common name, while being appropriate in that the species is found in Sulawesi (Celebes), would seem better suited to *N. celebensis*—also from Sulawesi—which is normally referred to as Northern Harlequin Halfbeak. Two subspecies of *N. liemi* are recognized: *N. l. liemi* (known as both Celebes Halfbeak and Southern Harlequin Halfbeak) and *N. l. snijdersi* (Snijder's Halfbeak).

MISCELLANEOUS FISH

In addition to the groups featured in the previous sections, there are many others represented in the aquarium hobby. Some have just a single representative or only a few, but like *Oryzias latipes* (Medaka), they are well known. In other instances, while the total number of species that can be obtained may be more numerous, many of them are little known. The pages that follow contain a selection of both types.

Below: *Scatophagus ornatus.* **Right:** *Dichotomyctere ocellatus.*

Blue-spotted Sunfish

Enneacanthus gloriosus

Family: Centrarchidae

Distribution: Atlantic and Gulf Slope drainages of the United States from New York in the north, south to Florida, and west to Mississippi and Louisiana.

Size: Up to 3¾in (9.5cm).

Behavior: A shoaling species except at breeding time, when males become highly territorial and aggressive.

Diet: Livefoods preferred, but deep-frozen, freeze-dried, and other commercial formulations accepted.

Aquarium: Spacious, heavily planted with cool-water species, and with numerous hiding places and a coarse sand or a fine gravel substratum. Neutral to slightly alkaline, medium-hard water preferred. Temperature range: 50–72°F (10–22°C).

Breeding: Lowering water level to around 6in (15cm) seems to enhance chances of success. Eggs are laid in a depression dug by male, who also defends the brood.

This sparkling silvery fish with reflective blue spots is probably the most attractive of the three species in its genus. It has been in the hobby since the early 1900s but, owing to its low temperature requirements, it has never acquired great popularity among tropical freshwater aquarists.

Redbreast Sunfish

Lepomis auritus

Family: Centrarchidae

Distribution: Eastern rivers of the United States and Canada.

Size: Approximately 9½in (24cm).

Behavior: Generally peaceful but territorial and aggressive during breeding.

Diet: Livefoods preferred, but deep-frozen, freeze-dried, and other commercial formulations accepted.

Aquarium: Spacious, heavily planted with cool-water species, and with numerous hiding places and a coarse sand or a fine gravel substratum. Neutral to slightly alkaline, medium-hard water recommended. Temperature range: 39–72°F (4–22°C).

Breeding: Lowering water level to around 6in (15cm) seems to enhance chances of success. Female lays approximately 1,000 eggs in a depression dug by male, who also defends the brood.

Characteristic of the Redbreast Sunfish is a yellow belly that is (as its common name implies) sometimes orange or rust colored. What is more distinctive, however, is the particularly long "ear" (opercle flap) that can reach in excess of 1in (2.5cm) long in some adults.

Pumpkinseed

Lepomis gibbosus

Family: Centrarchidae

Distribution: Widely distributed along the Atlantic drainages of the United States; also introduced into other areas of North America, Canada, and Europe, where it has become established in a number of locations.

Size: Up to 16in (40cm) but usually smaller.

Behavior: Generally peaceful but territorial and aggressive during breeding.

Diet: Livefoods preferred, but deep-frozen, freeze-dried, and other commercial formulations accepted.

Aquarium: Spacious, with large open swimming area; heavily planted with cool-water species, and with numerous hiding places and a coarse sand or fine gravel substratum. Neutral to slightly alkaline, medium-hard water is preferred. Temperature range: 39–72°F (4–22°C).

Breeding: Lowering water level to around 6in (15cm) seems to enhance chances of success. Eggs are laid in a depression dug by male, who also defends the brood.

First imported into Europe in 1877, this stunning species with its reflective blue speckling is the most frequently kept of all the sunfish species. Tough and adaptable, it is capable of becoming established in most temperate habitats, so it is essential to ensure that it neither escapes nor is released into nonnative waters. Such cautionary advice applies not just to the Pumpkinseed but to all other sunfishes and similarly adaptable species. Since the Pumpkinseed can attain a substantial size, it will outgrow most average-sized aquaria, a factor that requires consideration prior to purchase.

Everglades Pygmy Sunfish

Elassoma evergladei

Other common name:
Florida Pygmy Sunfish

Family: Elassomatidae
(referred to as Elassomidae
by some authors)

Distribution: From North
Carolina to Florida, including
the Everglades.

Size: Around 1½in (3.5cm).

Behavior: Timid, sometimes
retiring; best kept in a tank
specifically set aside for it;
males become territorial at
breeding time.

Diet: Livefoods preferred, but
other diets also accepted.

Aquarium: Heavily planted,
with hiding places, open
swimming area, and sandy
substratum. Mature, neutral
to alkaline, medium-hard
water recommended.
Temperature range:
46–86°F (8–30°C).

Breeding: Eggs are laid
among fine-leaved
vegetation. Hatching
takes 2–3 days.

The Everglades Pygmy Sunfish is the best known of the six species in the
genus. It has been available for nearly three quarters of a century and is
still much sought after by coldwater aquarists. It is not, however, a
community fish that can be kept with other, larger, cool-water fish
such as goldfish.

Perch

Perca fluviatilis

Family: Percidae

Distribution: Europe, but also introduced elsewhere.

Size: Up to 18in (45cm), but usually smaller.

Behavior: Shoaling predator during juvenile phase but tends to be a loner as it matures; can be kept only with tankmates too large for it to swallow.

Diet: Almost exclusively livefoods (invertebrates and fish).

Aquarium: Large, well filtered, well oxygenated with ample plant cover and gravel substratum. Neutral, soft to medium-hard water preferred, but some variation tolerated. Temperature range: 46–68°F (8–20°C).

Breeding: Very large setup necessary. Eggs are laid among plants or rocks and may take up to 3 weeks to hatch.

The Perch can be identified by its distinctive body markings. It has six or more bands on the sides of its body and a black blotch behind the first dorsal fin. Its pelvic, anal, and caudal fins have reddish coloration. Its back is humped behind the head, and it has a large mouth. The caudal fin is slightly forked and the first dorsal fin has up to 17 strong spines. However, although it can tolerate a wider temperature range than other members of its family, this beautifully marked species is best reserved for the specialist.

Marbled Sleeper

Oxyeleotris marmorata (previously Oxyleotris marmoratus)

Family: Eleotridae (subfamily Eleotridinae—*sensu* Hoese and Gill)

Subfamily: Butinae (*sensu* Nelson)

Distribution: Widely distributed in Southeast Asia.

Size: Up to 20in (50cm) but often smaller.

Behavior: Sedentary nocturnal predator; can be housed only with tankmates that are too large for it to swallow.

Diet: Wide range of chunky foods accepted, but livefoods preferred.

Aquarium: Spacious, well planted, with a fine-grained substratum, large hiding places, and subdued lighting. Neutral, medium-hard water recommended. Temperature range: 72–82°F (22–28°C).

Breeding: No documented accounts currently available.

The Marbled Sleeper is one of the very few members of its subfamily encountered in aquaria. (*Butis butis*—the highly adaptable, so-called Crazy Fish—is another occasional find). Like its relatives, Marbled Sleeper is predominantly a bottom-dwelling predator. It can grow to a large size and is not suitable for beginners.

Striped Sleeper Goby

Dormitator maculatus

Other common names: Fat Sleeper Goby, Spotted Goby

Family: Eleotridae (subfamily Eleotridinae—*sensu* Hoese and Gill)

Subfamily: Eleotrinae or Eleotridinae (*sensu* Nelson)

Distribution: Atlantic coast of tropical South America.

Size: Up to 10in (25cm) reported but usually smaller.

Behavior: Territorial predator that tends to dig.

Diet: Livefoods, including fish; invertebrate livefoods also taken as well as (more reluctantly) deep-frozen and freeze-dried preparations.

Aquarium: Spacious, with large, adequately spaced out shelters, e.g. caves, and a relatively fine-grained substratum. Salt-tolerant plants must be suitably protected against digging activities. Well-filtered, alkaline, hardish water, with about 2 teaspoonfuls of aquarium salt added to every 1 Imp. gal (1⅕ U.S.gal/4.5 l). Preferred Temperature range: 72–77°F (22–25°C).

Breeding: Challenging in aquaria. Eggs are laid on a pre-cleaned site, e.g. stone. Hatching takes about 1 day.

The Striped Sleeper Goby is a sturdy species that, despite its hardy appearance, is unable to adapt fully to pure freshwater conditions. It is, however, a good candidate for brackish water setups housing similar-sized tankmates. This is not a species for beginners.

Empire Goby

Hypseleotris compressa

Other common names: Empire Gudgeon, Carp Gudgeon

Family: Eleotridae (subfamily Eleotridinae—*sensu* Hoese and Gill)

Subfamily: Eleotrinae or Eleotridinae (*sensu* Nelson)

Distribution: Australia and New Guinea.

Size: Up to 4¼in (11cm), but often smaller.

Behavior: Territorial and predatory, but less so than some other family members.

Diet: Livefoods preferred, but deep-frozen, freeze-dried, and some other diets also accepted.

Aquarium: Spacious, well planted, with an open area containing some largish smooth-rounded or flat stones. Neutral or slightly alkaline, moderately hard water with 1 teaspoonful of aquarium salt to each 1 Imp. gal (1⅕ U.S. gal/4.5 l) is advisable, although this species will also accept freshwater conditions (carry transitions out gradually). Temperature range: 54–82°F (12–28°C).

Breeding: Eggs are laid on a pre-cleaned stone and protected by male. Hatching takes 1 day or slightly less.

Fully mature males of this species are spectacular, especially when in breeding colors. The Empire Goby is somewhat more flexible than many other sleepers; it is also more tolerant of tankmates, making it a better choice for mixed collections.

Purple-striped Sleeper Goby

Mogurnda mogurnda

Other common names:
Purple-spotted Trout,
Northern Trout, Sleeper
Goby/Gudgeon

Family: Eleotridae (subfamily
Eleotridinae—*sensu* Hoese
and Gill)

Subfamily: Eleotrinae or
Eleotridinae (*sensu* Nelson)

Distribution: Central and
north Australia, New
Guinea.

Size: Up to 7in (17.5cm), but
often smaller.

Behavior: Males become
aggressive and territorial
during breeding; less so
at other times.

Diet: Livefoods preferred, but
other diets accepted.

Aquarium: Sufficiently
spacious and planted,
with open area and with
strategically placed caves
or shelters around which
several males can establish
territories. Neutral to slightly
alkaline, hardish water
preferred. Temperature
range: 72–86°F (22–30°C).

Breeding: Eggs are laid in
caves or on flat surfaces
(including bogwood or even
the aquarium panes) and
are guarded by male.
Hatching can take 5–9 days.

Of the several common names for this beautifully marked species,
the Purple-striped Sleeper Goby and Sleeper Goby or Gudgeon are the
most appropriate; the connection with trout embodied in the others
is misleading because there is none. The slightly smaller but equally
beautiful *M. adspersa*, also known as the Purple-spotted Gudgeon
(from eastern and southeastern Australia), has similar requirements
but is less frequently available.

Peacock Goby

Tateurndina ocellicauda

Other common name:
Peacock Gudgeon

Family: Eleotridae (subfamily Eleotridinae—*sensu* Hoese and Gill)

Subfamily: Eleotrinae or Eleotridinae (*sensu* Nelson)

Distribution: New Guinea.

Size: Up to 3in (7.5cm) reported but usually smaller.

Behavior: Peaceful; should not be kept with boisterous tankmates.

Diet: Livefoods preferred, but a range of other diets accepted.

Aquarium: Well planted, with a number of hiding places or caves. Softish, slightly acid or neutral water preferred, though some deviation tolerated if adjustments are carried out gradually. Temperature range: 72–81°F (22–27°C).

Breeding: Eggs are laid on the roof of a cave or other hiding place (although spawning in the open also occurs). The eggs are guarded by male. Hatching takes about 7 days.

With its red markings brilliantly displayed against a blue background and yellowish belly, this species is the most colorful of all the sleeper gobies. The females of the species are rounder in shape than the males and the yellow banding on the edges of the dorsal and anal fins is more pronounced. The Peacock Goby achieved great popularity during the mid-1980s and the 1990s. It has now been widely bred in captivity and is one of the most often seen eleotrids.

Bumblebee Goby

Brachygobius nunus

Other common name:
Gold-banded Goby

Synonym: *B. doriae*

Family: Gobiidae

Subfamily: Gobiinae

Distribution: Southeast Asia.

Size: Around 1³/₄in (4.5cm), but often smaller.

Behavior: Peaceful and retiring toward other tankmates (which must be neither large nor boisterous), but territorial toward conspecifics.

Diet: Livefoods preferred, but deep-frozen and (sometimes) waterlogged freeze-dried formulations may be accepted.

Aquarium: Smallish, well planted, with several small caves or snail shells. Hard, alkaline water preferred, with up to 1 tablespoonful of aquarium salt per 1 Imp. gal (1⅕ U.S. gal/4.5 l) added. Temperature range: 75–86°F (24–30°C).

Breeding: Eggs are laid in caves or snail shells and are guarded by male. Hatching takes about 4 days.

The genus *Brachygobius* is in great need of closer study, since several similar-looking species appear under a number of (often disputed) names. *Brachygobius nunus*, for example, is regarded by some as synonymous with *B. doriae*, while some people doubt the validity of the most frequently encountered name, *B. xanthozona*. In addition, there is *B. aggregatus*. All species have the same basic requirements and characteristics.

Knight Goby

Stigmatogobius sadanundio

Other common name:
Spotted Goby

Family: Gobiidae

Subfamily: Gobionellinae

Distribution: Indonesia and Philippines.

Size: Up to 3¹/₂in (8.5cm).

Behavior: Males are territorial, in particular toward their own species but also (somewhat less so) toward other bottom-dwelling tankmates.

Diet: Livefoods preferred, but deep-frozen, freeze-dried, and other formulations may also be accepted; algal supplement recommended.

Aquarium: Well planted (with salt-tolerant species); a fine-grained substratum and several caves or shelters recommended. Well-filtered, hard, alkaline water with 1 teaspoonful of salt per 1 Imp. gal (1¹/₅ U.S. gal/4.5 l). Soft water must be avoided. Temperature range: 68–79°F (20–26°C).

Breeding: Eggs are laid on the roof of a cave, and they and the fry are protected by both parents.

This sturdy-looking fish can adapt to freshwater (it is often found in such habitats in the wild), but in aquaria it appears not to fare so well in the absence of salt. The male Knight Goby has a pale silver body dotted with black spots. Females have similar markings but with more yellow.

Blotched Mudskipper

Periophthalmus barbarus

Family: Gobiidae

Subfamily: Oxudercinae

Distribution: Widespread in estuaries in Africa, the Red Sea, Madagascar, Southeast Asia, and Australia.

Size: Up to 6in (15cm).

Behavior: Territorial; needs an exposed area onto which it can climb.

Diet: Livefoods taken, especially from the surface of exposed substrates.

Aquarium: Spacious, covered, with reduced water level and an exposed "beach" area or rocks and/or bogwood. Hard, alkaline water with 1 teaspoonful of salt per 1 Imp. gal (1 ⅕ U.S. gal/4.5 l) is necessary. Ensure that a high level of humidity is maintained above the water surface. Temperature range: 77–86°F (25–30°C).

Breeding: No documented accounts currently available.

Mudskippers are fascinating fish that live in burrows on mangrove flats and spend a great deal of time out of water grazing the mud surface for microalgae and other tiny organisms. All species can prove challenging to keep and are not suitable for beginners. Male Blotched Mudskippers have spectacularly colored dorsal fins that they flick open and shut during displays. Two other species are also occasionally available: *P. papilio* (Butterfly Mudskipper) and *P. vulgaris* (Blue Flagfin); both have similar characteristics and requirements to those of *P. barbarus*.

Emerald River Goby

Stiphodon elegans

Synonym: *Stiphodon ornatus elegans*

Family: Gobiidae

Subfamily: Sicydiinae

Distribution: Southeast Asia.

Size: Around 1³/₄in (4.5cm).

Behavior: Active but peaceful.

Diet: Livefoods preferred but other diets, including algae, accepted.

Aquarium: Well filtered, planted, with fine-grained substratum, some pebbles, and a water current (e.g. as produced by a powerhead outlet). Neutral, medium-hard water preferred, but some deviation (though not extreme) tolerated. Temperature range: 75–81°F (24–27°C).

Breeding: Challenging but achievable in aquaria. However, no documented accounts currently available.

The Emerald River Goby is one of the more recent species of goby to appear in the hobby. The lightish-colored body has a few irregular dark bands extending from snout to tail, but fully mature males develop the shiny emerald coloration indicated by the species' common name.

Japanese Medaka

Oryzias latipes

Other common names:
Golden Medaka, Japanese Ricefish, Geisha Girl

Family: Oryziidae (referred to as Oryziatidae by some authors)

Distribution: China, Japan, and South Korea; reported from Java and Malaysia.

Size: Around 1½in (4cm).

Behavior: Active shoaler.

Diet: Wide range of foods accepted.

Aquarium: Well illuminated, well planted, with open swimming areas, some clear surface area (i.e. free of floating vegetation), and water movement. Water chemistry not critical, but slightly alkaline, medium-hard water preferred. Temperature range: below 15°C (59°F) to above 28°C (82°F). These extremes should, however, be avoided in the long term.

Breeding: Eggs may be fertilized internally or externally; either way, the female carries them attached to the vent for a time before depositing them among fine-leaved vegetation. Hatching takes 7–10 days.

Virtually all the medakas currently in the hobby are golden—this being considerably more colorful than the wild type. Japanese Medaka is popular not just because of its color but because of its breeding behavior. Of the other ten or so species in the genus, the following are most often seen: *O. celebensis* (Celebes Medaka) from Sulawesi; *O. javanicus* (Javanese Medaka) from Java; and *O. melastigma* (Spotted Medaka) from the area around Calcutta (India). *O. nigrimas* (Black Medaka) from Lake Poso in Sulawesi—in which some males are jet black—is rarely seen. All have similar requirements.

Indian Glassfish

Parambassis ranga

Synonym: *Chanda ranga*

Family: Chandidae (referred to as Ambassidae by some authors)

Distribution: India, Myanmar, and Thailand.

Size: Up to 3in (8cm) but usually smaller.

Behavior: A somewhat territorial (but generally peaceful) and sometimes timid shoaler.

Diet: Livefoods preferred, but deep-frozen and freeze-dried diets readily accepted; dry foods reluctantly taken.

Aquarium: Heavily planted (with salt-tolerant or artificial plants), dark substratum, shelters, and subdued lighting. Mature, hard, alkaline water, with some salt added—(1–3 teaspoonfuls per 1 Imp. gal/1⅕ U.S. gal/4.5 l)—to maintain long-term health. Temperature range: 64–86°F (18–30°C).

Breeding: Challenging. Eggs are scattered among fine-leaved vegetation—often following exposure of the aquarium to morning sun. Hatching takes 1 day. Fry are difficult to raise because of their very small size.

This is the most naturally colorful of the three species that are generally available. *Parambassis (Chanda) commersonii* (Commerson's Glassfish) and *P. (C.) wolffii* (Wolff's Glassfish) are larger: in the wild—not in aquaria—the former attains around 4in (10cm) and the latter 7 in (20cm). During the 1990s "painted" glassfish—artificially colored (injected) fish — became widely available from Far East sources. Demand for them has declined dramatically both from consumers and dealers, with the natural types regaining some of their former popularity. Injected specimens lose most of their color after several months and also appear to be prone to lymphocystis (cauliflower disease), a nonlethal virus infection.

Archer Fish

Toxotes jaculatrix

Synonym: *Toxotes jaculator*

Family: Toxotidae

Distribution: Gulf of Aden to Australia, including India and Southeast Asia.

Size: Up to 10in (25cm) but usually much smaller.

Behavior: Generally tolerant of tankmates, including conspecifics; may be kept in a shoal if accommodation is sufficiently spacious.

Diet: Almost exclusively livefoods, but may accept floating freeze-dried and deep-frozen formulations. If flying insects can be provided, they will be shot down over a period of time.

Aquarium: Tightly covered. Deep-sided, but only partially filled to create an above-water space for twigs or branches that can act as perches for insects. Plants used for underwater decor must be salt-tolerant or artificial. Prefers neutral to alkaline, medium-hard water. Important to add 1 teaspoonful of salt per 1 Imp. gal (1 ⅕ U.S. gal/4.5 l). Temperature range: 77–86°F (25–30°C).

Breeding: No documented accounts of aquarium breeding available.

This is the most widely available member of its genus and family, although *T. chatareus* (Seven-spotted Archer Fish) is seen with increasing regularity. Two other species are also seen, but only rarely: *T. lorentzi* (Primitive Archer Fish) and *T. oligolepis* (Few-scaled Archer Fish). All possess the remarkable ability to eject powerful jets of water to shoot down prey, usually insects, from branches located as much as 5ft (1.5m) above the water.

Scat
Scatophagus argus

Other common name: Argus Fish

Family: Scatophagidae

Distribution: Widely distributed in brackish and marine waters in the Indian and Pacific Oceans.

Size: Up to 12in (30cm).

Behavior: Lively peaceful shoaler.

Diet: All foods accepted; a vegetable component is essential.

Aquarium: Large and deep, with clumps of salt-tolerant (or artificial) plants*, and substantial open swimming areas. Well-filtered, alkaline, hard water important. Add 1 teaspoonful of salt per 1 Imp. gal (1⅕ U.S. gal/4.5 l) to aquaria housing juveniles, gradually doubling this concentration as they grow. Eventually, nearly (or fully) saline conditions should be provided for adults. Temperature range: 68–82°F (20–28°C).

Breeding: No documented accounts available.

***NOTE:** It has been reported that the Java fern (*Microsorum pteropus*) is toxic to scats.

Juvenile scats are very attractively marked, although some of the intensity of coloration is lost as they grow. A reddish "species," or "subspecies," is also available and is referred to as *S. "rubrifrons,"* or *S. argus atromaculatus*. However, it is generally accepted that it is just a naturally occurring color variety of *S. agrus. S. tetracanthus* (African Scat) is only rarely seen in the hobby. *Selenotoca multifasciata* (Silver Scat) from Australia—also known as Striped Butterfish or Striped Scat—is occasionally available and has similar characteristics and requirements. In the wild, adult Scats are generally estuarine or saltwater fish. Juveniles enter freshwater, and are usually the Scats that are available in shops.

Mono

Monodactylus argenteus

Other common names:
Moon Fish, Finger Fish,
Silver Batfish, Butter Bream

Family: Monodactylidae

Distribution: Widely
distributed in brackish water
in tropical regions from
Africa to Asia and Australia.

Size: Up to 10in (25cm) but
usually smaller.

Behavior: Peaceful shoaler,
but larger specimens may
prey on small fish.

Diet: All foods accepted;
a vegetable component
is essential.

Aquarium: Large and deep,
with clumps of salt-tolerant
(or artificial) plants, and
substantial open swimming
areas. Well-filtered, alkaline,
hard water important. Add
1 teaspoonful of salt per 1
Imp. gal (1⅕ U.S. gal/4.5 l)
to aquaria housing juveniles,
gradually doubling this
concentration as they grow.
Eventually, nearly (or fully)
saline conditions should
be provided for adults.
Temperature range:
68–82°F (20–28°C).

Breeding: No documented
accounts available.

Usually sold as juveniles, Monos will—given appropriate conditions—
eventually grow into large fish. Juveniles often occur in freshwater, but
adults require brackish conditions. As juveniles grow, they lose their pelvic
fins either partially or entirely. In *Psettus (Monodactylus) sebae* (Seba
Mono), the body is deeper than it is long, particularly in young specimens.
It is also a little less tolerant of freshwater conditions than the Mono.

Green Puffer

Dichotomyctere fluviatilis (previously Tetraodon fluviatilis)

Family: Tetraodontidae

Distribution: Freshwater and brackish regions in Southeast Asia.

Size: Up to 6³/₄in (17cm).

Behavior: Increasingly intolerant and aggressive with age, particularly toward conspecifics; exhibits fin-nipping tendencies.

Diet: Wide range of foods accepted, including aquatic snails and succulent plants.

Aquarium: Spacious, with several shelters, fine-grained substratum, and tough and/or unpalatable plants— or their artificial equivalents —arranged in clumps along the sides and back, leaving an open swimming area along front. Neutral to alkaline hard water with about 1 teaspoonful of salt per 1 Imp. gal (1¹/₅ U.S. gal/4.5 l) recommended. Temperature range: 75–82°F (24–28°C).

Breeding: Challenging in aquaria; brackish conditions important. Eggs are laid on stone and are guarded by male. Hatching takes around 6–7 days.

This is probably the species of puffer most frequently seen in shops. As its species name indicates, Green Puffer can be found in at least some freshwater habitats in the wild. However, for peak long-term health, brackish conditions are recommended.

Butterflyfish

Pantodon buchholzi

Family: Pantodontidae

Distribution: West Africa: Cameroon, D. R. Congo, and Nigeria.

Size: Up to 10cm (4in).

Behavior: Surface predator; can be aggressive toward other surface swimmers but tolerant toward tankmates that occupy the lower levels of the aquarium.

Diet: Predominantly livefoods, but will take deep-frozen and freeze-dried diets, and may accept some floating dry formulations.

Aquarium: Spacious, well covered, with large open surface areas—but also incorporating some floating vegetation. Soft, slightly acid water, preferably tannin-stained, preferred, but some deviation tolerated. Temperature range: 73–86°F (23–30°C).

Breeding: Challenging in aquaria; floating eggs are produced over several days. Hatching takes 1½–2 days.

This challenging fish, known in the hobby since the early 1900s, has never been available in large numbers. Contrary to reports (and its common name), the Butterflyfish does not "fly," i.e. it does not flap its winglike pectoral fins. It is, however, able to glide for short distances.

Elephantnose

Gnathonemus petersii

Other common name:
Peter's Elephantnose

Family: Mormyridae

Distribution: Central and West Africa.

Size: Up to 9in (23cm) reported, but usually smaller.

Behavior: Predominantly a bottom dweller; crepuscular and nocturnal; territorial toward conspecifics; burrows in substratum in search of food.

Diet: Distinct preference for livefoods, but will also accept other formulations, particularly deep-frozen and freeze-dried diets.

Aquarium: Spacious, well filtered, with clumps of vegetation, open spaces, and fine-grained substratum (very important). A "moonlight" fluorescent tube to facilitate nighttime viewing is recommended. Softish, slightly acid to neutral water is preferred, but some deviation tolerated. Temperature range: 72–82°F (22–28°C).

Breeding: No documented accounts are available.

Elephantnoses use weak electrical pulses to communicate with each other and to find their way around in the often murky waters of their natural habitat. All species are challenging to keep, although modern-day foods and a deeper understanding of these somewhat unusual fish make their upkeep much easier than it used to be.

Clown Knifefish

Chitala chitala (previously Notopterus chitala)

Family: Notopteridae

Distribution: Widely distributed in Southeast Asia.

Size: Up to c.39in (1m) reported but usually smaller.

Behavior: Adults are solitary predators, active mainly at dusk and during the night. Juveniles may be kept together, at least for a time.

Diet: Large livefoods, including live fish, preferred —a factor that needs due consideration prior to purchase; chunky, meat-based or fish-based formulations also accepted.

Aquarium: Large, well covered, well filtered, well planted, with subdued lighting and large shelters, e.g. substantial pieces of bogwood. A "moonlight" fluorescent tube will facilitate nighttime viewing. Water chemistry not critical, but softish, slightly acid water preferred; quality must be good. Temperature range: 75–86°F (24–30°C).

Breeding: No documented accounts of aquarium breeding currently available.

The Clown Knifefish is generally available as small, very attractively marked juveniles. Adults are very large (a factor that should be borne in mind at the time of purchase). If their needs can be catered to, they make very interesting fish for aquaria, but they are not suitable for new aquarists. Two other species, *Papyrocranus (Notopterus) afer* (African Featherfin or Knifefish) and *N. notopterus* (Asian Knifefish), are also available. They have similar requirements to Clown Knifefish.

African Knifefish

Xenomystus nigri

Family: Notopteridae

Distribution: Nile River, Gabon, Liberia, Niger, and D. R. Congo.

Size: Around 12in (30cm).

Behavior: Adults are solitary predators, active mainly at dusk and during the night; juveniles may be kept together, at least for a time.

Diet: Large livefoods, including live fish, preferred —a factor that needs due consideration prior to purchase; chunky, meat-based or fish-based formulations also accepted.

Aquarium: Large, well covered, well filtered, well planted, with subdued lighting and large shelters, e.g. substantial pieces of bogwood. A "moonlight" fluorescent tube will facilitate nighttime viewing. Water chemistry not critical, but softish, slightly acid water preferred; quality must be good. Temperature range: 75–86°F (24–30°C).

Breeding: No documented accounts of aquarium breeding currently available.

While looking superficially similar to *Notopterus notopterus* (Asian Knifefish) and sharing a common name with *Papyrocranus (Notopterus) afer*—see under *N. chitala* (Clown Knifefish)—the African Knifefish can be easily distinguished by its total lack of a dorsal fin. This species is also considerably smaller than *Notopterus chitala* and can therefore be accommodated more easily.

Black Ghost Knifefish

Apteronotus albifrons

Family: Apteronotidae

Distribution: Widely distributed in northern South America.

Size: Up to 20in (50cm).

Behavior: Often timid but can become aggressive, particularly toward conspecifics.

Diet: Chunky livefoods and deep-frozen or freeze-dried formulations preferred.

Behavior: Adults are solitary predators, active mainly at dusk and during the night. Juveniles may be kept together, at least for a time.

Aquarium: Large, well covered, well filtered, well planted, with subdued lighting and large shelters, e.g. substantial pieces of bogwood. A "moonlight" fluorescent tube will facilitate nighttime viewing. Water chemistry not critical, but softish, slightly acid water preferred; quality must be good. Temperature range: 73–82°F (23–28°C).

Breeding: No documented accounts of aquarium breeding currently available.

This is a most attractively marked species whose jet-black body contrasts sharply with a white streak that runs from the snout to the top of the head, and two white patches in the caudal peduncular area. The somewhat less strikingly marked *A. leptorhynchus* (Long-nosed Black Ghost Knifefish)—which is smaller (around 10in/25cm)—is also available.

Green Knifefish

Eigenmannia virescens

Family: Sternopygidae

Distribution: Widely distributed in tropical regions of South America.

Size: Males reported up to 18in (45cm) but usually smaller; females are considerably smaller.

Behavior: Shoaler with crepuscular and nocturnal habits.

Diet: Large livefoods, including live fish, preferred —a factor that needs due consideration prior to purchase; chunky, meat-based or fish-based formulations also accepted.

Aquarium: Large, well covered, well filtered, well planted, with subdued lighting and large shelters, e.g. substantial pieces of bogwood. A "moonlight" fluorescent tube will facilitate nighttime viewing. Water chemistry not critical, but softish, slightly acid water preferred; quality must be good. Temperature range: 75–86°F (24–30°C).

Breeding: Adhesive eggs are laid among floating plants.

This is one of the so-called glass knifefishes grouped by some authors, along with other related species, within the family Rhamphichthyidae. However, according to the classification followed here (as in Nelson 1994), the Rhamphichthyidae are known as the sand knifefishes and contain only two genera. Green Knifefish look particularly impressive in a shoal, where the establishment of a strict pecking order prevents fighting and, thus, injuries. *Steatogenys duidae (elegans)* (Barred Knifefish), *Sternopygus macrurus* (Variable Ghost Knifefish), and various species of *Gymnotus*, especially *G. carapo* (Banded Knifefish), all of which have similar requirements, are occasionally available.

Silver Arowana

Osteoglossum bicirrhosum

Family: Osteoglossidae

Distribution: Amazon drainage, western Orinoco drainage, and Guyana.

Size: Up to c.39in (1m) reported but often smaller.

Behavior: Juveniles become progressively intolerant with age but may be kept with similar-sized tankmates; this species has exceptional jumping ability.

Diet: Large livefoods, including fish, preferred but a wide range of meat-based or fish-based formulations will also be accepted.

Aquarium: Large, well covered, well filtered, with plenty of open swimming spaces near surface. Soft, slightly to moderately acid water recommended. Temperature range: 75–86°F (24–30°C).

Breeding: Only occasionally achieved in aquaria. Eggs and (later) young are carried orally by male for up to 60 days.

Two species of Amazonian arowana are available, the Silver Arowana and *O. ferreirai* (Black Arowana) from the Río Negro. The adults are very similar, although Silver Arowana is somewhat sturdier looking, with fewer lateral line scales, dorsal and anal fin rays, and vertebrae. Juvenile *O. ferreirai* exhibit the characteristic black coloration responsible for the common name of the species. Both these arowanas are excellent jumpers that can pluck prey from branches above the water surface. This ability has earned them the local name of *macaco d'agua* (water monkey).

Red Arowana

Scleropages formosus

Other common names:
Dragon Fish, Asian Bonytongue, Asian Arowana

Family: Osteoglossidae

Distribution: Widely distributed in Southeast Asia.

Size: Up to 35in (90cm).

Behavior: Juveniles become progressively intolerant with age but may be kept with similar-sized tankmates; this species has exceptional jumping ability.

Diet: Large livefoods, including fish, preferred, but a wide range of meat-based or fish-based formulations will also be accepted.

Aquarium: Large, well covered, well filtered, with plenty of open swimming spaces near surface. Soft, slightly to moderately acid water recommended. Temperature range: 75–86°F (24–30°C).

Breeding: Eggs and (later) the young are carried orally by male for up to 60 days.

This legendary fish of the Far East is steeped in history and mystery and is one of the "greats" of the aquarium. In their native lands, Red Arowanas are said to bring health, wealth, and luck to their owners. As a result, they are highly sought after. The only specimens that can be legally traded are those bred in captivity and approved by the Convention in International Trade in Endangered Species (CITES). However, this species is now bred in such large numbers in captivity that current demand can be satisfactorily met. There are three main color varieties: silver/green, gold, and—the most highly prized and expensive—red. Several other varieties have been added and more are likely to follow. An Australian species, *S. jardinii* (Gulf Saratoga), is also now being bred in captivity, while another Australian species, *S. leichardti* (Spotted Saratoga), is only rarely seen.

Lesser Spiny Eel

Macrognathus aculeatus

Family: Mastacembelidae

Distribution: Southeast Asia.

Size: Up to 14in (35cm) reported, but usually smaller.

Behavior: Aggressive toward conspecifics when kept as pairs or trios; less so when kept in groups of about ten specimens; crepuscular and nocturnal burrower; may prey on small fish.

Diet: Bottom-dwelling livefoods preferred, but some commercial sinking formulations accepted; pellet/tablet diets may be reluctantly accepted.

Aquarium: Spacious, well covered, with fine-grained substratum, numerous hiding places, and clumps of plants protected from burrowing activities. A "moonlight" fluorescent tube will facilitate nighttime viewing. Neutral or slightly alkaline, soft to medium-hard water recommended. A small amount of salt, i.e. 1 teaspoonful per 2 Imp. gal ($2^2/_5$ U.S. gal/9–10) may be added (but not essential). Temperature range: 73–82°F (23–28°C).

Breeding: Rare in aquaria. Eggs are scattered and hatch in about 3 days.

Like all spiny eels, the Lesser Spiny Eel is an expert escape artist, so care should be taken to ensure the aquarium is well covered. The species is characterized by a number of prominent eyespots along the base of the dorsal fin and a series of darker and lighter bands running from snout to caudal peduncle. As in all spiny eels, the dorsal fin is preceded by numerous isolated small spines that can be raised, hence the common name for these interesting fish.

Fire Eel

Mastacembelus erythrotaenia

This is the best known and most colorful of all the spiny eels. It is also among the largest and perhaps the most sensitive to poor water conditions as well as parasitic infections and injuries. Special care must therefore be taken to ensure that its aquarium requirements are scrupulously met.

Other common names: Spotted Fire Eel, Asian Fire Eel

Family: Mastacembelidae

Distribution: Southeast Asia.

Size: Up to c.39in (1m) but usually smaller.

Behavior: Aggressive toward conspecifics when kept as pairs or trios; less so when kept in groups of about ten; a burrower that is most active at dusk and at night; may prey on small fish.

Diet: Prefers bottom-dwelling livefoods but will accept some commercial sinking formulations; may accept pellet/tablet diets.

Aquarium: Spacious, well covered, with fine-grained substratum, numerous hiding places, and clumps of plants protected from burrowing activities. A "moonlight" fluorescent tube will facilitate nighttime viewing. Neutral or slightly alkaline, soft to medium-hard water recommended. A small amount of salt, i.e. 1 teaspoonful per 2 Imp. gal (2²/₅ U.S. gal/9–10 l) may be added (but not essential). Temperature range: 73–82°F (23–28°C).

Breeding: No documented accounts currently available.

African Lungfish

Protopterus annectens

Family: Protopteridae

Distribution: Widespread in Africa.

Size: Up to 28in (70cm) reported.

Behavior: Intolerant and predatory.

Diet: Large livefoods, including fish; chunky meat-based or fish-based formulations also accepted.

Aquarium: Large, well covered, well filtered, with fine-grained substratum and large shelters and pieces of bogwood. Water chemistry not critical. Temperature range: 77–88°F (25–30°C).

Breeding: No documented reports of aquarium breeding currently available.

This tough large fish is, like all other lungfishes, able to tolerate a wide range of conditions. As their native pools dry up in the wild, all the African species bury into the substratum and secrete a mucous cocoon within which they estivate (undergo a period of summer dormancy) until the rains return. The pectoral and pelvic fins of African Lungfish are long and whiplike rather than finlike.

Ropefish

Erpetoichthys calabaricus

Other common names:
Reedfish, Snake Fish

Synonym: *Calamoichthys calabaricus*

Family: Polypteridae

Distribution: Cameroon and Nigeria.

Size: Up to 16in (40cm) reported but usually smaller.

Behavior: Peaceful toward tankmates that are too large to swallow; likes to burrow; active mainly at dusk and during the night.

Diet: Livefoods and chunky or meaty formulations.

Aquarium: Large, well covered, with several shelters/hiding places and fine-grained substratum. Protect plants against burrowing. A "moonlight" fluorescent tube to facilitate nighttime viewing is recommended. Slightly acid, medium-hard water preferred. Temperature range: 72–82°F (22–28°C).

Breeding: No documented accounts available.

Ropefish is closely related to the birchirs (*Polypterus* spp.), with which it shares several characteristics, such as the possession of a number of dorsal finlets (7–13) rather than a single fin, and the ability to use its swimbladder as an auxiliary respiratory organ. It is distinguished from its relatives by its extremely elongated snakelike body and the lack of pelvic fins. Ropefish can survive out of water for several hours, as long as the air is humid.

Ornate Birchir

Polypterus ornatipinnis

Family: Polypteridae

Distribution: Widely distributed in central Africa.

Size: Up to 18in (46cm) reported.

Behavior: Generally tolerant of large tankmates, but less so of conspecifics; will prey on small fish.

Diet: Large livefoods, including live fish; chunky, meaty formulations also accepted.

Aquarium: Large, well covered, with several shelters/hiding places and fine-grained substratum. Protect plants against burrowing. A "moonlight" fluorescent tube to facilitate nighttime viewing is recommended. Slightly acid, medium-hard water preferred. Temperature. range: 79–82°F (26–28°C)

Breeding: Tight spawning embraces—usually taking place among vegetation—are accompanied by egg release and fertilization. Eggs are abandoned and they hatch 4 days later.

This is the most widely available member of its genus. Although they have a number of characteristics in common with *Erpetoichthys calabaricus* (Ropefish), birchirs do not possess a snakelike body and do not lack a pelvic fin. Several other species are occasionally available: *P. congicus* (Congo Birchir), mainly from D. R. Congo; *P. delhezi* (Armored Birchir), also from D. R. Congo; *P. palmas* (Marbled Birchir) from Guinea, Liberia, Sierra Leone, and D. R. Congo; and *P. senegalus* (Cuvier's or Senegal Birchir) from Senegal, Gambia, the Niger, White Nile, and several major lakes, such as Lakes Albert, Chad, and Rudolf. All of these species have similar requirements.

Shovelnosed Sturgeon

Scaphirhynchus platorynchus

Family: Acipenseridae

Distribution: Mississippi River basin, Mobile Bay drainage (Alabama), and upper Rio Grande River (Texas).

Size: Around 39in (1m) but often smaller.

Behavior: Peaceful; burrows in the substratum in search of food, and may prey on small fish.

Diet: Chunky livefoods, deep-frozen and freeze-dried preparations, as well as sinking pellets and tablets.

Aquarium: Very large, well filtered, with open swimming areas and a fine-grained substratum. Neutral, medium-hard water is preferred, but some deviation accepted. Temperature range: 50–68°F (10–20°C).

Breeding: No documented accounts of aquarium breeding available.

Most sturgeons can grow to very large sizes—e.g. *Huso huso* (Beluga) can reach around 26ft (8m)—and are therefore totally unsuitable for aquaria. However, the Shovelnosed Sturgeon, along with *Acipenser ruthenus* (Sterlet) and *A. stellatus* (Stellate Sturgeon), are smaller and can be housed in aquaria as long as they are spacious enough. One of the reasons for their growth in popularity in certain countries—beginning in the late 1980s/early 1990s—has been the expansion of the pondkeeping/watergardening hobby in general, and that of Koi keeping in particular. Shovelnoses, Sterlets, and Stellate Sturgeons are transferred to outside ponds once they outgrow their aquaria.

Motoro Stingray

Potamotrygon motoro

Other common names:
Ocellated Stingray, Peacock-eye Stingray

Synonym: *Potamotrygon laticeps*

Family: Potamotrygonidae

Distribution: Widespread in tropical South America.

Size: Up to 20in (50cm).

Behavior: Tolerant; may be kept in a group; spends much time buried in the substratum with only the eyes showing.

Diet: Bottom-dwelling livefoods, chunky meat-based or fish-based formulations, and sinking deep-frozen diets.

Aquarium: Large, well filtered, with some floating vegetation, well-bedded rocks or bogwood pieces, and deep, fine-grained substratum. Slightly acid to neutral, soft to medium-hard water accepted. Temperature range: 75–79°F (24–26°C).

Breeding: No documented accounts of aquarium breeding currently available.

This is an extremely variable species that, along with other members of the family, is becoming increasingly popular. Stingrays are most definitely not suitable for new aquarists and should in any case be treated with caution because of the dangers posed by the sting. Seek specialist advice and consult specialist literature before purchase.

GLOSSARY

Words in SMALL CAPITALS can be looked up elsewhere in the Glossary.

acidic A reading on the pH scale below 7.0. (*See* pH.)

adipose fin Second DORSAL FIN.

adsorption The "adhesion" of molecules to a porous surface; no chemical transformation of these molecules occurs.

aeration The process of adding air to water in order to improve its oxygen content.

aerobic Chemical and biological processes (or reactions) that require oxygen.

air sac Structure connecting with the gut that evolved in primitive fish to provide buoyancy.

algae Microscopic plants present in water that can coat glass, rockwork, and other surfaces in the aquarium, especially under conditions of high light intensity.

alkaline A reading on the pH scale measuring above 7.0. (*See* pH.)

anaerobic Chemical and biological processes that can occur in the absence of oxygen.

anal fin Belly FIN.

andropodium Term often used for the GONOPODIUM of halfbeaks (family Hemiramphidae). (*See* SPERMATOPODIUM.)

annual Of fish species that live for only one season.

aquarium peat An additive-free peat that can be added to the aquarium filter to make the water more ACIDIC.

barbels Fleshy filaments growing around the mouth of a fish.

benthic Bottom dwelling.

brackish Water conditions that are more saline than freshwater, but not as salty as seawater. Typically encountered at the mouths of estuaries.

brood The number of young produced by a female at one time.

bubble nest The structure made from air bubbles encased in mucus, in which the eggs of certain fish are hatched.

cartilage Tough but flexible body tissue. The skeletons of some fish are made entirely of cartilage.

caudal fin Tail fin.

caudal peduncle Base of the CAUDAL FIN.

chemical filtration The use of chemicals to remove dissolved water by ADSORPTION.

community tank An aquarium used for keeping different species that are compatible with one another.

condensation tray Perspex or glass sheet installed between the aquarium and the hood to minimize evaporation and prevent electrical connections from getting wet.

conspecific Of the same SPECIES.

dechloraminator A chloramine-removing agent.

dechlorinator A chlorine-removing agent.

denitrification The conversion of nitrate to nitrite and thence to nitrogen. In aquaria this function is performed by anaerobic microorganisms.

diapause A period of dormancy, e.g., in the eggs of some killifish.

dorsal fin Back FIN.

dropsy Abnormal swelling of the body; may have infectious or noninfectious cause.

egg-layer A fish that lays eggs that are then fertilized outside the body.

egg spots Ovoid (egg-shaped) markings on the ANAL FINS of some male fish that resemble eggs and are significant in the breeding process, attracting the female so that fertilization can occur.

facultative viviparity Scientific term for SPECIES once regarded as ovi-ovoviviparous. (*See* OVI-OVOVIVIPARITY.)

family A TAXONOMIC grouping of fish consisting of several different genera. (*See* GENUS.)

fancy A STRAIN of fish selectively bred for characteristic features, such as coloration or FIN shape.

fins Projections on a fish's body, used for swimming and display, and in some cases for mating.

flake Very thin, waferlike, manufactured food for fish that floats well on the water surface.

flocculation Clumping of small particles into larger agglomerations.

fry Young fish.

gamete Reproductive cell, i.e., egg or sperm.

genital papillae Small projections found around the genital opening of some fish.

genital pore An opening that indicates the entrance to the genital tract, located on the underside of the body.

genus (pl. genera) A related group consisting of one or more SPECIES.

GH General or Permanent Hardness of a water sample, determined primarily by the chlorides, nitrates, and sulfates of calcium and magnesium.

gills The major means by which fish are able to extract oxygen from the water. They are located just behind the eyes on each side of the head.

gonopodium Copulatory organ possessed by males of livebearing families such as Anablepidae (e.g., Four-eyed Fish) and Poeciliidae (e.g., Guppy). It consists of highly modified RAYS of the ANAL FIN and is used as a means of introducing sperm into the VENT of the female during mating. (*See* ANDROPODIUM; SPERMATOPODIUM.)

gravel tidy Mesh sheeting that can be laid on top of UNDERGRAVEL FILTER plates to prevent grains of SUBSTRATE from blocking the plate slits or pores.

gravid The swollen appearance of female fish, indicating they are about to produce young.

gynogenesis Development of eggs after sperm penetration but without actual fertilization taking place (as in *Poecilia "formosa"*).

hard water Water that contains a relatively high level of dissolved calcium or magnesium salts.

hermaphrodite Animal possessing both male and female sex organs.

hybridization Successful mating of two different SPECIES, resulting in so-called hybrid offspring.

ichthyologists People who study fish.

KH A measure of temporary hardness of a water sample, caused by bicarbonates or carbonates of calcium and magnesium. Temporary Hardness, unlike General Hardness (GH), can be reduced or eliminated by boiling. (*See* GH.)

labial Refers to the lips.

labyrinth organ Specialized auxiliary breathing organ located close to the GILLS that enables fish to breathe atmospheric air directly.

lamella (pl. lamellae) Thin, platelike structure as found in the gills of mushrooms or fish GILLS, when it is often referred to as a gill filament.

lateral line system A system of pores that run along a fish's body. They lead to nerve endings that allow a fish to sense vibrations in the water and help it locate prey, detect predators, avoid obstacles, and so on.

length Measurement of a fish is usually carried out in a straight line from the snout to the base of the CAUDAL FIN, which is itself excluded from the figure.

lignin Hard "woody" material found in the walls of plant cells; some SPECIES of fish, notably Whiptail Cats (family Loricariidae), consume lignin as part of their natural diet.

livebearers Fish that reproduce by means of internal fertilization, with females retaining the eggs in their body.

livefoods Fish food consisting of live invertebrates.

metabolism The collective term for the biochemical reactions that occur in living organisms.

midline The central horizontal axis of a fish's body.

monogamous A one-to-one pairing system of a male and female. (*See* POLYGAMOUS.)

monotypic genus A GENUS that contains just a single SPECIES.

moonlight fluorescent lamp
A fluorescent tube that emits a weak bluish light that simulates moonlight. It is particularly recommended for aquaria housing fish that are active mainly at night.

morph Any different form of a SPECIES that may occur.

mouthbrooder A fish that retains its fertilized eggs in its mouth until they hatch. It may also allow its young back there for a period afterward to escape danger.

mulm The debris that can accumulate on the floor of the aquarium.

mutation A genetically induced change in color or appearance.

neoteny The retention of larval characteristics in sexually mature adults, e.g., external GILLS in Axolotls.

neuromast A "pore" of the LATERAL LINE SYSTEM.

nitrification The conversion of ammonia to nitrite and then to nitrate. In aquaria this function is carried out by AEROBIC microorganisms.

nocturnal Fish that are active when it is dark.

nuchal hump In male cichlids the swelling found on the forehead of mature specimens.

omnivorous Fish that eat both plant and animal matter.

operculum Cover, consisting of bony plates, that encloses the GILLS.

ovarian follicle Egg sac.

ovi-ovoviviparity Term (no longer widely used) to describe reproductive strategies that consist of internal fertilization with subsequent release of the fertilized eggs.

oviparity Egg-laying.

ovoviparity Livebearing reproductive strategy that includes internal fertilization, with most of the embryo nourishment originating from egg yolk. (*See* LIVEBEARERS.)

peat sandwich A layer of AQUARIUM PEAT sandwiched between two layers of a different medium (e.g., gravel) or wrapped in muslin. It can be laid as the SUBSTRATUM of the aquarium or within a filter (for peat filtration).

pectoral fin Chest FIN.

pelvic fin Hip FIN.

pH A value indicating levels of acidity/alkalinity. The scale is logarithmic, i.e., each "unit" represents a tenfold increase or decrease. A value of pH 7 represents neutral conditions; lower values indicate increasing levels of acidity, while higher ones indicate increasing levels of alkalinity. (*See* ACIDIC; ALKALINE.)

pharyngeal teeth Sharp projections used for rasping food, located in the throat region of some fish.

photosensitive Affected by light.

piscivorous Describes fish that hunt other fish for food.

pit Area in the SUBSTRATE where SPAWNING takes place and some young fish are corralled by their parents.

plankton Microscopic plant and animal life in the water.

polygamous Describes a male that mates with several females rather than living as a member of a pair. (*See* MONOGAMOUS.)

polymorphism Occurrence of the same SPECIES in recognizably distinct forms.

quarantine The complete isolation of newly acquired fish for a period of time to ensure that they are healthy before introducing them to other fish; or the isolation of a sick fish.

raw water Household water that comes direct from a faucet.

rays Bony framework that provides structural support for the FINS.

scales Protective covering present over the bodies of most fish.

schools Groups of fish, usually of one SPECIES, swimming together.

scute A type of scale found in some fish, especially certain catfish, that is modified into a bony plate.

sexual dimorphism A difference in appearance between the two sexes.

shoal A group of fish, usually of the same SPECIES, that swim together. (*See* SCHOOL.)

soft water Water that is low in dissolved salts, as typified by rainwater.

spawning The process of mating and egg-laying.

spawning mop Strands of nontoxic material (e.g., wool) attached to a floater (e.g., a piece of cork). Mops are frequently used in killifish breeding aquaria to provide a SPAWNING medium for SPECIES that (in the wild) deposit their eggs among vegetation (rather than in the SUBSTRATUM).

species A group of fish that closely resemble each other and can interbreed.

specific gravity (SG) The mass ("weight") of a volume of liquid as compared to an equivalent one of pure water. Pure water has an SG of 1.000, while seawater has an SG of around 1.020, which varies according to the concentration of salts it contains.

spermatopodium The notched ANAL FIN in males of livebearing SPECIES of the family Goodeidae. It is used to carry out internal fertilization of eggs during mating. (*See* ANDROPODIUM; GONOPODIUM.)

strain A line of fish specifically developed for particular characteristics such as color or FIN shape; may be named for the breeder who created it.

subspecies A genetically distinct and interbreeding group of individuals found in the wild within a SPECIES. It is allocated a separate Latin name—e.g., *Symphysodon aequifasciatus aequifasciatus* and *S. a. axelrodi* are two subspecies of a single species.

substrate 1. A substance on which an enzyme acts, e.g., carbohydrates are acted upon by enzymes during respiration and are therefore substrates. 2. A medium to which: (a) fixed animals are attached, e.g., rocks onto which barnacles and mussels are attached; (b) plants are anchored or attached, e.g., a piece of bogwood on which an aquatic fern grows, or gravel/mud/silt in which aquatic plants have their roots embedded. Used in the latter sense, substrate is interchangeable with substratum.

substratum *See* SUBSTRATE.

superfetation Strategy exhibited by some LIVEBEARERS in which a female can simultaneously carry several small BROODS of embryos at different stages of development.

surfactant Proteins, fats, and other compounds that are attracted to or trapped by the interface between water and gas.

swimbladder The fish's air-filled organ of buoyancy.

taxonomy The science of identifying fish and tracing their relationships.

T.D.S. Total Dissolved Solids (or Salts) in a water sample. It is the equivalent of TOTAL HARDNESS.

territorial Describes fish that establish and defend a territory.

toothcarps Members of the order Cyprinodontiformes, made up of LIVEBEARERS and their egg-laying relatives, often called killifish.

Total Hardness The sum of all the dissolved salts in a water sample, i.e., Temporary/Bicarbonate/Carbonate Hardness, plus Permanent/General Hardness.

tubercles White protruberances present on the body of male cyprinids before SPAWNING.

undergravel filter A plate filter that fits right across the bottom of the aquarium.

variety A subdivision of a SPECIES with uniform characteristics; most often applied to forms specially bred artificially by breeders.

vent Ano-genital opening behind the ANAL FIN.

ventral fin Another term for PELVIC FIN.

venturi An aeration device incorporated within powerheads or power filters. It drags air from the atmosphere via a tube into the water, and dispels it in a stream of bubbles.

viviparity Livebearing, i.e., giving birth to live young.

zoonosis (pl. zoonoses) Disease that can be transmitted from animals to humans.

FURTHER READING

Alderton, D. *Bettas and Gouramis* (Bowtie Press, Irvine, CA, 2004).

Alderton, D. *Cichlids* (Bowtie Press, Irvine, CA, 2002).

Alderton, D. *Livebearers* (Bowtie Press, Irvine, CA, 2004).

Alderton, D. *Starter Aquarium* (Bowtie Press, Irvine, CA, 2002).

Alderton, D. *The International Encyclopedia of Tropical Freshwater Fish* (Howell Book House, New York, 1997).

Allgayer, R., and J. Teton. *The Complete Book of Aquarium Plants* (Ward Lock Ltd., New York, 1987).

Andrews, C., Exell, A., and N. Carrington. *The Manual of Fish Health* (Tetra Press, Morris Plains, NJ, 1988).

Axelrod, H. R., and W. E. Burgess. *African Cichlids of Lakes Malawi and Tanganyika* (TFH Publications, Neptune City, NJ, 1988).

Axelrod, H. R., Burgess, W. E., Pronek, N., and J. G. Walls. *Dr. Axelrod's Atlas of Freshwater Aquarium Fishes* (TFH Publications, Neptune City, NJ, 1985).

Baensch, H. A., and R. Riehl. *Aquarium Atlas* Vols. 1–3 (Baensch, Melle, Germany, 1987, 1993, 1996).

Banister, K., and A. Campbell (eds.). *New Encyclopedia of Aquatic Life* (Facts On File Inc., New York, 2004).

Barlow, G. W. *The Cichlid Fishes: Nature's Grand Experiment in Evolution* (Perseus Publishing, Cambridge, MA, 2000).

Bassleer, G. *Colorguide of Tropical Fish Disease [on Freshwater Fish]* (Bassleer Biofish, Westmeerbeek, Belgium, 1997).

Britchard, P. *Cichlids and all the Other Fishes of Lake Tanganyika* (TFH Publications, Neptune City, NJ, 1989).

Burgess, W. E. *Colored Atlas of Miniature Catfish: Every Species of* Corydoras, Brochis *and* Aspidoras (TFH Publications, Neptune City, NJ, 1992).

Dakin, N. *The Questions & Answers Manual of The Marine Aquarium* (Tetra Press, Morris Plains, NJ, 1996).

Dawes, J. *Livebearing Fishes: A Guide to their Aquarium Care, Biology and Classification* (Blandford, London and New York, 1991).

Dawes, J., Lim, L. L., and L. Cheong (eds.). *The Dragon Fish* (Kingdom Books, Havant, U.K., 1999).

Glaser, U., and W. Glaser. *Loricariidae: All L-Numbers and all LDA-Numbers* (Verlag A.C.S. GmbH, Germany, 1996).

Glaser, U., and W. Glaser. *South American Cichlids: I, II, and III* (Verlag A.C.S. GmbH, Germany, 1996).

Glaser, U., Schifer, F., and W. Glaser. *All Corydoras* (Verlag A.C.S. GmbH, Germany, 1996).

Göbel, M., and H. J. Mayland. *South American Cichlids: IV—Discus, Scalire* (Verlag A.C.S. GmbH, Germany, 1998).

Goldschmidt, T. *Darwin's Dreampond: Drama in Lake Victoria* (MIT Press, Cambridge, MA, 1998).

Goldstein, R. J. *Bettas: A Complete Pet Owner's Manual* (Barron's, Hauppauge, NY, 2001).

Helfman, G. S., Collette, B. B., and D. E. Facey. *The Diversity of Fishes* (Blackwell Science, Malden, MA, 1997).

Hieronimus, H. *Breathtaking Rainbows* (Verlag A.C.S. GmbH, Germany, 1999).

Hieronimus, H. *Guppies, Mollies, Platys—A Complete Pet Owner's Manual* (Barron's, Hauppauge, NY, 1993).

Hiscock, P. *A Practical Guide to Choosing your Aquarium Plants* (Barron's, Hauppauge, NY, 2001).

Hiscock, P. *Creating a Natural Aquarium* (Interpet, Dorking, U.K., 2000).

Hoese, D. F., and A. C. Gill. Phylogenetic Relationships of Eleotrid Fishes (Perciformes: Gobiodei), *Bull. Mar. Sci.* 52 (1) (1993); 415–440.

Houde, A. E. *Sex, Color, and Mate Choice in Guppies* (Princeton University Press, Princeton, NJ, 1997).

Jepson, L. *A Practical Guide to Keeping Healthy Fish in a Stable Environment* (Interpet, Dorking, U.K., 2001).

Jinkings, K. *Bristlenoses: Catfish with Character* (Kingdom Books, Havant, U.K., 2000).

Kempes, M., and F. Schäifer. *All Livebearers and Halfbeaks* (Verlag A.C.S. GmbH, Germany, 1998).

Konings, A. *Back to Nature Guide to Malawi Cichlids* (Fohrman Aquaristik AB, Jonsered, Sweden, 1997).

Konings, A. *Back to Nature Guide to Tanganyika Cichlids* (Fohrman Aquaristik AB, Jonsered, Sweden, 1997).

Konings, A. *Cichlids and All the Other Fishes of Lake Malawi,* (TFH Publications, Neptune City, NJ, 1990).

Konings, A. *Cichlids from Central America* (TFH Publications, Neptune City, NJ, 1989).

Linke, H. *Labyrinth Fish: The Bubble-Nestbuilders* (Tetra Press, Morris Plains, NJ, 1991).

Meffe, G., and F. F. Snelson (eds.). *Ecology and Evolution of Livebearing Fishes (Poeciliidae)* (Prentice Hall, Englewood Cliffs, NJ, 1989).

Nelson, J. S. *Fishes of the World* (3rd edition) (John Wiley & Sons, Inc., New York, 1994).

Parenti, L. R. A Phylogenetic and Biogeographic Analysis of Cyprinodontiform Fishes (Teleostei, Atherinomorpha), *Bull. Am. Mus. Nat. Hist.* 168 (4) (1981); 335–557.

Richter, H-J. *Complete Book of Dwarf Cichlids* (TFH Publications, Neptune City, NJ, 1989).

Ross, R. A. *Freshwater Stingrays of South America* (Verlag A.C.S. GmbH, Germany, 1999).

Sandford, G. *The Questions & Answers Manual of the Tropical Freshwater Aquarium* (Tetra Press, Morris Plains, NJ, 1998).

Scheel, J. J. *Atlas of Killifishes of the Old World* (TFH Publications, Neptune City, NJ, 1990).

Scheurmann, I. *Aquarium Plants Manual* (Barron's, Hauppauge, NY, 1993).

Seegers, L. *Killifishes of the World—New World Killies* (Verlag A.C.S. GmbH, Germany, 2000).

Smartt, J., and J. H. Blundell. *Goldfish Breeding and Genetics* (TFH Publications, Neptune City, NJ, 1996).

Smith, M. P. *Lake Tanganyikan Cichlids* (Barron's, Hauppauge, NY, 1998).

Smith, M. P. *Lake Victoria Basin Cichlids* (Barron's, Hauppauge, NY, 2001).

Staek, W., and H. Linke. *Cichlids from Eastern Africa* (Tetra Press, Blacksburg, VA, 1994).

Tepoot, P. *Aquarium Plants: The Practical Guide* (New Life Publications, Homestead, FL, 1998).

Vierke, J. *Bettas, Gouramis and Other Anabantoids: Labyrinth Fishes of the World* (TFH Publications, Neptune City, NJ, 1988).

Wischnath, L. *Atlas of Livebearers of the World* (TFH Publications, Neptune City, NJ, 1993).

Zurlo, G. *The Tanganyika Cichlid Aquarium* (Barron's, Hauppauge, NY, 2000).

USEFUL WEB SITES

http://aagb.org/
Web site of the Anabantoid Society of Great Britain.

http://www.aqualink.com
This currently represents one of the largest fish-keeping Web sites. A useful starting point, it includes beginner information in Basic Resources.

http://www.aquariacentral.com/
An aquarium-related site with plenty of information and a large fish species database.

http://lists.aquaria.net/fish/livebearers/
A discussion forum about livebearers and their care.

http://www.aquarium-dietzenbach.de
A German site with information in English as well. General, but useful for photographs of new species and details about established ones.

http://www.aquariumsite.com/
A general introduction to the hobby.

http://www.aquaticcommunity.com/
A resource and meeting place for tropical aquarium fish keepers. Useful for those considering their first tropical fish aquarium as well as experienced aquarists.

http://www.aworldoffish.com/
A general site containing useful information for aquarium enthusiasts at all levels.

http://www.caoac.on.ca
Web site of the Canadian Association of Aquarium Clubs.

http://www.cichlid.org
Web site of the American Cichlid Association.

http://cichlidresearch.com/links.html
Cichlid research homepage, with useful links to other fish resources.

http://www.cichlasoma.nl/
The largest resource concerning cichlids of Central America, including practical information for aquarists.

http://cichlid-forum.com/articles/
A good cichlid site, with articles and advice on getting started.

http://www.duboisi.com/
Provides information about various aspects of keeping fish from Lake Tanganyika in Africa.

http://www.fishbase.org/
A comprehensive taxonomic resource.

http://www.fishlinkcentral.com/
A guide to aquarium resources on the Internet.

http://www.flmnh.ufl.edu/fish/
Homepage of the Florida Museum of Natural History Department of Ichthyology. Follow the links to freshwater research.

http://cil.france.free.fr/index.html
Communauté Internationale pour les Labyrinthidés (CIL)

http://ibcbettas.com/
International Betta Congress.

http://igl-home.de/
Internationalen Gemeinschaft für Labyrinthfische (IGL). German Web site.

http://www.livebearers.org/
Home page of the American Livebearer Association. Essential for photos and information about this group of fish and for contacting fellow enthusiasts, as well as how to join the ALA.

http://www.suite101.com/linkcategory.cfm/14243/24419
General tropical fish site with links to other useful sites.

http://www.thekrib.com/
Provides information about tropical fish aquaria, particularly freshwater aquatic plants and dwarf cichlids.

http://www.thetropicaltank.co.uk/links.htm
Fish and aquarium-related links, with plenty of information about tropical fish and aquaria.

INDEX

Bold common names and page numbers, e.g., **Acara, Blue 20** indicate the illustrated main entry for that species. Italic page numbers, e.g., Aphyosemion, Red *14*, indicate an illustration that is not part of a main species' entry.

G